Dear Guideposts Friend,

Want to know the secret for taking ten years off your appearance? Smile!

Yes, you can look younger by simply smiling! A cheerful face can take years off our appearance—without the pitfalls of plastic surgery. A youth-seeking makeover might promise a younger look, but some people have so much work done that their facial muscles don't operate correctly anymore. They think they're smiling, but no one would know because nothing on their face moves! I say, keep it simple and keep on smiling.

I like to think we're a lot like books. Our pages may tear or turn yellow and our binding become loose. Some of our ideas may even sound dated or passé. But if we can somehow hold ourselves together, survive the elements to which life exposes us, and keep most of our pages intact, we'll become a rare and special book indeed.

The best way I know how to keep those pages intact is to see the humorous side of life. It's right there in front of us; all we have to do is let ourselves laugh. It's a God-given ability, and He must have realized how much we would need it. If I had to come up with a mission statement, I think it would be this: Life's tough. God's good. And laughter's calorie-free!

I sincerely hope you'll enjoy a laugh or two by reading this book. If it reminds you that God is always giving us something fresh and new to smile about, that's the best advice I can give you on how to stay young—at heart.

Sincerely,

Martha Bolton

Martha Bolton

The BEST of
Martha Bolton

THREE BOOKS COMPLETE IN ONE VOLUME

Didn't My Skin Used to Fit?

• • •

Cooking with Hot Flashes

• • •

Growing Your Own Turtleneck

Guideposts®

CARMEL, NEW YORK 10512

CONTENTS

MARTHA BOLTON is a full-time comedy writer and the author of over fifty books. She was a staff writer for Bob Hope for fifteen years along with writing for Phyllis Diller, Wayne Newton's USO show, Ann Jillian, Mark Lowry, Jeff Allen, and many others. Her material has appeared in *Reader's Digest*, *Chicken Soup for the Soul* books, and *Brio* magazine, and she has received four Angel Awards and both an Emmy nomination and a Dove Award nomination. Martha and her husband live in Tennessee.

DIDN'T MY SKIN USED TO FIT?

To Dr. Robert Rood,
my doctor and friend,
for keeping me together
all these years.

ACKNOWLEDGMENTS

A special thanks . . .

To my husband, Russ, whom I met when I was fifteen years old and married when I was eighteen . . . back when my skin used to fit.

To my family: Russ II, Matt, Tony, Nicole, Crystal, and Kiana, who try their best to keep me dressing young and in style. (Now, where did I put those bell-bottoms?)

To my friends Linda Aleahmad and Mary Scott, for never letting a birthday pass without getting our annual dose of laughs. Despite what the rest of our bodies are doing, I'm glad none of us has developed a wrinkle in our sense of humor.

To the memory of my father and mother, Lonnie and Eunice, who taught me how to find the humor in all circumstances . . . even crow's-feet.

To my "adopted" mother, Diantha Ain, whose energy and youthful appearance continue to defy the aging process. What's your secret, Di?

To my editor, Steve Laube, who didn't send even one threatening e-mail while waiting for me to finish this project. (Changing my address four times might have had something to do with that.)

And finally, to all my friends and relatives, who've made this life the wonderful journey it is, I thank you from the bottom of my murmuring heart.

CONTENTS

1

Hangin' Loose

I began noticing it several years ago. The skin I had worn for most—no, make that all—of my life suddenly didn't fit anymore. It used to fit. Rather snugly, as a matter of fact. It was tight around the eyes and mouth. There wasn't any extra under my chin or any hanging down from the sides of my cheeks. There was just enough to make one pass around my entire body. One trip was all that was required, and the exact amount was provided to do the job. Not too much, not too little. It was a perfect fit.

It even stretched. If I gained a pound or two, or twenty, my skin easily expanded to accommodate the increased territory. It wasn't judgmental. It didn't condemn me for that third trip to the food bar. It never tried to knock the brownie out of my hands or shame me into putting back that super-sized scoop of banana pudding. It simply stretched and accommodated. It met the challenge of whatever was required and never once complained.

If I lost weight, my skin was equally accommodating. It would easily return to its original size as though nothing had ever happened. I could gain weight or lose to my heart's content, or discontent, and it would adjust, snapping right back into place when the time was right.

Well, it doesn't snap back anymore. In fact, it doesn't do much of anything except hang there, looser in some places than in others. Like under my chin. That's where a lot of it seems to gather and hang. I'm not very happy about that. It's disconcerting when people stare at my neck and I know they're thinking about Thanksgiving.

Frankly, I think someone should come up with a choker necklace that could be worn just below the chin and would keep all that extra skin tucked neatly in place so it doesn't hang down like loosened upholstery under an antique chair. Whoever designs the first necklace like that will make a fortune.

Little folds of flesh have started to gather around my eyes, too—wrinkles that won't minimize no matter how much wrinkle minimizer I apply. They call it "crow's-feet," but my face doesn't have just a few of them. It has a whole chorus-line thing going on! Every time I squint, my skin seems to fanfold itself into a neat little stack, like pulled taffy, right beside my eyes. It's orderly, but not very attractive. I don't know about you, but I don't want tidy little stacks of pulled taffy next to my eyes. I'd much rather go back to the days when crow's-feet were something you only worried about in an Alfred Hitchcock film.

For some reason, my upper arms have fallen to this extra-skin curse, as well. Don't ask me why, because I haven't a clue. What I do have, though, is a nice swag look every time I raise a hand. I've measured, and there is a good two inches of loose skin under each arm. If a strong wind kicks up, I could be flapping for hours.

I don't think I'd ever actually become airborne, but given the right aerodynamic circumstances, I wouldn't bet against it. That's the reason I wear long sleeves most of the time. They help keep me grounded and save the embarrassment of having to explain a sudden and unscheduled flight to air traffic controllers. What would I say?

"I know I should have radioed in my flight pattern, sir, but this was one of those spur-of-the-moment trips. And besides, that 747 could easily have gone around me."

I'm sure I'd get into some sort of trouble with the Federal Aviation Administration.

Personally, I believe that's why Renaissance clothing sported those long, flow-y sleeves. The women back then had a problem with loose underarms, too.

I've also been noticing the skin beginning to bunch up around my ankles. I thought about painting the little rolls of flesh to match my outfits, passing them off as slouch socks, but decided against it. Even slouch socks aren't supposed to go *that* far up your legs. Besides, if I wear real tight nylons, I can usually push the extra skin back up to my knees, where people *expect* to see extra skin.

Wouldn't it be great if we could unzip our skin, take it to the dry cleaners, and let them shrink it back into shape? They shrink everything else! I suppose that's not an option, though. When's the last time you saw a dry cleaner coupon that read, "While-U-Wait Epidermis Pressing. Save 20%"?

An elderly movie star I once worked with had a good idea. She pulled all the loose face skin up under her bangs, then taped it back by her ears. Amazingly enough, it gave her the illusion of being thirty years younger! I was so impressed with the results, I tried it myself, but it didn't work as well for me. All we had in the house at the time was duct tape, and the silver kept showing through my hair.

Skin that doesn't fit is just one of the symptoms of growing older. There are plenty more, of course. Symptoms that, for the most part, we can't stop no matter how much we'd like to or how hard we try, so we might as well laugh about them. And laughing about them is what this book is all about.

YOU KNOW YOU'RE GETTING OLD WHEN ...

getting "in the groove" means your walker hit a crack in the sidewalk.

2

Yo Quiero
No Discount

I always feared it would happen someday, and there it was—in
black and white. All I had done was walk into a Taco Bell in
east Tennessee and give my order to the teenager behind the
counter.

I wasn't trying to cause any trouble, or pick a fight, or be
disruptive in any way. I was just trying to get a couple of tacos
and a seven-layer burrito. *That's all*. It was lunch. There was no
justification for what the clerk did. He should have handed me
my order and let me pay for it, and I would have been on my
way. A simple transaction. But *noooo*. This guy had to take it
one step further. He had to be confrontational. He had to take
it upon himself to ruin my otherwise happy and peaceful day.
He had to keep going until he pushed my buttons. All right, *his*

button—the one on the cash register *that printed out the words "SENIOR DISCOUNT" on my receipt!*

SENIOR DISCOUNT! I almost dropped my tray! The nerve of that acne-faced troublemaker! Had I not been so hungry, I would have taken him on right then and there. I would have put my tray down, told him to meet me outside, then paper-cut him to a pulp with my birth certificate! I may have been over forty, but I was a *long* way from a senior citizen discount!

But I calmed down, decided to turn the other wrinkle—I mean, cheek—and forgive him. It was a simple oversight, after all. I went ahead and gave him the benefit of the doubt. It was the right thing to do. And besides, *a 10 percent discount is a 10 percent discount!*

Maybe he had a migraine headache and his vision was temporarily impaired, I reasoned. Or maybe it was Taco Bell's own version of *Candid Camera.* That's what that little video camera above the cash register was all about. Or, what was most likely the case, the young man's finger slipped, causing him to inadvertently hit the senior discount key instead of the coupon key. That had to have been it. Both keys were probably in the same general area. One little slip is all it would have taken.

That would have been the end of it, except I realized I

hadn't ordered a drink and had to go back.

"Diet Pepsi, please," I said, watching his every move this time. His finger hit the Diet Pepsi key, then without even getting anywhere near the coupon key, it went straight for the one marked "senior discount." He didn't hesitate for a second. He was confident. He was beyond confident. He didn't even bother to ask my age. If you're in doubt about something, you usually ask first, don't you? Like if you're not sure if someone's pregnant or if she's just put on a few pounds, most people ask before throwing a baby shower. It's the same principle.

But apparently this guy had no doubt. He was so confident I deserved a senior discount, he announced it as he handed the receipt to me.

"Here's your drink, ma'am," he said. "And with the senior discount it comes to $1.09."

I didn't have a choice now. I had to stop him before he dug his hole even deeper.

"*Excuse* me," I said, "but I'm not really a senior. I'm not entitled to a discount. In fact, I shouldn't have gotten a discount on my first order, either."

There, I thought to myself, *I've set the record straight. That should make him think twice before giving away Taco Bell's profits to some other undeserving patron.* I smiled, feeling vindicated and proud of myself that I had made the world a safer place for those of us past the forty mark.

"Aw, close enough," he said. "What's a couple of months?"

It had to be the lighting.

You grow up on the day you have your first real laugh at yourself.
—Ethel Barrymore

3

Walk a Mile in My Feet

They were by far the most comfortable pair of shoes I'd ever tried on. They were made of soft leather, and their built-up arches supported mine—which, like the Roman Empire, had long since fallen. There was plenty of room to stretch my toes, and they even had tiny air holes that helped the shoes—and my feet—to breathe.

They came in a variety of colors—okay, white, black, and brown—and were available in all the hard-to-find sizes. They weren't cheap, either. About eighty bucks, to be exact. If you want quality, though, you have to pay for it, or at least that's what the salesman kept telling me.

What I'm referring to, of course, is corrective footwear. There, I've said it. I recently had to start wearing corrective shoes because I was developing what is known as a Taylor's bunion on my left foot. I don't even know who Taylor is or why he had the nerve to park his bunion on my foot, but it appears I am stuck with it.

Now, corrective footwear may not represent the latest look on the Paris fashion runways, but who knows, it might catch on someday. And I for one am doing my part to bring corrective footwear into the forefront of the designer world.

I've decided against surgery. Actually my doctors decided against it. Their recommendation was corrective shoes together with a set of custom-made inserts that compensate for every flaw in my feet.

I'm pleased with the results, but let's face it—corrective shoes could use a little updating. They may be comfortable to walk in and give my feet plenty of room, but most of the styles are rather matronly.

We have the power to change that, though. All we bunioned people need to do is *unite*. It's up to us to demand better representation in the fashion world. We need to stand up on our Taylor's bunion, or whoever else's bunion we happen to have, and protest. We deserve stylish sandals and adorable pumps. We're bunioned, not dead. We have the power to make

Dr. Scholl as popular a designer as Bill Blass or Oscar de la Renta. All we need is the chance.

Not only do our feet go through changes as we grow older but our toenails do, as well. In case you haven't noticed it yet, something happens to toenails on a forty-plus body. They start doing what old envelopes do—curl up around the edges and turn yellow. They also tend to thicken and grow to incredible lengths. Howard Hughes' toenails were a perfect example of this. For some unknown reason, he decided to let his toenails and fingernails grow into all sorts of interesting shapes. Maybe he didn't have enough whisks around the house and decided it was just as easy to grow his own.

Long toenails aren't very attractive and limit your choice of footwear, but there are some advantages. Walking barefoot in your backyard could easily take care of that Rototilling job you've been putting off for months. And think of all the fun you can have going swimming and spearfishing at the same time. And then, of course, there are all those cans that you'll be able to open should your electric can opener ever go on the blink.

Other changes that happen to the middle-aged foot have to do with bone structure. Sometimes foot bones start doing strange things when they pass their fortieth birthday. My own feet started growing bony extensions out their sides a few years ago. I'm not sure why they're doing this, but if I ever go to the backwoods of Canada and leave my footprints, we could start a whole new Sasquatch rumor.

Many of the foot problems that we suffer later in life, though, are our own fault. Perhaps they're the result of repeated sports injuries, improper nail care, or years of cramming a size nine foot into a size seven shoe. I used to do that myself, so I guess I shouldn't be surprised if today I've got a Taylor's bunion. In fact, I shouldn't be surprised if I'm carrying around his whole family on my feet. After all, if the shoe fit, I really should have worn it.

If I'd known I was going to live this long, I'd
have taken better care of myself.
—Eubie Blake, at the age of 100

4

And He Huffed and He Puffed . . .

In the story of *The Three Little Pigs*, the big bad wolf gave the three little porkers a threat. He said that if they didn't cooperate and open up their doors, he would huff and puff and blow their houses in.

It's obvious from the verbs "huff" and "puff" that we're talking about a middle-aged wolf here. Middle-aged wolves and middle-aged people do a lot of huffing and puffing. For some of us, it has become a second language. I myself am trilingual—being equally fluent in wheezing.

In our youth, we "huffers" could run, jump, climb, race up stairs, even skip a step or two in the process. We didn't have to make six rest stops in the 100-yard dash or send out for oxygen at the halfway point of a flight of stairs. We could have walked up the steps of the Taj Mahal with very little effort.

As soon as we hit forty, though, it's a different story. A fifteen-step staircase suddenly looks like Mount Everest. Before even attempting to scale something of that magnitude, we search the entire area for an elevator, a ramp, a rope, a search and rescue team, a St. Bernard, anything to make our task easier.

Running, jumping, and stair climbing aren't the only activities that can start us huffing and puffing. We huff and puff getting out of our cars, too, especially if those cars are so low to the ground only an ejection seat could get us out without effort. Frankly, I don't understand why car manufacturers make car seats that low anyway. Maybe it's so that after a test drive the client can't get out and has to buy the car.

Answering the telephone can leave us huffing and puffing, especially if the call comes in the middle of a shower. I'm sure more than a few callers have hung up on a middle-aged huffer, mistaking his gasps for heavy breathing.

A few of us even huff and puff putting on our shoes. You thought tying your shoelaces was a challenge when you were four? Try it when you're forty. That's probably why so many seniors opt for slip-ons. Tying shoelaces just isn't worth the battle.

Opening things can leave us huffing and puffing, too—things like potato chip bags, vacuum-packed cookies, vacuum-sealed cans of cheese puffs, or a membership account at the gym. I don't see why manufacturers have to package their foods so tightly anyway. Is keeping us out of the package the only way they can get away with the nutritional benefits printed on the back?

Now, contrary to what you might think, not all huffers and puffers are smokers . . . or even ex-smokers, for that matter. I'm a huffer even though I've taken very good care of my lungs. I've never smoked and I'm very careful not to inhale too much of my own cooking. And although I did grow up in the Los Angeles smog, I held my breath during most of my formative years. Yet even after taking all these precautions, I still huff and puff. The bottom line is lungs are delicate and susceptible to routine damage over the years no matter what you do to protect them.

So, you see, it had to have been a middle-aged wolf chasing those three little pigs. No teenage wolf would huff and puff that much after going to only three houses. And to huff and puff hard enough to blow two houses in? Why, the poor beast should have been carrying a portable oxygen tank! The story's been told wrong all these years. That wolf didn't want those pigs' houses; he needed mouth-to-mouth resuscitation, and not one of those pigs would help him. Not a good-hearted Babe in the bunch. That poor wolf had to keep going from house to house, huffing and puffing and wheezing. Then, when he finally climbed down the chimney of the third house to personally plead for help, what did they do? They lit a fire in the fireplace, which took up even more oxygen! The story ends there, of course, but it makes its point: middle age? It's rough on both man *and* beast!

YOU KNOW YOU'RE GETTING OLD WHEN ...

the brand new house you remember moving into as a child is now protected by the historical society.

5

Hey, Brother, Can You Spare a 401K?

Many middle-aged people have planned well for retirement. Their savings accounts have grown, their stock investments have paid off, and their retirement plans are all set to kick in. They're prepared.

This chapter is for the rest of us. We who have $2.48 in our savings account, didn't invest in Microsoft because we thought it was a hand cream, and will probably get to our senior years, reach for our nest egg, and realize we already fried it years ago.

I've never been much of a financial wizard. The only portfolio I have is the one I bought at OfficeMax. I have, however, watched everyone around me get rich off their stock market or other investments, while I'm busy looking for a grocery store that has a coin machine where I can cash in my quarters.

Not that my husband and I haven't tried our hand at investing. We have. We just haven't been very successful at it. Take, for instance, the piece of desert property we bought over twenty-five years ago as a retirement investment. It's five and a half acres, and we were told it would eventually be worth well over $100,000.

Today it's not worth much of anything because it has been turned into a sanctuary for an endangered insect. I believe it's in the gnat family. So much for making our fortune there. We've listed it for sale a couple of times, but not many people want to own a government-protected five-and-a-half-acre gnat grazing ground.

Whatever porcelain collectibles I've managed to accumulate over the years haven't paid off either. They actually were increasing in value, but the last Northridge, California, earthquake turned them into mosaic pieces.

How about a game show called *Wheel of Missed Fortunes*? Contestants could spin the wheel for a dollar amount— $10,000, $50,000, $100,000, and so on. A lovely blonde could stand by the answer board while contestants guessed the cost of their missed investment opportunities or bad business decisions. It might be a depressing show for the contestants, but the viewing audience would feel a lot better about their own bad investments.

It's hard to predict which "sure deal" really will be a sure deal. We don't know if a piece of real estate will cost us a fortune or make us one. The stock market carries no guarantees, either. Gold might be devalued; the company handling our retirement account could default; we could be hit with a catastrophic illness that depletes every dime of our savings. There are no fail-safe ways to wealth, no assurances that the money we save is going to be there for us when we need it. That's why the most important investments we can make aren't financial. They are the ones we make in the lives around us.

AN ADVANTAGE OF POVERTY:
Your relatives gain nothing by your death.
—Hebrew proverb

6

Out of Style

I'm not against people dressing younger than their age, but there are some who go to extremes to look young. At some point we have to accept the fact that we're not teenagers anymore. We really *do* need diffused lighting.

Just so there's no misunderstanding, I should clarify that I'm not talking about the person who *acts* young. Being young at heart is a healthy attitude that will add quality to your life and maybe even years.

This chapter is about that individual who blots out her age on her driver's license with Wite-Out, reinvents her personal history to cover her age tracks, and shops in the youth department of clothing stores while complaining to the clerk that the loud music is giving her hearing aid feedback.

I'm glad I don't do things like that. Okay . . . there was that one weekend when my niece, Lisa, gave me a temporary tattoo just above my right ankle. It was one of those fun things you do when your sixteen-year-old niece is staying with you for the weekend. It was a rose in full bloom, but it took several weeks to completely wear off. When people saw it in its varying stages of decomposition, they probably thought I had gotten a real tattoo on the installment plan.

But it was just for fun. Don't get me wrong, I'm not condoning or condemning tattoos. Personally, I'd never get a real one, but that's me. I get enough ink on me when I write. And to be perfectly honest, I can't see varicose veins going that well with body art.

What I am saying, though, is this: In our quest for a more youthful appearance, moderation should be our goal. The following guidelines are provided as a public service:

MIDDLE-AGE FASHION FAUX PAS
The following combinations DO NOT go together:

- A nose ring and bifocals
- Spiked hair and bald spots
- A pierced tongue and dentures
- Bikinis and liver spots
- Miniskirts and support hose

- In-line skates and a walker

- Ankle bracelets and corn pads

- Speedos and cellulite

- A belly button ring and a gall bladder surgery scar

- Unbuttoned disco shirts and a heart monitor

- Hot pants and varicose veins

- Midriff shirts and a midriff bulge

I'm not saying the above is the last word on the subject. Simply use it as a guideline. The fashion police will thank you for it.

All men should strive to learn before they die
what they are running from, and to, and why.
—James Thurber

7

Changing With the Times

I've yet to go through the change of life. I know it's coming—
those night sweats that flood the lower floor of your home, the
hot flashes that keep three fire stations on standby, and the
mood swings. Oh, the mood swings—those hormonal changes
that make you weep like a baby because Grape-Nuts just went
on sale or turn you into a raging lunatic when the telephone
cord gets tangled around your ankles.

I'm not looking forward to menopause. Night sweats don't
sound like a lot of fun to me. I had them once after a bout with
the flu, and it was a lot like taking a shower with your clothes
on only the water was coming from the inside out. I prefer the
traditional shower. I don't like waking up in a water bed when I
didn't start out in one.

And hot flashes—whose idea were those? Frankly, I think they should be called "in-law flashes" since they come totally unannounced and seem like they're never going to leave.

They say irritability is also a common side effect of the change. IRRITABILITY? CAN YOU BELIEVE THAT?! THAT'S THE MOST RIDICULOUS THING I'VE EVER HEARD! THEY'VE GOT NO . . . Sorry. I don't know what came over me.

Men go through a change, too, but they call it a mid-life crisis. Some make it through this period unscathed. Others? Well, you've seen them. Those perfectly stable, well-adjusted men who suddenly go out and buy a Harley-Davidson motorcycle, get a tattoo that says, "AARP RULES," and start listening to the same music they've been telling their kids to turn down for years.

I only mention the Harley-Davidson because it's so symbolic. Many men have their identity tied up in the kind of vehicle they drive. In fact, you can usually tell what stage of life a man is going through by his mode of transportation:

MALE TRANSPORTATION THROUGH THE YEARS

Teenager: take the bus, or ride with your parents

Twenties: borrow Dad's car

Thirties: family van

Forties: sport utility vehicle or truck

Fifties: cherry red convertible capable of going from 0–60 in
    two tickets or less

Sixties: Harley with a sidecar for grandchildren

Seventies: fifty-miles-to-the-gallon subcompact vehicle

Eighties: take the bus, or ride with your kids

Now, there's nothing wrong with buying a hot new cherry red convertible or the sleekest motorcycle you can find for your mid-life crisis. But be forewarned: While convertibles and motorcycles can give you that renewed youthfulness and excitement your life has been needing for a long time, you might have to stop every couple of miles or so to go back and pick up your hair.

The meaning of life is to give life meaning.
—Ken Hudgins

8

A Handout

Remember when you were little and someone would ask you your age? You'd hold up three fingers, or four, or five, and say, "This many."

When you get up in years, you still give away your age by your hands, only now it's not intentional. No matter how many face-lifts you undergo, how many laser surgeries you sit perfectly still for, or how much duct tape you've got holding back loose skin, your hands will still betray you. Hands give away age secrets as freely as the rings of a tree trunk or a former best friend.

You could wear gloves, of course, but you might look a little overdressed at your grandson's soccer game. You could keep your hands in your pockets, which is what Napoleon used to do, probably for the same reason, but sooner or later you're going to have to take your hands out to applaud, scratch your nose, or write a check. You can sit on your hands, too. It's not very comfortable and tends to stop the flow of blood, but this is America. You're free to do those kinds of things.

I've also heard lemon juice will help fade age spots, but I don't know how true that is. I tried it once and all it did was make my hands sticky. I don't like sticky hands. I don't mind being friendly, but when I shake someone's hand, I'd like to eventually let go.

A popular dish soap company used to have a mother-daughter team wash dishes together to see if viewers could tell by the look of their dishpan hands which of them was the mother and which was the daughter. It was always difficult to tell since both sets of hands looked terrific. Their soap, they said, was the reason for this. In other words, they were saying to women everywhere that we have to do dishes to get younger looking hands.

I think a husband wrote that commercial.

Age spots, wrinkles, and prominent veins are all telltale signs that we've been putting, as Sheriff John used to say, "another candle on your birthday cake" for quite a while now. And I suppose someday some plastic surgeon will make a lot of money doing wrist lifts or palm pulls to help people hide their age. But until then, I guess our only option is to keep doing those dishes and try to keep our hands as soft and youthful looking as possible. Personally, though, I've given up trying to

hide my age spots. I'm just going to wait for all of them to con-
nect—then I can pass it off as a tan.

What if "Hokey Pokey" really *is* what it's
all about?
—saying on a T-shirt

9

Tan Your Hide

Speaking of tans, I watched a television commercial today for a new instant tanning cream. The pitch seemed to be aimed at those of us who want younger looking skin and are willing to pay three payments of $39.95 each for it. The spokesperson said that a nice golden tan is the secret to looking younger. Face-lifts, laser surgery, and even duct tape were not the answer.

It seems the sun, nature's usual tanning device, does a good job of browning our skin, but it also tends to age it. Harmful sunrays can damage skin so much that instead of our looking younger we actually end up looking older.

The commercial said tanning beds can be harmful to our skin, as well. They didn't have to spend too much airtime talking me out of that. I don't think I'd ever resort to a tanning bed. I'd feel too much like a croissant going into an oven, and since I know all too well what happens to croissants in my oven, I know I'm better off passing on that.

So what's the answer? Well, according to this advertisement, the answer is simple—their instant tanning cream, at $39.95 a month for three months. That's a lot of money, but I'm tempted to order it anyway.

My natural skin tone has always been Clown White, and it'd be fun to have some color for a change. (I'm on the list for a tan transplant, but so far there haven't been any donors.)

So I suppose an instant tanning cream is the only way to go. I just hope they've improved since the days when I was a teenager. I tried one back then and it turned my skin a beautiful shade of Tang orange. I don't think I want to be orange again. It really isn't my color.

But the ad said their instant tanning cream wouldn't do that. In fact, not only did it make those swimsuit-clad fifty-year-old men and women look younger, it also gave them the energy to play a round of beach volleyball. That's some tanning cream!

And while we're on the subject of swimsuits, why doesn't someone make a style that those of us over forty would actually wear? I for one don't like pleats. My skin already has enough pleats; why would I want them in my beachwear? I don't like plunging necklines, either. Enough of me is plunging on its own. And who told anyone that black is the favorite color of those over forty? Our skin might not fit anymore but we're not in mourning over it.

But first things first. No matter what kind of swimsuit I wear, I still need a tan, so I've decided to go ahead and order the tanning cream. And if it doesn't work this time, and I still turn orange, well, I guess that's okay. I live in Tennessee, and orange is one of the colors of the Tennessee State University football team!

Go, Vols!

Therefore we do not lose heart. Though outwardly we are wasting away, yet inwardly we are being renewed day by day.
—2 Corinthians 4:16, NIV

10

Infomercial Paradise

Some say the older you get the less sleep you need. At fifty, you might be getting by on only six or seven hours of sleep. By the time you reach sixty, four or five hours may be all you need. Get to seventy, and not only are you staying awake at night watching every infomercial on television, you're probably squeezing in a 3:00 A.M. trip to the twenty-four-hour Wal-Mart, too.

One reason we require less sleep as we grow older could be all the naps we take throughout the day. I'm not talking about those after-lunch comas that hit people of all ages. I'm talking about that uncontrollable dozing off that seems to hit middle-aged people without warning. It's that overwhelming urge to get in a few winks, whether you're having a root canal, talking on the telephone, or running for a bus.

My husband takes a lot of naps. He can sleep virtually any-where, but his lounging areas of choice are the sofa, the easy chair, the car, the floor, the pew, airline seats, the desk at business meetings, and once in a while, the bed. He can get by on a twenty-minute nap here, a thirty-minute nap there, and only four or five hours of sleep at night.

Another reason we sleep less as we grow older is because we know the party's almost over and we don't want to miss out on a single thing. It's the same reason football fans stay at the game until the very end, even when their team's losing 49–0. It's why people don't sleep through the last fifteen minutes of a good movie. They're afraid they'll miss the best part.

Do the math. If we're in our forties now and are lucky enough to have the genes to make it to our eighties, our lives are already half spent. We should be savoring these days, hours, minutes, even seconds, not sleeping through them. Who wants to oversleep and wake up just in time to hear, "Your life will be closing in ten minutes. Please take all your purchases to the nearest counter and exit through the main doors on your left"?

Life's too important to snooze our way through it. There's too much to do, too much to see, too much to be a part of. If the food processor they're featuring on that 3:00 A.M. infomercial really does dice, slice, chop, mince, puree, and provide therapeutic counseling for my vegetables, I want to know about it. If there's a store open twenty-four hours within a ten-mile radius of my house, I'm going to be out there in the wee hours of the morning supporting it. After all, the people working in the twenty-four-hour Wal-Marts and Kmarts, all-night restaurants, and gas stations are no doubt just like us. They're trying to stretch every moment they've got left, too. I think "Attention Kmart shoppers" has a subliminal message. It's a code for "Life's too short. Stop and smell the roses . . . in our Garden Center at the rear of the store, for $12.98 a dozen."

Time is going to steadily tick by—ticktock, ticktock—and there's nothing we can do to stop it or slow it down. If we're going to live this life to its fullest, and if we're going to do the work that God has for us to do, we need to do it now, not later—today, not tomorrow. After all, we don't want to get to the pearly gates and have to stand before God and say, "Sorry, Lord, I was sleeping. Can you tell me what it was I missed?"

The tragedy of life is not that it ends so soon,
but that we wait so long to begin it.
—Anonymous

11
Making Memories, Not Regrets

My mother dreamed her whole life of going to Washington, D.C. Almost every summer my family traveled from our home in California to Arkansas, where my grandparents lived. One of those summers we probably could have driven up to Washington, D.C., and fulfilled her lifelong dream, but we never did. For whatever reason (no doubt financial), she denied herself that pleasure.

When my father passed away, the one regret I had was that I had not taken him on more trips. So after his death, I made a vow to myself that my mother would see Washington, D.C. Fulfilling that dream didn't come easy. I had to save the money, make adjustments to my work schedule, book all the necessary flights and hotels, and—hardest of all—get Mother to agree to the vacation. She thought she couldn't take that much time off work. I tried to convince her that she could, but when that didn't work, I called her boss and arranged for her to have the time off, then basically "kidnapped" her.

We had a wonderful time visiting the White House, the Capitol, the FBI headquarters, Arlington Cemetery, the Smithsonian, and just about everything else there is to see there. And although the trip took some extra effort and planning, it was well worth it. The pictures and memories I have of our time together are irreplaceable.

After that trip, I planned as many weekend jaunts with my mom to as many different places as I could. These trips quickly became a highlight of both our lives.

A few years ago I decided to fulfill one of my own lifelong dreams. I had always wanted to see the Indian dwellings at Mesa Verde, Colorado. Using the same strategy I had used with my mother, I decided I was going to *make* it happen. I would create my own memories instead of waiting for them to come to me. I saved the money, made the arrangements, and soon my family and I were standing among Indian ruins. Seeing those dwellings gave me a sense of completeness. Once again I had made a memory instead of a regret.

Life is unpredictable. My mother's life came to an end before any of us expected. She was seventy-two and, except for the lymphoma, which had only appeared eight months before, she had hardly been sick a day in her life. I miss her terribly, but every time I run across my pictures of our trips together, they remind me of a few of her dreams that I didn't allow to die with her.

Where is it that you've always wanted to go? What is it you've always wanted to do? Is there some place you've longed to take a loved one? Quit making excuses. Make plans, make the sacrifices, and do it!

Life is made up of ever so many partings welded together.
—Charles Dickens

12

Gravy Is Not a Food Group

It doesn't matter how many deep-fried onion rings we've consumed over the years, how many pecan pies we've inhaled, or how much gravy we've allowed to dam up our arteries, when we pass forty, all of a sudden we become obsessed with eating healthy foods. We don't necessarily change our diet, but we become obsessed with the *idea* of changing it.

It's all those public service announcements that start getting to us:

> Ben thought he was going to live forever. He believed he was invincible. He was convinced his fatty, cholesterol-filled, salt-laden diet wasn't hurting him. Ben was wrong. At

forty-three, he now has to work at home. His desk at his job wasn't equipped to handle the life-support apparatus. Don't be like Ben. Don't wait until it's too late to make those lifestyle changes you've been wanting to make. Unless, of course, you've got a bigger desk than Ben.

We hear Ben gasp for breath in the background as he reaches for that last bag of potato chips. *Gasp, crunch, gasp, crunch.* It's enough to drive anyone to the treadmill.

Health food stores play on our fears, too. They convince us to buy extracts of vegetables we didn't even know existed and make us believe that if pureed and blended together, they're somehow going to taste better. They don't. I'm sorry, but a rutabaga-leek-broccoli-cauliflower swirl is still going to taste pretty much like rutabagas, leeks, broccoli, and cauliflower. A blender and crushed ice isn't going to make them taste like a hot fudge sundae.

But we also know that our bodies need those vitamins, minerals, and, of course, the roughage. The older we get, the more maintenance our bodies require. After forty-plus years, we've had one too many medical tests that show exactly where all that fat we've been consuming over the years has deposited itself. We've seen the ultrasounds, the echocardiograms, the Post-it Notes on our medical reports. We know the blood in our arteries and veins isn't flowing like it did in our youth. We're not fools. Nor are we suicidal. We know if we're going to make it to a ripe old age, we've got to make some changes in our eating habits. We've got to start thinking of that cheesecake as the enemy instead of our reward for doing those three push-ups. We need to start reaching for that bowl of stewed prunes instead of that leaning tower of brownies. And instead of ordering the fried mozzarella sticks, we need to take a second look at those alfalfa sprouts and tofu squares. (Maybe we don't have to go so far as to eat them, but we should at least give them a second look.)

We have to make a commitment to be kinder, gentler to our bodies. We don't want to overwork our hearts or place any unnecessary strain on the rest of our vital organs. One way is to limit our intake of red meat. Cutting out red meat is no problem for me. Most of the meat I serve is black anyway, not red. Including more fish in our diet is a good way to become healthier, too. We should be filling our freezers with rainbow trout, mahimahi, orange roughy, and salmon. They sit nicely on top of the Ben and Jerry's.

You see, there are plenty of ways to improve our eating habits and insure a long, healthy life. But a rutabaga-leek-broccoli-cauliflower swirl? I don't think so. Unless they add a scoop of Rocky Road.

And in the end it's not the years in your life
that count. It's the life in your years.
—Abraham Lincoln

13

I've Only Got Eyelids for You

My good friends Linda Aleahmad, a licensed marriage and family therapist, and Mary Scott, a poet and administrative assistant to a Southern California newspaper editor, and I celebrate our birthdays together each year. We usually go out to a nice restaurant and talk about things like life, work, children, and of course, growing older. No matter how much we don't want to be reminded of it, the subject of aging almost always comes up, and we spend the rest of the evening comparing our latest physical changes and laughing about them as much as possible.

Tonight the physical change du jour was droopy eyelids. Each of us noted that our once perky eyelids had recently unperked themselves, and as Joshua might have said at the wall of Jericho, "They've come a tumbling down!" Not that we're tripping over them or anything, but they've drooped enough to give us that half-open, half-closed look that so many of us had through high school and college.

It seemed to happen to each of us overnight. Eyelids are sneaky that way. You go to bed with all your body parts exactly where they're supposed to be: Chin in place? *Check*. Lips in place? *Check*. Eyelids where they're supposed to be? *Check*. But when you wake up in the morning and look in the mirror, you notice that the rest of your body is exactly where it was eight hours ago, but your eyelids are now drooping like Deputy Dawg's, and you're just about as excited as he is about it.

I suppose we shouldn't be surprised. Our eyelids can't be expected to stay at attention forever. Forty or fifty years is long enough. They're pooped. They're ready for a break. They've faithfully served at their post and now they deserve a rest.

Unfortunately, though, their early retirement begins to place undo pressure on the eyelashes. They are the only things between the avalanche of flesh and our cheekbones.

A business associate of mine had her eyelids pulled back surgically. That's one solution, I suppose. And yes, it worked, but now she has that wide-awake look, like someone just said, "Boo!"

My friends and I spent the evening together weighing the pros and cons of getting our eyelids done but decided against it. We opted to keep the skin we're in and let nature take its course. We would be thankful for our health, our families, and all our blessings. It seemed like the right thing to do—especially when we remembered that Thanksgiving was just around the corner.

I think there was something about my neck that reminded them.

There's more to life than increasing its speed.
—Gandhi

14

Death Doesn't Become Us

Since my friend Mary had recently attended a family funeral, the subject moved from fallen eyelids to funerals, wills, and last wishes. Linda was the first to share what she wanted done with her remains.

"I want to be cremated," she said, "and my ashes placed inside a firecracker and shot into the air in one spectacular send-off."

We figured it must be the cheesecake gone to her head.

Mary said she wanted to be cremated, too, but she also wanted a memorial service in which people said nice things about her. She also wanted a good picture on display, and she'd like her ashes scattered in the barranca in Ventura, California.

I opted for a more traditional funeral. I want nice things said about me at my funeral, too (I'll write them up ahead of time), but I also want the service to be full of funny remembrances. I've embraced laughter my entire life. I wouldn't want it to be missing from my funeral. I want tears, too, of course (who doesn't want to be missed?), but I would hope there'd be lots of laughter to balance things out.

I also asked them to help my husband with the telephone calls. I know him too well. He'll have every intention of calling all my friends listed in our telephone book, but he won't make it past the Cs. It'll be wearying to keep relating the same story over and over again, reliving all the details of how I left this world—especially if I go in some bizarre way like "The manager at the skating rink said it was the first time they'd ever lost anyone during the Hokey Pokey, but they're still going to award her the free CD posthumously for all her efforts." Or "We told her not to use the computer while in the bathtub, but she just mumbled something about a deadline, plugged it in, and deleted herself. We tried to save her as a text file, but we got there too late."

However it happens, my husband will get tired of telling the same tale again and again and again, so he'll just quit—right after the Cs. My friends whose last names begin with the letters *D* through *Z* won't find out about my demise until I'm missing from the family-photo Christmas card. I can hear the phone calls now.

"Where's Martha? I didn't see her by the tree."

"Oh, didn't you know?" my husband will say. "She passed on six months ago."

"Why didn't anyone tell me?"

"I would have, but you weren't in the front of the phone book."

Linda and Mary understood my dilemma (most women can) and agreed to help my husband with the phone calls.

The three of us then moved on to discuss where we wanted our remains to be buried. Living in both Los Angeles and Nashville, I wasn't sure where I'd want my services, so I left the options open. I even entertained the idea of having a service in both places. I didn't see a problem with that, especially since Linda, being shot off in a firecracker, would be having multiple resting places, too. Linda and Mary both opted for California since that's where they live.

Mary wanted the songs "In My Life" by the Beatles and Van Morrison's "Have I Told You Lately That I Love You?" played at her service, and she wanted someone to read several poems, which she has selected. Linda mentioned she wanted "Muskrat Love" sung at hers, but I think she was kidding. I'm still deciding on the songs I want played, but "No One Ever Cared for Me Like Jesus" is definitely one of them.

Next we talked about our choice of flowers. Mary wants irises or tulips. Linda's favorites are daisies and pansies. Mine are magnolias.

We also talked about whether or not we wanted to be organ donors and what parts of our bodies we would be willing to give to science. Not liking the prospect of science returning some of these parts (as defective), we decided not to worry about making these plans right now.

In fact, we decided to change the subject altogether. It was getting way too maudlin. We each felt we had plenty of life left to live, and most of our plans still needed tweaking anyway. Especially Linda's. She wants her funeral in Los Angeles, where fireworks are illegal. That would mean Mary and I would either have to get special clearance or get into a lot of trouble fulfilling her last wishes.

And to tell you the truth, we're not about to get arrested for shooting off a firecracker illegally, even if our best friend is in it.

Despite the high cost of living, it remains a popular item.

—Anonymous

15

Are We Having Fun Yet?

My husband and I spent last Fourth of July doing laundry at the local all-night Laundromat. What can I say? We're still party animals after all these years.

Actually it was my husband's idea. I was ready to celebrate our nation's birthday like it should be celebrated—an old-fashioned barbecue, picnic games, fireworks, a nap. But no, we had laundry to do.

My husband didn't see any problem with doing our laundry on the Fourth of July. He's of the impression that the older he gets the less holiday excitement he can handle. He prefers nice quiet evenings with the History Channel or curling up with a good book (the Best Buy catalog counts). If my husband had his way, New Year's Eve would be spent getting the transmission fluid checked on our car, Valentine's Day reseeding the lawn, and Christmas morning the perfect time to shampoo the carpets.

His main problem with holidays is he doesn't like crowds. According to him, two's company and three's an unlawful assembly. So since the Fourth of July meant crowds, we did laundry.

Unbeknownst to us, though, the parking lot of the Laundromat happened to be the ideal location for local residents to watch the city's fireworks display. While we were busy fluffing and folding, cars began filing into the parking lot one by one, staking claim on the spaces with the best views. Not that all those people were in for any more excitement than we were going to experience *inside* the Laundromat. Until you've watched a Maytag hit the spin cycle and start shaking in time to "God Bless America" being played over the Laundromat TV, you haven't celebrated the Fourth of July. And if one of the dryers happens to develop an electrical short and the sparks start to fly, well, even Bob Hope would have a hard time beating a finale like that.

So there we were celebrating the Fourth of July in style. No, we wouldn't be seeing the Blue Angels in a flyby (although there were a couple of wasps inside that were putting on quite a show). There wouldn't be a marching band or rockets going off or even sparklers. It was just the two of us with a pocketful of quarters and five loads of laundry needing to be done.

Now that I look back on it, it was a pretty enjoyable evening. We actually got to see some of the fireworks through the reflections in the washing machine portholes, and my husband found a quarter behind one of the chairs. As Yakov Smirnoff would say, "What a country!"

YOU KNOW YOU'RE GETTING OLD WHEN ...
you start buying Geritol by the six-pack.

16

Thanks for the Memory ... Loss

Memory is another thing that dulls with age. But more importantly, memory is another thing that dulls with age. As you grow older, you'll find yourself repeating things and forgetting where you put your glasses, your car keys, your checkbook . . . your teeth. I heard of one older gentleman who looked all over the house for his dentures. He finally found them hours later when he sat down on his sofa. Imagine explaining that one to the emergency room team: *"I don't care if it is physically impossible, doctor, I'm telling you the truth. The bite was self-inflicted."*

We all know the negatives about losing our memory, but believe it or not, there are some positives. For one thing, think of all the new cars you get to drive home.

"Whaddya mean we don't own a Lexus, honey? It was parked in the same parking space I distinctly remember parking in. It's got to be our car!"

One night you get to drive home a Lexus, the next night a Suburban, the next night a BMW convertible. For some reason, though, if you find a Yugo parked in your spot, your memory usually comes back to you.

Another plus to memory loss is the fact that there always seems to be more money in your checkbook than there should be. That's because you don't remember to record amounts written and to whom. I'm still working off the deposits I made six months ago. I think I've spent the same money five or six times. Maybe that's why my bank keeps sending me all those letters . . . and here all this time I thought they were just being neighborly!

There are other good things about losing your memory. When your memory goes, your Christmas list gets cut in half. "How many kids did you say we had again?"

And without a good memory, you only have to mail in your taxes *every other* April 15 or whenever you happen to remember you've got an Uncle Sam. That alone should take some of the sting out of aging.

You even start visiting your neighbors more often. Of

course, it's because you think that's where you live, but they don't know that. They might, however, get a little suspicious when an entire season passes before you say you need to go home.

It hasn't been proven yet, but I'm fairly certain our memory cells die faster with physical exertion. They must. Think about it: How many times have you walked into a room to get something only to stand there looking around wondering what it was you went into the room to get?

I think it's the walking that does it. If you would have stayed in your chair just thinking about getting up to get whatever it was you needed to get up and get, you would have remembered what it was you were going to get up and get in the first place.

Memory cells die off while using the telephone, too. Has this ever happened to you? You dial a number, then completely forget who it is you're calling. You don't hang up, of course, because you're sure you'll remember who you called the minute you hear the voice on the other end of the line. Unfortunately, though, a six-year-old answers, and you're still clueless. The kid doesn't help you out, either, when you ask him who his parents are because he's been taught not to talk to strangers. So you simply pretend to have dialed the wrong number, until the six-year-old finally recognizes *your* voice and says, "Grandpa!"

What I don't get is why our memory has to go on the blink at a time when we're given so much to remember. Our doctors tell us to take three of one pill four times a day, four of another pill three times a day, and one of yet another every ten hours for twelve days. How are we supposed to remember all that? Why can't they just put all our medications into one giant capsule that's set to release the proper dosage at the proper time? Sure, they make those little containers marked Sunday, Monday, Tuesday . . . but what good are they if you don't know what day it is?

Then there are all those other numbers we have to memorize nowadays: our bank account number, our driver's license number, our Social Security number, the PIN numbers for twelve credit cards, our previous three addresses, our age, and our frequent-flyer account numbers. I don't know why we can't be assigned one number for all of it and stay with that for the rest of our lives. Like twenty-five. I'd be happy to keep the number twenty-five for my PIN, my phone card number, and my permanent age.

Long-term memory doesn't seem to be as big a problem as short-term memory. While we may not be able to remember what we said to someone five minutes ago, we can clearly recall the hurtful comment our spouse made back in 1984, what he was wearing at the time, and the barometric pressure that day.

Some people call that selective memory. Maybe it is. Maybe as we grow older we get better and better at selective memory. We remember in vivid detail those few things that brought us pain, while forgetting the hundreds of blessings that come our way every day.

I think we've got it backward.

None are as old as those who have outlived
enthusiasm.
—Henry David Thoreau

17

You Don't Bring Me Flowers Anymore

It happens over a period of time, a change so slow you hardly notice it. First, it's your birthday gift. Instead of getting that cute little nightie with the embroidered hearts, you open the gift bag and discover a lovely pair of flannel pajamas, complete with feet. You tell your husband you love them, and to a certain extent, it's true.

You appreciate the fact that the pajamas will keep you warm when he sets the thermostat to twenty degrees (minus-four degrees wind chill factor with the ceiling fan). But flannel pajamas, no matter how well crafted, could mean more than toasty warmth on those chilly summer nights. They could be a warning sign that something has changed in your relationship—not a serious change, just a notable one.

Christmas gifts are affected next. Maybe you get an egg poacher instead of those marcasite earrings you had your heart set on. Or maybe it's an industrial-size container of Spray 'n' Wash instead of the perfume you wanted.

Anniversary presents are the last to change. Instead of pearls, it's plumbing supplies; a makeup kit is replaced with oven cleaner; and that romantic weekend getaway you've been hinting about for months has become a pass for an all-night bowling session.

When these gift changes start to happen in a relationship, there's no denying it—you have a problem. It's called practicality. Now on the surface there's nothing wrong with practicality. After all, why buy your sweetheart a box of chocolates when you really need a new toilet plunger? And with roses costing up to seventy-five dollars a dozen, why waste that kind of money when you can rent a carpet shampooer for half the price?

If we're not careful, by the time we reach middle age the romance in our lives can be virtually nonexistent. We can become too comfortable with our spouse, taking him or her so much for granted that we stop doing those little things that are so necessary to keep love alive. We can easily fall into the trap of never paying attention to our loved ones until they walk in front of the TV while we're watching our favorite show or tie up the telephone when we're expecting a call.

Think about it—when was the last time you went for a walk with your husband? (Helping him take out the garbage doesn't count.) Did the last note you left on the dresser tell him you love him or was it a reminder to pay the electric bill? And husbands, when was the last time you brought your wife flowers, besides that packet of seeds you gave her to plant last spring?

The good news is your romance doesn't have to grow cold. You may not be the young starry-eyed couple you used to be, but you're still a couple. Some of the most romantic couples I've seen are in their seventies and eighties.

There's something wonderful that develops between a man and a woman who have survived all the storms of life together. They can celebrate their fortieth, fiftieth, or even their seventy-fifth wedding anniversary and look back on a *good* marriage—no marriage is perfect—to which they have stayed true. Their disagreements taught them how to compromise, and through their disappointments they learned to appreciate the good times. Instead of growing out of marriage, they persevered and grew in it.

To endure is the first thing a child ought to
learn, and that which he will have the most
need to know.
—Jean-Jacques Rousseau

18

Regrets

One of my favorite songs is George Burns' "I Wish I Were Eighteen Again." It's the kind of song that makes you feel good and sad at the same time. ("You're the Reason Our Kids Are Ugly" does that, too, but in a different way.)

Whether you've just turned forty or you're nudging one hundred, by now you've no doubt accumulated your share of regrets. When you look back on your life, there are things you'd do differently if you were eighteen again. Or twenty-five. Or thirty. You know the things you wish you had done but didn't and the things you wish you hadn't done but did. There are people you'd like to have spent more time with and a few with whom you might regret having spent so much time. There are places you wish you had visited and a few you might wish you had skipped.

Maybe you regret having taken so many risks. Maybe you wish you had taken more. Now that you see the bigger picture, you wish you hadn't wasted so much time worrying, because what you worried about never came about and the difficulties you did face never could have been imagined.

If you could do it all over again, maybe you'd want to make more money, save more money, or give more away. Maybe you'd have the same friends; maybe you'd choose different ones. You'd surely trust some people more because you can see now that they are trustworthy and you'd trust some people less because of your experience with them. Maybe this time around you wouldn't treat each day as cavalierly as you have in the past.

As much as we'd like to do a better job the second time around, the truth is *this is it*. Whatever regrets we have now are going to go with us into eternity unless we take steps now to change them.

I have regrets I need to deal with.

I regret the time I spent waiting for the other person to call when I had the power to pick up the phone myself.

I regret not verbalizing my opinions instead of verbalizing my frustration with not being able to verbalize my opinions.

I regret not keeping more journals. I had plenty of blank books but usually forgot to write in them. Journals are not meant to remain blank. A blank journal gives the impression you've had a blank life. Nobody leads a blank life. Even if it feels blank some days, it's really not. If you woke up on Wednesday morning, May 14, that's noteworthy. If you didn't wake up, you wouldn't be able to write that in your journal; in fact, it's the only viable excuse for not writing in your journal.

I regret not trying out all the recipes I tore out of magazines. What was I saving them for?

I regret the time I wasted wishing I had more time.

I regret not standing up to the bullies who crossed my path. It takes a lot of courage to confront a bully. That courage never came easy for me.

What I don't regret is the time I've spent with my family and friends. I don't regret anything I've ever done that might in some small way have had an eternal significance in someone else's life. And I don't regret dedicating my life to God at the age of six and the fact that I am still trying my best to honor that commitment today at age . . . well, you know, somewhere over forty.

We make a living by what we get, we make a
life by what we give.
—Winston Churchill

19

The Gravity of
the Situation

I doubt if I'll ever forget it. It was one of those images that burn
in your memory like a scene from a low-budget horror film. I
couldn't sleep for days, and if I've ever been certain of anything,
I'm certain of this: I never want to see it again.

It was early in the morning, an ordinary day—nothing
much planned except a business meeting I had to attend in
about an hour.

I curled my hair with my curling iron just as I do every
morning, then began to brush it out. Having read somewhere
that brushing your hair upside down gives it more body, I
decided to give it a try. Fat hair should be everyone's goal in
life,

right? So I bent over and brushed . . . and brushed . . . and brushed. I could feel my hair thickening with each stroke. Not being able to resist the temptation, I turned my head to the side and peeked at the mirror. I caught a glimpse of my hefty hair in all of its glory all right, but I also saw something else. I hadn't bargained for this. It was a complete shock. To this day it sends shivers up and down my spine.

What the "Ambassador of Obese Hair" forgot to mention about upside-down brushing was the fact that a woman over the age of forty should never look at herself in the mirror with her head down. If you're over forty and you bend over, all forty years bend with you, believe me. Gravity kicks in, and every fold of skin that has ever thought about becoming a wrinkle suddenly gets its wish. Your hair may look great, but your face looks like Methuselah's mother on her second week without sleep—during allergy season.

This is why when an older movie star is interviewed she tilts her head back in an unnatural position. Notice this the next time you see one on a talk show. Her head is tipped back so far you could give her a sinus exam. No doubt she's had the experience I had the day I bent over and then looked in the mirror. Stephen King may have gotten his inspiration for his last three novels after doing this himself.

I don't recall this phenomenon occurring when I was

younger. I could bend over and tie a shoe, bend over and scratch my leg, bend over and take the dishes out of the dishwasher, and my skin stayed pretty much in place. I'm sure I could look at myself in the mirror upside down or right side up and know beyond a shadow of a doubt who I was.

But the person I saw that day was someone else entirely. Someone who looked about fifty years older and a lot scarier than the right-side-up version. Thus, I've decided to stick with my anorexic hair.

I suppose it has something to do with the law of gravity. Gravity affects our whole body, skin included, and there's not much we can do about it. Areas that used to hold their own now seem to be falling faster than the stock market after an interest hike. Gravity affects men and women alike. It strikes people of every race, creed, and regional setting. You may be a northerner, but by the time you hit middle age, your body will be heading south.

For all its negative effects on the body, though, gravity does have its advantages. For one thing, it's what keeps us from floating off into outer space. And since there aren't any outlet stores on Mars, that's a good thing.

I can't retire. Who'd support my mom and dad?
—George Burns

20

All Grown Up

I distinctly remember the last Christmas my mother gave me a doll. Being a junior-higher, I considered myself much too grown up for dolls. Dolls were for little girls, not young adults. I tried to act pleased but I was more embarrassed than pleased. Couldn't Mom have given me something more appropriate to my age? Something more mature? Something like a nice sweater, a daily planner, or maybe even a pair of high heels?

After all, I had just turned thirteen. *Thirteen.* How much more grown up could I get? It was time for me to put away childish things, to move from Barbie to Bach, or at least to rock. I was growing up and needed grown-up gifts. I didn't play with dolls anymore. I hadn't played with dolls in several weeks, at least. Hadn't Mom noticed that?

I was a young adult. I wanted to be included in adult conversations about news events. I knew who the president of our country was, and I was part of the working class—I had a job babysitting twice a month. I was certain I could hold my own on any adult topic. I had even been watching TV like an adult. No more cartoons except on Saturdays and after school three or four times a week. Instead, I was tuning in to shows like *Meet the Press* and *60 Minutes*. You won't hear a single "Yabba-dabba-do" or "Th-th-that's all, folks!" on either of these award-winning programs. (OK, maybe between takes, but that's different.)

I was dressing like an adult, too. Instead of cut-off jeans and a T-shirt, I was wearing more sophisticated attire—skirts, blouses, and formal T-shirts. I was changing right before Mom's eyes, yet had she picked up on even one of the signals? Apparently not.

So there I was—holding the newly unwrapped doll in my lap and trying desperately to release the words "Thank you" from my lips. When I finally did, it wasn't very convincing.

Don't get me wrong. I realize many perfectly well adjusted adults still have dolls, and that's fine—for them. I have a lot of my dolls on display in my home, too. But at this particular point in my life I was trying desperately to be accepted into the adult world, and Mom's gift set all my efforts back an eternity, or at least a couple of years. All I wanted was to be treated as the intellectual, deep-thinking thirteen-year-old I was so certain I had become.

Mom, on the other hand, was trying her best to hang on to

the child in me. I was the youngest of her five children, her last baby, and the fact that I was growing up meant she was getting older, too. It was a truth she may not have wanted to face—not yet anyway.

None of us can control our own aging process, so we sometimes do what we can to delay the aging process of others. We think if we can just slow the clock for them, our own clock might slow down, too. We do this with TV and movie stars. We don't want to admit they're aging at all. It threatens our own youth. So through the miracle of film and videotape, we trap them in their younger days, before gray hair and gravity set in. And we make them stay there. We place an unfair burden on them to always look young, act young, and sound young, while our own aging process continues unabated.

The simple truth is we're all growing older, even those we so desperately wish wouldn't. So, yes, I forced a smile, said thank you once again, and went to my room. If she didn't want me to grow up, who was I to take that away from her?

Later that evening, after I had sufficiently displayed my dissatisfaction with the doll, at least in the privacy of my room—I took it out of its package and started playing with it. I even had fun.

I guess I didn't really want to grow up so fast, either.

YOU KNOW YOU'RE GETTING OLD WHEN ...

you find yourself wishing recliners had ejection seats.

21

A Hairy Experience

I don't know why, but for some reason, as we grow older we
start growing hair in places where hair never grew before. I'm
not sure what the medical term for this is, but I'd hazard a
guess that the words "Big Foot" are in there somewhere.

I have a hair on my cheek that can grow two inches long if
I let it. It's blond, so I can't always see it when I look in the
mirror. Most of the time my husband will notice it first.

"If you're going to keep that," he'll say, pointing at the stray
hair, "don't you think you oughta perm it?"

He's such a romantic.

There's a hair on my chin that can take a growing spurt,
too. I usually don't notice that one until it's curling itself into
my bowl of cereal.

I'm not sure why aging makes previously well mannered
hair start doing these kinds of strange things, but it does.
Maybe it's a hormone thing. Hormones like to act up at this

particular time in our lives, so if our ankles start growing side-burns, we shouldn't panic. It might just be a side effect of per-fectly normal hormonal changes.

I am actually having the opposite problem now. For some reason, when I hit thirty-five the hairs on my legs stopped growing altogether. I don't mind, of course. Shaving was always a high-risk ordeal for me. I'd end up with more cuts and slashes than a Republican budget. So who knows, not having to shave my legs may have increased my life expectancy by ten years.

The hair on my head is getting thinner, too. I first noticed something was happening when I was able to fit all of it onto one large curler. And brushing my hair out each morning was taking less and less time. Even my bangs are thinning out. They look like a little blond picket fence that's missing more posts than it started with.

Not only does the volume of our hair change as we get older but also the color. My husband's hair is almost all gray. I've been trying to get him to use a permanent hair color for men, but so far he's holding out. He thinks leaving work on Fri-day with gray hair and returning on Monday with black hair might not be as undetectable as the TV ads imply. He feels he can't explain the younger look as having simply caught up on his sleep.

Another thing that hair starts to do, especially on men, is back up, turn inward, and start to grow out of their ears. Most men don't mind. To them, hair is hair no matter where it grows. Some men even go so far as to grow out their ear hairs and comb them up over their bald spot. I think that's carrying things a bit too far. If it gets that bad, maybe they should just go ahead and shave their whole head. It didn't hurt the careers of Yul Brynner, Telly Savalas, or Michael Jordan.

My father was able to keep a full head of hair into his seventies. The hair on his head stayed put, but he developed a receding eyebrow, forcing him to color it in with an eyebrow pencil. He wasn't happy about it, but he did what he had to do. Well, guess who inherited his unnatural hair loss? I started losing my left eyebrow about a decade ago. Of all the things I could lose, I suppose an eyebrow isn't so bad. At least I can color it in. It's harder to color in a gall bladder.

No matter what color our hair is, whatever unnatural place it's started to grow, or how much of it we have left, the most important thing to remember is this: it doesn't work that well as dental floss, so try to keep it out of your cereal.

He is so old that his blood type was
discontinued.
—Bill Dana

22

A Cut Above

After grocery shopping today, I walked to my car and found an ad for the services of a plastic surgeon tucked under the left windshield wiper. I didn't take it personally. I really doubt that a plastic surgeon was lurking in the bushes waiting for a good candidate to happen along. Yet there it was in black and white—telling me how I could take five, ten, twenty years off my appearance with the mere snip of some surgical scissors.

Now, as tempting as a more youthful look sounded, the word "snip" gave me pause. I don't like that word used in conjunction with one of my body parts. Snip and clip is what we do to hedges, tree limbs, and chicken parts. We even snip and clip our hair, but it doesn't involve anesthesia, bruising, or a four-week recovery period (unless, of course, it's a really bad haircut).

But a lot of people are opting for plastic surgery these days. I guess they're not buying into the notion that wrinkles add character. They're going the snipping, clipping, reshaping, moving-this-here-and-that-there route. They rearrange their faces like some people rearrange their furniture. One thing that gets interesting is their photo Christmas cards. It's almost like going through a family album in reverse.

Plastic surgeons now offer all sorts of new procedures, so no matter what you're unhappy with, they can fix it. They can even lift the whole face, make the necessary adjustments, and reattach it again. A friend of mine had something like this done and the end result was terrific. Even so, it sounds a bit drastic for me. I'd probably get a surgeon with a sense of humor who'd put my face back on upside down to see how long it took for people to notice.

Laser surgery and chemical treatments are getting popular, too. Some of the results can be quite remarkable, but again, I'd be afraid something would go wrong. What if I ended up with a cute little chin cleft right where my nose used to be?

So, after reading the advertisement on my windshield, I tossed it on the passenger's seat and drove home. I knew I'd never call for an appointment, but I thought about calling to offer a good business tip: Leaving flyers on cars parked in grocery store parking lots isn't going to gain a lot of new clients. If this guy really wants his phone ringing off the hook, he needs to place his ad where it will get some attention: the mirrors in ladies' dressing rooms. Everyone knows that when a woman looks at herself in dressing room lighting, she always looks at least twenty years older. We forget all about the outfit we're trying on and gaze in disbelief at the decrepit stranger staring back at us in the mirror. If a plastic surgeon's business card were taped there, we might rush to the nearest pay phone. Better yet, he could move his office to the mall and save us all a lot of time and effort.

Grow old with me. The best is yet to be, the last of life, for which the first was made.
—Robert Browning

23

Old Friends

New jobs, new homes, new churches—all bring the possibilities of making new friends. And making new friends is one of the things that keeps life exciting. But there's something to be said for old friends—friends who have been there through the good and the bad: a wedding, a divorce, the births of our babies, child-rearing, illness, hospital stays, job loss, moving, birthdays, funerals. Friends who've remained close no matter how many miles have come between us. Friends who have stuck by us even when it was difficult to do so.

Some of the following may apply to new friends, too, but they definitely describe old friends.

Old friends know just when to call.
Old friends don't need an excuse to drop by.
Old friends can be trusted with secrets.
Old friends know what you're thinking even before you speak.

Old friends aren't jealous of your successes or pleased with your failures.

Even when years have passed, old friends can pick up right where they left off.

A stroll in the park, lunch, or a day of shopping—it doesn't take much to have fun with an old friend.

Old friends don't have to ask, "What can I do to help?" They just know.

Old friends don't only know the real you, they prefer it.

When disagreements arise, old friends don't have to be right.

Old friends overlook your faults instead of keeping a list of them.

Old friends treat you the same behind your back as they do when they are with you.

Old friends give you the benefit of the doubt.

Old friends have stood the test of time, time and time and time again.

Old friends are like antiques—the longer you have them, the more valuable they become.

Old friends are what friendship is all about.

YOU KNOW YOU'RE
GETTING OLD WHEN ...

your grandchild asks you to close your eyes so
she can give you a surprise, and you don't wake
up until the following afternoon.

24

Blisters, Sweat, and Tears

Exercise is important at any age, but it's especially important for those of us who are over forty. Lucky for me, there's a fully equipped state-of-the-art YMCA gym about a mile or so from my home. It has everything—rowing machines, exercise bicycles, an Olympic-size swimming pool, aerobics classes. I know this because I drive by it every night on my way to Baskin Robbins. I looked into joining it, but they suggested I wait until they opened their new Intensive Care Unit (I think that's their code name for advanced classes).

Physical exertion has never been high on my priority list, so it's a good thing I became a writer. Producers and editors don't often ask you to "drop and give me two hundred push-ups." (Well, maybe during contract negotiations, but that's all.)

Realizing the importance of exercise, I have managed to work some of it into my daily routine. Whenever possible, I take the stairs instead of the elevator, especially if I'm going down. And now I *run* to the ice cream truck instead of walking to it. It's a good workout and easier to catch up to it that way.

I enjoy bowling, which is good exercise, especially since I prefer to walk down to the pins before releasing the ball. Not only do I burn more calories this way but I also better my score.

Tennis doesn't work as well for me. I find it too difficult to keep track of the ball, and it's much too tempting to use the net as a hammock.

I've tried working out on various forms of exercise equipment, but they're not my cup of sweat, either. The idea of lifting weights doesn't appeal to me in the least. I figure carrying junk mail into the house every day and tossing it into the wastebasket gives my muscles all the workout they need.

My experience with a treadmill was less than beneficial. I had one for a while, and my cardiovascular system might have gotten a good workout on it, but my pillow kept getting stuck on the conveyor belt.

Since I don't like traditional forms of exercise, someone

once asked me if I'd ever thought about giving clogging a try. Other than my arteries, I had to say no. Clogging does appear to be a great workout, though, so I've ordered a couple of videotapes to learn how to do it. I figure if it doesn't get me into shape, at least it'd be a fun way to strip the varnish from my hardwood floors.

Walking is still one of the safest and most effective forms of exercise for those of us over forty, so I try to do a little each day. My favorite place to walk is the airport. If you've never tried it, you should check it out sometime. It's air-conditioned, you get to meet a lot of different people from all over the world, and if you walk on the moving sidewalks, you can do two miles in nothing flat.

Even though I don't exhibit much energy on the outside, in my mind I'm a workout fool. There's absolutely no exercise I can't picture myself doing. Mention aerobics, and in my mind I'm Jane Fonda. Gymnastics? I'm Mary Lou Retton. Swimming? I'm one of the lifeguards on *Baywatch*. But that's just in my head. In reality, I'm more like Aunt Bea, Grandma Moses, and one of the near-drowning victims on *Baywatch*.

One of the reasons I don't exercise is because of a bad experience I once had. Someone told me a vibrator belt was good for shaking your body into shape. You just wrap it around yourself, turn it on, and let it shake you like a bowl of Jell-O. It sounded simple enough. Besides, they also said it would help get rid of my cellulite, so I decided to give it a try. I used it on my hips and my legs, and when they suggested I try it on my arms, I gave those a good shaking, too. It worked, but not in the way I had imagined.

When I woke up the next morning, I looked in the mirror and noticed something odd, something very different from the firm image I expected. For some reason, all my upper arm fat had slid down to my elbows. There were huge indentations in my upper arms—sinkholes, if you will—that dipped almost to the bone. I had fat-free upper arms and elbows the size of swim floats. In short, I looked like Popeye. The cellulite didn't go away, it just went south for the winter.

I made an appointment with Dr. Robert Rood, my longtime physician, who after a thorough examination explained that it was some sort of medical oddity. People have used vibrator belts for years, and he had never seen anything like this.

After two years of stares, questions from curious people, and, of course, the Popeye references, I awoke one morning to discover that my upper arm fat had mysteriously returned to where it came from. It had been two long years, but now the fat was back in its rightful place, along with the cellulite, but this time I decided to leave well enough alone.

The rest of my body could still use some work, though.

And since I'm in my forties, I figure it's time to make those changes. It's time to develop an exercise program and stick with it. It's time to . . . I'll get back to this later. I think I just heard the ice cream truck.

You are never too old to set another goal or to dream a new dream.
—Les Brown

25

You're So Vein

My varicose veins are starting to spell out my name. Not my whole name, of course, just my initials. The *M* is pretty easy to make out, and right now the *B* looks more like a *P*, but it's well on its way. I'm just waiting for the people from *Ripley's Believe It or Not!* to contact me, and I'll be rolling in the dough. Unless, of course, someone else has already beat me to it.

A lot of people over forty have varicose veins. Some even have what they call "spider veins"—the network of veins that look a lot like a spider web. I don't have spider veins yet. I guess God figures I have enough webs around my house to deal with—why make me wear them, too?

My mother had varicose veins. I'm sure there was a medical reason for them, but I personally attributed her condition to the fact that she worked at a department store and was on her feet most of the day. It doesn't seem fair, does it? Hard work should result in a strong heart, good muscle tone, and healthy lungs, not the alphabet suddenly appearing on your calves.

Today there are various treatments for varicose veins, some simple, others more extensive. So far, I think I'll keep mine. They don't actually hurt, and, lucky for me, the blue stripes only clash with a few of my outfits.

I've got so many liver spots I should come
with a side of onions.
—Phyllis Diller

26

Where's Your Drive?

I don't believe age should be a determining factor in issuing a driver's license. One's driving skill, reflexes, and knowledge of the highway laws are what should be held up to scrutiny. Age is nothing more than a number.

At the age of seventy, my mother scored 100 percent on her driving test. She was an excellent driver who preferred to drive in the slow lane whenever possible. When making left turns, her motto was "If you wait long enough, it'll eventually be clear." Having to drive the streets of Los Angeles, this motto often kept us waiting at intersections into the night, but Mother was emphatic. Whenever risk could be avoided, she avoided it.

The rules of the road have changed so much lately, I wonder if she'd even pass the test today, much less get another perfect score. Remember the good ol' days when the potential answers to a question like "What do you do when someone is tailgating you?" used to be: (a) slow down, (b) swerve to avoid his hitting you, or (c) gently honk your horn? There wasn't any (d) draw a gun on him, or (e) pull over and beat him to a pulp.

The test is more difficult because of so many societal changes, but as I said, age shouldn't be a determining factor in driver's license renewal. If, however, any of the following apply to you, you might want to consider voluntarily surrendering yours.

IT MIGHT BE TIME TO GIVE UP YOUR DRIVER'S LICENSE IF . . .

- you've ever waited in an intersection through three or more light changes before making your left turn;
- you consider the raised median your personal driving lane;
- you've ever worn out a new brake light on a two-mile trip to the store;
- you refer to going thirty-five miles per hour as "flooring it";
- you've ever honked at a pedestrian and said the words, "Move it, buddy! You think you own the sidewalk?";
- a tractor has passed you on the freeway, and it was being pushed;
- you've ever used a stoplight to get in a short nap;

- you've ever made more than three U-turns within a single block;
- you've driven for more than twenty-five miles with your left turn signal on;
- you've ever tried to report a fire truck for tailgating you.

You're only as old as you feel . . . and I don't
feel anything until noon. Then it's
time for my nap.
—Bob Hope

27

Beside Myself

I don't like the idea of my skin cells dying every day. I suppose it's perfectly natural; it happens to everybody. We do grow new ones, but it still seems a bit morbid.

What is it that's killing them off anyway? Are they looking at themselves in the mirror every morning and committing suicide? (If you saw how I looked in the morning, you might not blame them.) Whatever it is that's making them die off, shouldn't we be doing something about it? Oh, I realize there are facial masks, skin cleansers, astringents, and all sorts of other skin care products on the market that supposedly do a good job of removing dead skin cells, but I'm talking about something a bit more organized.

Perhaps we could hold fund-raisers or weekend telethons. After all, this is a problem affecting the entire human race. I know I'd rather not have to worry about thousands of cells falling off my body every day and forming a microscopic pile at my feet. If I could save one skin cell from an untimely death, it would be worth whatever work it took to achieve that goal.

But it's hard getting others to feel equally passionate about my cause. All they want to do is scrub dead cells off and let them slide down the drain rather than do anything to save them. I once knew a lady who got so into scrubbing dead cells from her face, she actually drew blood. Obviously she went a bit overboard. She probably took out some cells that were merely in critical condition. I'm sure her intentions were good, but someone needed to tell her there's nothing attractive about raw flesh.

Skin is a good thing. It helps people recognize us, and it keeps the dust out of our vital organs. Even as I'm writing this, though, my own skin cells are continuing to die despite all my efforts to intervene.

I suppose one day they'll try cloning new human beings from dead skin cells. Scientists have already taken the DNA of sheep and cloned exact replicas. Not that I'm saying it's the morally correct thing to do, but there has been a lot of experimentation going on lately. I don't know about you, but I wouldn't want an exact replica of me walking around, especially one that looks younger than I do! And who's to say the clone wouldn't start charging up all my credit cards? Or worse yet,

charging *less* than I do? My husband might want to trade me in
for the cheaper model.

No matter how much a clone may look like us, though, it
can never actually *be* us. For one thing, it wouldn't have our life
experiences, and knowing what we do, we'd want to save it
from every difficult situation it might have to face. But it's the
unique combination of both the difficult times and the happy
times in our lives that have made us who we are. So instead of
having another "you" running around, all you'd get in a clone is
a shallow look-alike.

That's why if my skin cells have to die I'd rather they stay
dead. I hate to lose them, but they did their tour of duty. They
were faithful to a point, and now it's time for them to say their
farewells and go to that big loofah sponge in the sky.

Age should not have its face lifted, but it should
rather teach the world to admire wrinkles as the
etchings of experience and the firm
line of character.
—Ralph B. Perry

28

Happy Birthday to Me

Birthday parties are fun, but they remind us that . . . well, you know—we're getting older. Most of us loved celebrating our birthdays when we were two, eight, sixteen, and even twenty-one. But when we get past forty, we might not want to be reminded of the number of years we've lived.

Surprise birthday parties can be deadly the older you get. Imagine poor Grandpa walking into the kitchen on the evening of his ninety-ninth birthday. All he wants is that slice of apple pie he's had his eye on all week. He doesn't suspect a thing, and with his impaired eyesight, he certainly can't see the shadows of eighteen people hiding under the counter. He feels along the

wall, turns the lights on, and all of a sudden hears, "Surprise!!"
The rest of the story can be read in the coroner's report.

Then there are the gifts. Ah, the gifts. After forty, you no
longer receive gifts that you really want. Unbeknownst to you,
you've suddenly crossed over into a different realm, you've
entered into what is known as *The Medical Gift Zone*. You're getting things like medical dictionaries, callous removers, and bas-
kets filled with an assortment of Bengay products.

I suppose to a certain extent it's understandable. After all,
nothing says "I love you" like a blood pressure cuff or one of
those new at-home cholesterol tests.

When my husband turned forty, the only thing he wanted
for his birthday was a full body scan. He didn't have a single
symptom, but if something was getting ready to go haywire, he
didn't want to be the last to know about it. His reasoning was
this: What good is a new power tool if your triglycerides are on
a roller coaster ride? A new tie means nothing to someone
whose thyroid gland is about to poop out.

A full body scan was what he wanted, and it was my duty
as a wife to get it for him. But you can't just go to aisle 14 at
Kroger's and pick up one. And if you go to a hospital to buy
one, they'll tell you you need a doctor's order.

So I got him a tie . . . and a doctor's appointment. I do want
to keep him around for a lot more years. I want to be able to

watch him blow out seventy, eighty, or even ninety candles.

It's funny, isn't it? The older we get, the more candles we're expected to blow out. If you ask me, it should be turned around. At our first birthday party, there should be eighty candles to blow out. We've got breath then. We're full of energy and should be able to handle it without having oxygen on standby. Then we could start removing the candles, one per year. That way, by the time we reach eighty we'd have only one candle left to blow out. And if that's too much, we could call in a tag team.

Live your life and forget your age.
—Norman Vincent Peale

29

The Good Ol' Days

If you've lived more than forty years, chances are you've seen a lot of changes. In my lifetime I've seen the advent of the personal computer, the information highway, e-mail, the fax machine, the cell phone, space travel, and pet rocks.

I've seen changes in clothing, too. I've watched bell-bottoms come into style, go out of style, and come back in again. I've seen torn and holey jeans graduate from being a financial statement to a fashion one. I've seen hemlines go up, down, and even shred themselves.

I've seen hairstyles go from long to short to blue to purple to spiked to bald. And that's just the women.

Body piercing used to be something you only saw in *National Geographic* or when you accidentally pierced yourself putting on a new shirt before taking out all the straight pins. Now some people are piercing every body part they can think of. I don't get it. I had two amniocenteses done while pregnant with my last child, and that was all the body piercing I needed for a lifetime.

I've witnessed a lot of changes on the political scene, too. I've seen a president impeached, a president resign, a president assassinated, and one lose his meal in a dignitary's lap at an overseas state dinner.

We've traveled to the moon and had plenty of public figures we'd like to send there.

I've watched dissatisfied, unfulfilled stay-at-home moms join the work force and dissatisfied career women quit their jobs to become stay-at-home moms.

I've seen dads become Mr. Moms when they realized that their children are only young once.

I've seen good changes and some that weren't so good. Changes we've fought against and plenty we've had to learn to accept. But if life is about anything, it's about change. We don't have a choice in that. We do, however, have a choice as to how much *we* change with it.

In three words I can sum up everything I've
learned about life: It goes on.
—Robert Frost

30

Extra! Extra!

I've stopped reading the newspaper. Not all of it. Just certain parts of it. OK, just *one* part of it—the "obit" column, otherwise known as the obituaries. Most of the news ruins my day anyway, but the obituary column can ruin it the fastest.

The problem is this: instead of reading the deceased's name, accomplishments, and who they are survived by, my eyes are immediately drawn to their age. I can't help it.

I've talked to other people who do the same thing. If the age of the deceased is anywhere near our own age, give or take twenty years, we spend the rest of the day wondering what it was that took the person. If the poor guy walked in front of a bus and was run over, then we'll be more careful the next time we cross the street, but we won't lose sleep over it. If he slipped at the grocery store, slid into a giant pyramid of canned pinto beans, and was hit square in the temple with the jumbo-sized one, causing a massive brain hemorrhage, we'll feel bad and probably skip that aisle the next time we go grocery shopping, but we're not going to become paranoid over it.

But if they're dropping like flies from things that could easily strike us, too, then we start to worry. That pain in our back suddenly becomes cancer instead of the muscle strain the doctor told us it was. The discomfort in our chest that comes right after eating that fifth slice of sausage, onion, and bell pepper pizza becomes the heart attack we're sure is going to take us. Don't get me wrong. Any persistent symptom should be checked out by your physician, but sometimes we write ourselves off when we've still got plenty of life left.

Personally, I don't want to go until I'm 110. It sounds like the perfect age to leave this world. You've seen it all. You've had fun. It's time to move on. No one talks about a 110-year-old man or woman being "struck down in the prime of life." You won't hear phrases like "It was so sudden. Nobody saw it coming." At 110, everyone sees it coming. You're wearing a sweatshirt that says, "Life—Been There, Done That." You're probably on your third heart and fourth kidney by then.

But the majority of those listed in the obituary column aren't over 100. Most of them are substantially younger than that. That's why I've quit reading it.

One obituary recently caught my eye, though. It was that of Sarah Knauss, who died on December 30, 1999, at the tender young age of 119. Her daughter, Kathryn Sullivan, ninety-six, attributed her mother's longevity to the fact that she was a tranquil person. Nothing could faze her.

So maybe that's the secret to longevity. That and a good sense of humor. George Burns, who also made it past his 100th birthday, used to say that every morning he'd get up and read the obituary column. If his name wasn't there, he'd make breakfast.

According to the U.S. Census Bureau, by the year 2050 the number of people over the age of 100 will be nearly 834,000. That's pretty encouraging. Just imagine all the things you could do if you lived to be over 100 years of age. You could wait until you're fifty to get married and still live long enough to celebrate your golden wedding anniversary (that is, if your spouse lived that long, too). You could put off college until your forties, then get your doctorate and still put in a fifty-year career. You could attend your eightieth high school reunion and take any seat you wanted. You'd probably have to dance by yourself, and your class photo might be of you and the waiter, but you could still have a great time.

Do you realize that at 100 years of age, you could conceivably see the birth of your great-great-great-great-grandchild? What kind of gift do you buy a great-great-great-great-grandchild?

By the time you reach 100, you could have cashed in three consecutive thirty-year bonds and paid off three thirty-year mortgages.

If you live to be 100, chances are you've outlived your parents, your siblings, your doctors, most of your friends, and a lot of your enemies. Your diary would read like a history book, and you wouldn't have any elders to look up to except God.

So if you're lucky enough to live as long as Sarah, or even George, don't just sit there reading the obituary column every morning, wondering whether or not you should get up and make breakfast. Put on your in-line skates and roll on down to the Waffle House.

If I had my life to live over again, I wouldn't have the time.
—Bob Hope

31

Aka Doughgirl

Lately my cheeks have been looking puffy. I look like the CBS eye—with hair. I don't know why I'm filling out this way. The fact that I've gained fifteen pounds could have something to do with it, I suppose, but I'm not a doctor.

Maybe I got bit by something. Insect bites can make you swell. Or maybe it's an allergic reaction. I could have been allergic to that box of Krispy Kreme donuts I ate the other night.

The thing I don't understand about weight gain is why it takes place in just one or two parts of your anatomy. For some people, it's the hips; for others, it's the stomach; for me, it's the cheeks . . . What's going on? Do all our fat cells gather together in one place and hold meetings? Do they send messages to each other like "Union meeting today, right hip, two o'clock. Be there"? I'm pretty sure my fat cells held a meeting there last week while I was busy eating at an all-you-can-eat buffet. After that third plate, I glanced down at my right hip and it looked like a 100 percent turnout! In fact, it looked like they might have been holding a regional convention.

The way my cheeks have puffed up, I have a feeling they're gathering for the Million Man Fat Cell March. But why my cheeks? If they really felt the need to congregate somewhere, why didn't they go where my body could use some added cells? I have a few suggestions, and I'd be more than happy to direct them there, but so far I haven't been able to figure out how to crash one of their meetings.

In the meantime, if CBS ever needs a double for its logo, they know where to find me.

Life is a great big canvas, and you should throw
all the paint on it you can.
—Danny Kaye

32

Impatiently Ever After

We don't only lose hair and teeth as we grow older, many of us start losing our patience. We just don't put up with as much as we used to. That's why you hear about so many "grouchy old men" or "cranky old ladies." By the time you're sixty or seventy years old, you've had enough. You don't always know what it is you've had enough of, you just know you've had enough of it.

Traffic jams never used to bother me. Now I find myself wishing I had multiple personalities so I could at least drive in the carpool lane.

Slow food service didn't affect me either. But lately I've noticed when my husband takes me to our favorite romantic restaurant, I start honking the minute I don't think their drive-thru lane is moving fast enough.

Perhaps you can identify with what I'm saying. When you're

reading *Snow White and the Seven Dwarfs* for the fourth time to your grandchild, do you find yourself editing the story down to *Snow White and the Four Dwarfs* just to get it over with sooner? Have you been making Cinderella leave the ball by ten o'clock just because *you* can't stay awake until midnight? Has Little Red Riding Hood had to take a taxi to grandmother's house rather than waste time walking through the forest?

If the answer is yes to any of the above, your patience level has reached the danger zone. You can help yourself by (1) buying shorter books to read to your grandchildren, and (2) avoiding things that could possibly make your blood pressure rise. These include but are not limited to . . .

- political campaign speeches;
- people who never put their cell phone down;
- telemarketer calls during dinner;
- broken postage stamp machines;
- businesses that refuse to put you through to a live person no matter how many buttons you press;
- dogs who perform barking concerts at two in the morning;
- closed-minded people who refuse to agree with you no matter how many times you tell them you're right;
- people you let cut in front of you who are so impressed

with your kindness they let twelve people cut in front of them, too;

- door-to-door salesmen who spend more time on your porch than the family cat;
- relatives or friends who only seem to remember your phone number when they need a favor.

The list of things that cause us to lose our patience continues to grow with each passing year. But there are a few things left that most of us can still be patient about. For one thing, I don't have any problem with my dentist taking as long as he needs before calling my name—I could wait for hours and never complain. I'm never in a hurry for April 15 to roll around either. And those February deferred credit card statements? They could arrive in August and you wouldn't hear a peep out of me.

So you see, impatience doesn't have to be an inevitable result of aging. It's up to us whether or not we slow down and enjoy life to the fullest. The sun is going to continue to rise and set at the same speed every day no matter what. So relax and enjoy.

I love long walks, especially when taken by
people who annoy me.
—Fred Allen

33

Life of the Party

I used to be the life of the party at amusement parks. I don't know what happened, but I'm no fun anymore. I know this because everyone else brings home souvenir pictures of themselves on the newest roller coaster ride, right in the middle of the upside-down triple loop. I bring home souvenir pictures of me on one of the stationary animals on the carousel.

It's not that I don't want to ride the roller coaster. I do. I used to ride all those wild rides, but the older I get, the more safety-minded I've become. You can get hurt on a roller coaster, for heaven's sake. Sure, millions ride them every day, and there have been only a few incidences of a person falling out, but it could happen. If I'm riding the roller coaster, I really don't want to end up in the sky buckets. You have a much better time when you get off the same ride you got on.

My day at an amusement park usually goes something like this:

9:00 A.M.—Arrive at park. Discuss renting locker. Everyone convinces me we don't need one.

9:15 A.M.—Buy tickets.

9:30 A.M.—Restroom break

9:40 A.M.—Pass on virtual reality ride. Afraid shaking
might throw my back out.

9:55 A.M.—Walk by log ride. Decide to pass. Getting wet
could give me a chill. Hold jackets and cameras of family and friends (the same ones who
said we didn't need a locker) while they go on
log ride.

10:33 A.M.—Snack break

11:05 A.M.—Walk by roller coaster. Hold jackets, cameras,
and cups of soda of family and friends while
they ride roller coaster.

11:58 A.M.—Lunch break

12:48 P.M.—Ride train after conductor guarantees in writing
that the ride only moves in a forward direction
and absolutely no water is involved.

1:36 P.M.—Restroom break

2:00 P.M.—Stop at souvenir store. Insert quarter and use
the electric foot massage machine. Get a little
dizzy, but it's worth it.

3:05 P.M.—Walk by spinning teacups. Pass on spinning
teacups (I forgot my Dramamine). Hold jackets, cameras, cups of soda, and bags of souve-

nirs of family and friends while they ride spinning teacups.

3:45 P.M.—Restroom break

4:00 P.M.—See stage show. Try to convince family and friends that it should count as a ride since a slight aftershock hit while we were there, but they don't buy it.

6:10 P.M.—Dinner break

7:35 P.M.—Ride bumper cars

7:45 P.M.—Still trying to figure out how to get my car to move.

8:11 P.M.—Restroom break

8:25 P.M.—Hold jackets, cameras, souvenirs, and doggie bags of friends and family while they ride dinosaur ride. I pass on the ride. (I watched *Jurassic Park* one too many times.)

9:30 P.M.—Walk by lockers on our way back to the car. Family and friends remind me how smart we were to not waste our fifty cents on a locker.

10:45 P.M.—Arrive home. Sit in vibrating recliner. It's exhilarating, free, and I didn't even have to wait in line for it.

To err is human. To forgive is simply
not our policy.
—Source unknown

34

Is There a Doctor in the House?

There's nothing that'll make a person feel older than having to deal with a young professional. The older we get, the younger pilots, police officers, lawyers, and doctors look. Especially doctors. I don't know about you, but I feel uncomfortable going to a doctor who has a Scooby Doo sticker on his residency certificate.

But regardless of how young he looks, we still see him regularly. Why is this? Because medical care is important to us. It's important at any age, but it's especially important as we get older. We're hoping to hold up, but just as a car needs repairs and replacement parts as it ages, so do our bodies. We could be chugging along fine on our factory-installed original equipment, but after those first one hundred thousand miles or so, things could start to go haywire. Our battery doesn't charge like it used to, our fan belt gets a little frayed, and we might even discover a crack in our engine block. And if that's not bad enough, we can develop an embarrassing leak in our transmission. We need help, maybe even a complete overhaul.

Fortunately, I've only had a few things go wrong with my engine over the years. I've had a couple of benign breast cysts removed, some laser surgeries performed on my eyes, and my pancreas needs a little help to work properly. Other than that, I haven't had to spend too much time in the pit, and for that I'm thankful.

But since ours is the age when things can start to go wrong, good health insurance is important. If you don't have private insurance, chances are you have an HMO. I've had both. One thing I've learned about HMOs is that they aren't all the same. Some are terrific and are equipped to meet whatever medical need might arise. Others fall short of the mark.

To aid you in your search for a good HMO, the following list is provided:

YOU KNOW YOU'VE JOINED A CHEAP HMO WHEN . . .

- Resetting a bone involves duct tape.

- For a second opinion, they refer you to last week's episode of *ER*.

- Their EKG machine bears a striking resemblance to an Etch A Sketch.

- Their IV solution looks an awful lot like Kool-Aid.

- They get their X rays developed at Walgreen's.

- They recycle their tongue depressors.

- You get a discount if you make up your own hospital bed.

- Their ambulance rents itself out as an airport shuttle on the off-hours.

- Their thermometer reads to 400 degrees and tastes an awful lot like turkey.

- Their mammogram machine doubles as the waffle iron in the hospital cafeteria.

All the flowers of all the tomorrows are in
the seeds of today.
—Source unknown

35

It's All in the Attitude

Getting older is beyond our control. No matter how much we'd like to, we can't stop time from marching on. However, *growing old* is something we can control. That's where attitude enters in.

When we look in the mirror, we can either see a life that's half over or a life that's half begun. We can spend all our time dwelling on the mistakes of our past or we can spend it focused on the hope of the future. We can count our wrinkles or count our blessings. The choice is ours.

It's been said that we live the first half of our life for success and the second half for significance. I agree. In our twenties and thirties, most of us were consumed with our careers, attaining financial stability, and perhaps raising a family.

By the time we reach the second half of our life, our priorities change—or at least they should. Many of us have had to watch our parents' health decline or fail. At this juncture, we are forced to face the cruel reality that our time on this earth is limited. When we fully realize this, the reports and meetings that seemed so important and pressing suddenly lose their urgency. We spend less time thinking about the mortgage on our home and more about the people in it.

When I was driving my mother to her chemotherapy treatments, she would often remark about the flowers along the side of the road. She noticed them as if for the first time. Of course, she'd driven that road many times before, and the flowers were there each spring, but she wasn't looking at them then. She was usually on her way to work and had a host of other things on her mind. Now, battling cancer, she appreciated their beauty to the fullest.

The second half of life is a chance to get our priorities straight. It's a time to realize that having the last word isn't as important as having a conversation. It's time to quit trying so hard to get ahead of the Joneses and to try a little harder to walk beside them and be their friends. It's time to realize that it's not going to matter how much money you leave your family when you die. What is important is how much of yourself you leave with them.

By the time you're eighty years old, you've learned everything. You only have to remember it.

—George Burns

36

I'm My Own Grandma

There's an old country song titled "I'm My Own Grandpa." If my memory serves me correctly, it's about a man whose relatives have married people they're already related to by law—in-laws, stepparents, step-siblings, etc., eventually making him his own legal grandfather.

Now, while the story in the song may be highly unlikely, there's another way to become one's own grandfather, grandmother, mother, or father. Just live long enough.

They say as we grow older, we begin to look and act like those who've gone on before. My sister, Melva, is becoming my mother right before my eyes. Not only does she look like her, she has her expressions and even sounds like her. I wish she would have sounded like her years ago when I was in high school, then when my teachers called the house, they could have talked to Melva instead of Mom and I wouldn't have gotten grounded so often.

One of my mother's favorite sayings was "Food takes the place of sleep." There's absolutely no official documentation to this, but Mom said it as though it were the latest finding of the American Medical Association. She honestly believed that if you had to work late, a meal was as good as a nap. (Maybe that's why I gained those fifteen pounds.)

My sister says things like that now. She reacts to situations as Mother would have, is a hard worker, and has a heart for others. She may not be her own grandpa, but in so many ways she has become her own mother.

I don't remember seeing my mother in my sister in her younger years. When my sister was a teenager, she was just Melva. Even in her twenties she was Melva. She didn't start turning into Mom until recently. The forties seem to be about the time this phenomenon hits. We're going along fine, being our own person, and then one day we look in the mirror and are suddenly struck with the image of one of our parents staring back at us.

I have some of the characteristics of both my parents. I've already mentioned that I inherited my father's eyebrows, but I also have his sense of humor. I have my mom's appreciation for a good joke, her smile—slightly tilted to one side—and I have her almond-shaped blue eyes. Both of my parents were tall with high cheekbones, and I've inherited those qualities, as well. But the person I believe I'm starting to look like the most is my maternal grandmother. I have a picture of her over our bed, and the resemblance between the two of us is becoming more apparent with each passing day.

When you get down to it, we're all a combination of all our ancestors. We might have our father's nose, our mother's eyes, our grandmother's ears, and our great-grandfather's chin. Depending on our family, this could be a good or a bad combination. Yet no matter what physical characteristics we've been blessed with, or stuck with, our inner qualities are what are most important. In other words, heirs should be more grateful for the good judgment they inherited from their father, the gentle spirit they got from their mother, the sense of fairness that was passed down from their grandfather, and the self-esteem imparted to them from their grandmother than they are for whatever physical characteristics they may have inherited.

For the things which are seen are temporal, but
the things which are not seen are eternal.
—2 Corinthians 4:18 KJV

37

When You've Got It, You've Got It

I couldn't believe the nerve of this guy. Had he no manners? Didn't he realize his Neanderthal behavior wasn't appreciated in the least? Did he not know he was being obnoxious and making a scene? Couldn't he see that I had a cell phone and could call 9-1-1 at a moment's notice?

Perhaps I should start at the beginning. It happened at the post office near my house. I had driven there to mail a letter, and as soon as I got out of my car, he started howling and making wolf calls at me. They were loud, they were rude, and they were annoying.

I walked to the post office entrance, trying my best to

ignore his junior high behavior, but it was becoming increasingly more difficult.

"Grrrowwwwooofff!" he howled loud enough for anyone within a two-block radius to hear. "Grrrowwwwooofff! Grrrowwwwooffff!" The guy was pathetic.

Finally, I'd just had it. I was ready to give him a piece of my mind or at least shoot him a look that said exactly what that piece of my mind was thinking. But when I turned to glare in his direction, I saw something totally unexpected. That howling wasn't coming from a man. It was coming from a dog—a very large dog upset about being left in a very small car.

I was laughing so hard at myself when I stepped into the post office, the clerks must have thought they had another crazed lunatic on their hands. But I couldn't help it. Here I had thought I was attracting the unwanted advances of a man, when I was merely attracting the attention of a canine who only wanted his freedom. No wonder they say it's not a good idea to jump to conclusions. How we interpret a situation might have very little to do with reality.

So now when I hear someone make some sort of verbal advance at me, I turn to look before I start judging. After all, the next whistle I hear might be coming from a parrot, and it's not easy to press harassment charges against fowl.

YOU KNOW YOU'RE GETTING OLD WHEN ...

you need a running start to go for a walk.

38

Plenty to Smile About

The ad read, "Do your teeth make you look ten years older than you really are?" Now, *there's* a side effect of aging I hadn't even considered.

The advertisement went on to say that as we age our teeth can darken, our gums recede, and our breath start smelling like last week's laundry. I guess wrinkles and age spots weren't enough, now our teeth have to get into the act.

And what's this about receding gums? Why would they want to do a thing like that? There's nothing honorable in receding. Can't they hold on for another twenty or thirty years and then retreat?

None of it seems quite fair, does it? After all the attention we've given our teeth all these years, when we need them most, they're going to start jumping ship one by one.

From as far back as I can remember, my father wore a full set of dentures. I know this because whenever he sneezed they'd fly out of his mouth and land some ten feet away. I don't know if there's ever been an Olympic event for this, but if there were, he would have taken home the gold.

My father even made his own denture repairs. If they didn't fit just right (which was obvious since they were on the frequent-flyer program), he'd heat them over the kitchen stove, remolding them to whatever size or shape was needed. My father was creative that way. He probably could have set up a business fixing dentures for other people, but we lived in a residential area and I doubt if he could have gotten a zoning permit.

But Dad's philosophy was why pay for dental work when you could just as easily do it yourself? Luckily, he didn't have the same attitude when he had to have his appendix removed. I don't think our butter knives could have done the job.

I'm not sure if I'd like having to wear dentures. There's something about putting your teeth in a glass at night and waking up to their smiling back at you that's unsettling. It's a little Stephen King-ish, if you know what I mean.

Darkening teeth and receding gums aren't the only mouth problems we have to be concerned about as we grow older. Over the years my jaw has developed a malady known as TMJ. Because of this condition, my jaw makes a popping sound whenever I eat. Sometimes the popping is so loud a seven-course meal can sound like a reggae concert. One of these days I might look into getting my jaw fixed, but until then I'm still looking to land a recording contract.

We should never allow ourselves to fall into the trap of thinking we're too old to correct mouth or dental problems, however. Some people in their forties or fifties are getting braces for the first time. They're correcting something that has bothered them for years. Too often by the time we reach middle age we tell ourselves, why bother? We figure if we've put up with something this long, why not put up with it for the rest of our lives? That's limited thinking. No matter how old we are, chances are we still have some good years left, so why settle for dingy teeth, receding gums, or loose-fitting dentures?

We should all do what we can to improve our smiles. After all, it's one of the most important aspects of our appearance.

Do not worry, saying, "What shall we eat?" or "What shall we drink?" or "What shall we wear?" . . . your heavenly Father knows that you need them.
—Matthew 6:31–32 NIV

39

Seasons

Growing up in the Los Angeles area, I didn't really get to experience the changes of seasons. The only variation we had was going from wearing long sleeves in winter to short sleeves in spring to no sleeves in summer to three-quarter sleeves in the fall. The only big changes in our weather reports were the jokes.

When I moved to Tennessee, I finally got to see what a real change of seasons looks like. It snows in Tennessee—just enough to remind you that the white stuff exists. After a few months the winter cold gives way to spring with all the dogwoods blooming in bright splashes of pink and white. Summer has a different kind of beauty, with more shades of green than you could imagine. To me, the most beautiful of all seasons here is the fall. I think no matter where I might live in the future, I'd always want to spend some of the fall in Tennessee. The drive from Nashville to the Smoky Mountains is breathtaking. It's as though someone came along and aerial-sprayed barrels of orange, yellow, red, and brown paint all over the countryside.

Being over forty is like being in the fall of your life.

Spring, of course, is the time when new life is birthed, and one can't help but be filled with anticipation for what each new day will bring. It's a period of firsts: the first smile, the first tooth, the first steps, and the first time to shave the cat. A few bruises are earned learning to walk, words are jumbled learning to talk, and a few plates of spaghetti are dumped learning to eat, but eventually these tasks are mastered and one moves on.

The summer of life—the teenage–young adult years—is full of fun and wonder. You experience life on a new level, making your own decisions and having to live with the outcomes. Life is an adventure, and you want to enjoy every minute of it. You might stumble once in a while getting your footing, but you've been around long enough to realize the importance of getting up and trying again.

Fall is the season of change—in nature and in life. Your children are moving out and going away to college or getting married and having children of their own. You might be changing jobs or retiring, downsizing your home, reevaluating your priorities, and altering your opinions on a thing or two. Age tends to mellow all but the most closed-minded individual.

Winter is a time for reflection, a time to look back and smile about the good times and assess what you've learned from the not-so-good times. A tree doesn't fear when winter's coming. It doesn't lower its head and cry because most of its leaves have dried up and fallen off. (OK, maybe a weeping willow cries in winter, but it probably has other issues it's dealing with.)

A tree knows that every season of its life is equally beautiful. That's why it stands just as proudly in the fall as in the spring. It's content no matter what the season. It doesn't try to change its fall colors into summer colors or wear its spring colors after autumn has set in. It takes each season as it comes and appreciates its beauty for what it is.

We could learn a lot from a tree.

There are only two ways to live your life. One is as though nothing is a miracle. The other is as though everything is a miracle.
—Albert Einstein

40

The Search

I tried killing a spider today. I squashed it three times with my shoe but it bounced right back. That's when I realized it was a dust ball.

I think my age is starting to affect my eyesight.

Mistaking a dust ball for a spider may be a more common occurrence than one might think. I'm sure many middle-agers have made the same incorrect assessment. Mistaking a dust ball for a cat, however, would not only mean I need a new pair of glasses but also the entire crew of Molly Maids.

A good friend of mine warned me that sometime after forty my eyesight would change. He said I would be reading the newspaper, a magazine, or a book and all of a sudden the letters would start running together. "Congress passes tax cut" would become "Fuphmfi hkswop ruilizhs." Either version would still be hard to believe.

My friend was right, though. Once I hit forty, my vision did change, and it seemingly happened overnight. I went to bed with 20/20 vision, and by breakfast I couldn't read the morning paper unless someone was holding it ten feet away.

OK, it's not quite that bad, but I am up to a 2 percent magnification in drugstore glasses. My optometrist is the one who recommended I buy my glasses at the drugstore. He told me if 2 percent was all the magnification I needed, why not spend $10 instead of $100? I like my optometrist. Of course, he's one of the last medical professionals still driving a Pacer.

My biggest problem with glasses is remembering to keep them with me. I've left them at work, at church, at restaurants, at department stores, at gas stations. The most common place I leave them, though, is on top of my head. I can never find them there. It's the last place I look.

What I want to know is why we don't lose other things on top of our head. When's the last time you saw someone walking around with a curling iron on her head, looking for her curling iron? Or her brush. Or a football helmet. That's because you usually don't forget when those things are up there. The curling iron is a bit unwieldy, a brush might be a possibility, but a football helmet? Well, you'd just know. So why is it so easy to lose our glasses up there? I guess it's just one of those unexplained phenomena of life.

I should probably buy one of those little dishes they make

especially for glasses. You know, the ones that say something clever like "Here they are, stupid." But I'm afraid a dish to hold my glasses would be just as easy to misplace.

Maybe they should start equipping eyeglasses with tracking devices. Then as soon as we realize our glasses are missing, we could call a central number, report the disappearance, and within seconds our glasses would start beeping.

Of course, if they are on top of your head, all the beeping could really give you a migraine.

I would never have amounted to anything were it not for adversity.
—J. C. (James Cash) Penney

41

Scars

Most of us don't make it through life without a few scars. Over the years we've scraped a knee or two, maybe even broken a few bones. Life, though full of wonder and excitement, also comes with its share of pain.

When our youngest son was just two years old, he had to undergo two separate heart surgeries. The first was to repair what is called a patent ductus; the second was open-heart surgery to repair a ventricular septal defect.

After the first surgery was performed successfully, the doctor informed me in the Intensive Care Unit that the second surgery needed to be done within a few weeks. I wasn't prepared for that news. We had just made it through one grueling ordeal and now we were going to turn around and do it all over again. I had been hoping for more of a breather. I couldn't understand why the second surgery couldn't wait for at least a year or so.

One of the reasons the medical team felt they couldn't wait any longer than a few weeks was the fact that adhesions would start to form after the first surgery and these make a second incision more difficult. So we braced up for the second go-around in a few short weeks. Thankfully it was the right decision and all went well.

Did you know that the emotional wounds we suffer in life can also form adhesions around them? These make it difficult for help to get through—not impossible, however. God's love can cut through even the toughest scars.

If you've been scarred by an abusive or controlling parent, sibling, spouse, or even a friend, or if you've suffered some other traumatic incident in your life, chances are you've developed some adhesions to protect that wounded area. These may prevent further injury, but they also keep you from making repairs on the inside. In this second half of your life, maybe it's time to allow God to do what he does best—cut through those adhesions and mend your heart and spirit. The longer you wait, the tougher the scars become.

An unexamined life is not worth living.

—Socrates

42

Hold Your Tongue

I remember the very first time someone called me "ma'am." I was only in my twenties, but it felt like I had just been wished a happy birthday by Willard Scott.

Until that night, I had always been referred to as "girl," "hon," "sweetie," maybe even an occasional "Hey, you!" But now I was being called ma'am. *Ma'am*. There's no way to put a youthful spin on ma'am.

"Lady" is about as bad. The first time I heard "lady" in reference to me was jarring, too.

"Hey, lady, do you know that's wet cement you just parked in?"

I looked around. *Surely he can't be talking to me*, I thought. I was no lady. I was a *girl*. But since he was looking straight at me, and since my car did indeed seem to be just spinning its wheels, obviously stuck in something, I figured the title must have been intended for me.

Men don't have this problem. Addressing a teenage boy as "sir" is usually considered a compliment. You can be a sir at six as easily as at sixty.

We women, however, aren't in that much of a hurry to get to the "ma'am stage," so don't rush us.

I suppose it all evens out when we get into our senior years. People go back to calling us "sweetie," "hon," and "Hey, you!" again.

We might even get a few "Hey, babes" tossed in our direction. I wouldn't mind that. It would remind me that I've still got it. Now, if only I could remember what "it" is and where I put it!

Youth is happy because it has the ability to see beauty. Anyone who keeps the ability to see beauty never grows old.
—Franz Kafka

43

Running Hot and Cold

Circulation problems can sometimes develop as we grow older. Our blood still flows, it just takes it a little longer to make its rounds.

Lately I've started having some mild circulatory problems. I've got body parts falling asleep at all hours of the day and night, which I don't really think is fair. Why should I be getting only seven or eight hours of sleep a night while my right leg is getting twelve?

Circulation problems can also cause our body's thermostat to malfunction. We'll often find ourselves feeling colder than anyone else. You start to realize this when you look around and notice you're the only one on the beach wearing a parka.

I'll admit my body temperature runs substantially colder than anyone else in our house. My teeth will be chattering and I'll have lost all feeling in my feet while everyone else is opening windows and putting ice packs on their heads to cool off.

I get cold everywhere—the house, the car, lava pits. Frankly, I think someone should come out with a personal mini-heater. You know, like those mini-fans you can hold in your hand. Personal mini-heaters could be used on airplanes, in cars, at the workplace, and most importantly, in grocery stores—they could distribute them to customers just before they embark down the frozen-food aisle.

I could really use a mini-heater at home. My husband, lord of the thermostat, likes to keep our house set at sixty-eight degrees. When he's not looking, I usually turn it up just a bit, somewhere between "Three Mile Island" and "Volcano."

Thus begins our "Dance of the Thermostat." My husband takes the lead. First, he turns, slides four steps to the left, stretches his arm up John Travolta-style, and deftly turns the thermostat down. I pivot on one foot, take three steps to the right, do a backbend, and turn it back up. He takes my hand, twirls me in two complete revolutions, leads me eight steps away, and moonwalks back to the thermostat to turn it down again.

The dance is really quite interesting to watch. Once in a while one of the kids will try to cut in and set the thermostat where they want it, but it's not long before it's just my husband and me again, freezing and sweating and dancing until dawn. How romantic!

It's too bad Arthur Murray never offered courses in the Dance of the Thermostat. He could have made a fortune.

Lord Tyrawley and I have been dead these two years, but we don't choose to have it known.
—Lord Chesterfield

44

That's Entertainment?

My taste in music has changed over the years. Not that I've become a die-hard polka fan or have the world's largest collection of Lawrence Welk music videos or anything like that, but I don't listen to the same music I used to listen to, either.

These days I prefer "easy listening"—that's all those songs you hear while riding elevators or getting your teeth drilled. I'm not all that fond of most of today's rock music. Often the lyrics are too explicit, and I don't like all that bass. If I want to get my heart pounding, there are other ways to do it, like finishing that sit-up I started last week.

I don't think I'd ever be able to get into the punk rock scene, either. Mosh pits don't entice me in the least. All that pushing and shoving and bumping into each other. I get enough of that at after-Christmas sales.

I do like country music, though. I like songs that tell a story, even if it is about some poor guy's wife getting trampled to death by an elephant at the circus and how the ringmaster sends him the bill for the elephant's therapy sessions after such trauma. Life's tough. Singing about it is how we cope.

My taste in movies has changed, too. I don't enjoy sophomoric humor or watching the antics of some seventeen-year-old heartthrob who thinks a liver spot is a stain you get on your shirt during dinner. I prefer complicated plots, good dialogue, and a forty-year-old heartthrob.

And there's been a change in what I read. I've traded in *Teen Beat* and *Seventeen* for *Newsweek* and *Time*, and I'll take an occasional peek at *Modern Maturity* (in a plain brown wrapper, of course).

Yet even though my taste in entertainment has changed over the years, I'm still the same person. The basic elements of one's personality don't change. If we were easygoing and reserved in our youth, we'll probably be easygoing and reserved in our later years. By the same token, if we were the adventurous daredevil type in our twenties, we'll still be the adventurous daredevil type when we reach our seventies. In other words, we'll be the one hang gliding off the patio at "the home."

Experience is the name that everyone gives to
their mistakes.
—Oscar Wilde

45

Made to Last

I recently attended the thirty-third California International Antiquarian Book Fair, which was held at a hotel near Los Angeles International Airport. My friend Cynthia Christenssen had invited me to go along with her. I had never been to an antiquarian book fair before, and it was fascinating to see the vast collection of rare and antique books.

One display especially caught my eye. It was a handful of pages from an old writing book that had been used by Mark Twain. There in his very own handwriting was part of one of Twain's manuscripts, complete with corrections. It was fascinating—and, of course, priced well into the thousands of dollars.

Many of the books at the show were in the same price neighborhood. There was one collection by Chaucer that was selling for, I believe, $250,000. My Visa card doesn't go that high. I couldn't have bought the bookmark that went along with it.

It was interesting, though, to watch people walk from booth to booth, surveying the rare and old books with respect and excitement. One book was 350 years old. Another was 200. There were books we remembered from our childhood (not the 200 one, of course). Rare book dealers had come from as far away as England, Germany, Spain, and countless other countries to display their collections and offer them for sale. If anyone had brought a book in that was less than ten years old, I don't think it would have gotten past the front gate.

So what makes these old and used books so valuable? Much of the reason has to do with the simple fact that they've survived. It's not easy to preserve a book for forty or fifty years, much less hundreds. They've seen too many yard sales, swap meets, and, of course, two-year-olds. Many books can't take it and eventually succumb to the wear and tear.

People are like books. Our pages may tear or turn yellow and our binding become loose. Some of our ideas might even sound dated or passé. But if we can somehow hold ourselves together, survive the elements to which life exposes us, and keep most of our pages intact, we'll have become a rare and special book indeed.

Keep away from people who try to belittle your ambitions. Small people always do that, but the really great make you feel that you, too, can become great.

—Mark Twain

46
What'd You Say?

My husband suffered some hearing damage in his years of service with the Los Angeles Police Department. Today officers are required to wear ear protectors while qualifying with their service revolver. That wasn't the case when my husband joined the department, so the monthly visits to the firing range took their toll, and now he's paying for it.

High-pitched sounds are what give him the most trouble, especially background noises at restaurants and women's voices. Even with hearing damage, though, he refuses to get a hearing aid. I don't understand this thinking, but he's not alone. A lot of people think a hearing aid will make them look older than they want to look. Frankly, I don't get it. Does answering the question "Did the mail come?" with "No, I didn't see the cow" really make a person look younger?

Though my husband's hearing was damaged years ago, hearing loss is also a side effect of aging. And we don't only start losing our hearing, but our ears seem to get bigger, too. They continue to grow as we age, some of them even turning outward. Maybe that's to give us more access for trimming ear hairs?

I've found, though, that what most middle-aged and older people suffer most from is selective hearing. They hear what they want to hear. My husband can hear me whisper a Home Shopping Network order into the telephone from two rooms away, but he can't hear me calling him to dinner.

He can hear the rear fender of my car barely tap the planter as I'm backing out of the driveway—while he's taking a shower in the house—but he can't hear the telephone ringing when he's two feet away from it.

One of these days someone's going to come out with a chip for hearing aids that would work like the V-chip in a TV. It could be programmed to edit out all the things you don't want to hear: "Honey Do" lists, mother-in-law visiting plans, and long distance service sales pitches, to name a few. The advantages would be endless.

Until then, if we want to get out of uncomfortable situations, I guess we'll just have to keep on faking it.

He's so old that when he orders a three-minute egg, they ask him for the money up front.
—Milton Berle

47

Who Unplugged the Fountain of Youth?

People have searched for it for years, and in case you're one of those still looking for it, I'm sorry to inform you that there is no fountain of youth. There is no pool of magical water where you can go for a dip and regain your youthful vitality. There are no water springs that will grant sharper memory or tighter skin. And if there were such a place, we wouldn't be able to get near it anyway. Can you imagine the parking problems?

No matter how badly we may want our youth to return, it's not coming back. Oh, we can snip a little here or tape a little back there, successfully taking a decade or so off our appearance, but we're not fooling Mother Nature. Once spent, youth can't be recaptured. We only get one dip in it, one go-around. Fountains of youth and time machines make interesting books and movies, but they are purely fictional.

I'm not so sure a fountain of youth would be a good idea anyway. Would we really want a world in which no one grew old? What kind of an existence would it be where we were all eternally adolescent? After a while we'd get tired of the childish games and rock music. We'd long for more variety, more substance, and some of the wisdom that only comes with age.

I once attended a church that had a young pastor and only a handful of older members. There was plenty of youthful energy there, but something important was missing. I like to call it the "been-there-survived-that mentality." I don't know about you, but I appreciate it when I'm going through a difficult time and an older adult shares with me that she, too, went through a similar difficulty and made it to the other side. It gives me hope.

So don't waste your time searching for the fountain of youth. Youthfulness isn't what you're seeking anyway, it's usefulness, and that isn't found in a fountain. It's only found within yourself.

The minute you settle for less than you deserve, you get even less than you settled for.

—Maureen David

48

Evading the Obvious

I once attended a memorial service in which the person delivering the eulogy did everything she could to avoid saying the word "dead." She used words like "departed, passed on, no longer with us, away, on the other side, gone to a better place, at peace, at rest, sleeping, walking with the angels"—well, you get the idea.

Most of us are uncomfortable talking about death. It's not something we put on our list of New Year's resolutions of things we want to do. We realize it's a natural part of the life cycle, but we don't like to dwell on it.

As we get older, though, the concept of death becomes harder and harder to ignore. We've attended far more funerals than we would have liked, and the fact that life has no guarantees is a truth that always seems to be slapping us in the face.

We may have even experienced a few brushes with death. My first close call came when I was only three months old. It was Christmas Eve, and my family had just left my uncle's house, heading for our home just a few miles away. While stopped at an intersection, we were struck head on by a drunk driver and knocked off the road and down an embankment.

Our car was totaled, and our injuries ranged from my father's critical condition to broken bones and bruises for most of the rest of us. One of those broken bones happened to be my arm. I easily could have been killed, though. But obviously God had a different plan for my life.

Then on a youth retreat as a teenager, I nearly drowned while playing underwater tag with our youth pastor. I didn't know how to swim, so every time he'd dive under the water to grab me, I'd take refuge by standing on his back. This seemed like a good idea to me at the time, but he was of a different opinion. Something about needing to breathe. Each time I stood on his back, he'd carry me for as long as he could, then finally knock me off so he could—breathe.

Once when he knocked me off, though, we were in nine feet of water, and down I went. I could hear voices laughing and talking in the background, but no one seemed to notice I was drowning. All I could do was pray and try not to open my mouth while doing so. The only parts of my body I could raise out of the water were my hands. I tried waving them, but still no one noticed my plight.

On my fourth attempt to rise to the surface, no part of my body cleared the water. That was when I began to accept the fact that it was over. I wasn't happy about it, mind you. Drowning was not on the list of retreat activities. But there wasn't a thing I could do to help myself.

Finally, someone yelled, "Hey, look, she's drowning!" From the moment I heard those words, I knew everything was going to be OK. I was still sinking like a rock in nine feet of water, but I now had hope.

Our youth pastor swam over to me and pulled me up and to the side of the pool, thus saving my life. I easily could have drowned that day. But God had a different plan for my life.

In the years that have followed, I've had other brushes with death. I'm sure you could relate some of your own. Arriving at an intersection four seconds earlier, you might have been hit by that car running the red light. Taking a closer look at the prescription spared you from swallowing someone else's medication.

Each of us may have missed death hundreds of times without even being aware of it.

Only God knows precisely how much time he's assigned us. There's no drop-in company in heaven. We're not going to get there a day sooner than he's expecting us. So whether we've been given forty-five years or ninety, it's up to us not to waste a single second of it.

Many of life's failures are people who did not
realize how close they were to success
when they gave up.
—Thomas A. Edison

49

And Another Thing ...

A character's dying words are usually pretty moving—in the movies. Their lines have been brilliantly scripted by a screenwriter. They are concise yet poignant. There's no redundancy or bad grammar. You won't hear any clichés uttered on a deathbed on the big screen. The writer will give his character something memorable to say, something that will put the audience in awe of his wisdom at such a time.

It doesn't always happen that way in real life, though. Most of us don't wax eloquent when we're taking that final breath. On his deathbed, H. G. Wells uttered these memorable last words: "Go away. I'm all right." Pancho Villa was even less prepared for his final sentiment. He said, "Don't let it end like this. Tell them I said something." Convicted murderer James Rodgers had a little more time to think about what he would say before his death. When asked for his final request before facing the firing squad, he said, "Why, yes—a bulletproof vest."

Dying people have left us with brilliant insights as to the meaning of life. They've used their final words to reconcile broken relationships not only with people but also with their God. They've even used their last breath to utter revisions to their will, especially if their beloved beneficiary is standing at their bedside with a date.

When it comes time for me to utter my last words, I'm afraid I won't be able to do it. As a writer, I know I'm going to keep wanting to do a rewrite. I can hear myself now: "Take time to stop and smell the roses." Too cliché. "I regret that I have but one life to give for my cooking." No good either. That would force an investigation into my refrigerator and perhaps even an autopsy. "Life—live it, love it, give back to it." Ummm . . . now that has some promise. But with my luck, when that time comes there won't be a single pen in the house.

I am a part of all that I have met.
—Lord Alfred Tennyson

50

Priorities

A lot of what we allow to consume our time and energy isn't really important, at least not in the big picture. So just in case we ever question whether or not something is worth all the attention we're giving it, the following chart is provided:

WORTH OUR TIME	NOT WORTH OUR TIME
A good book	A TV show with no redeeming qualities
Thankfulness	Selfishness
Appreciating others	Petty jealousies
Friends who stand by you	Friends who desert you
Helping others	Getting even with others
Encouraging people	Discouraging people
Spending time with family	Working unnecessary overtime

Taking a long walk	Waiting in long lines
Having a pet	Fretting over a neighbor's pet
Love	Hate
Striving for excellence	Striving to bury your competition
Peace of mind	Worry over things you can't control

What Youth deemed crystal,
Age finds out was dew.
—Robert Browning

51

The Ride

I remember as a child going to carnivals and amusement parks
with my family. After waiting in long lines, some for nearly an
hour, I'd climb onto the ride with so much excitement I could
barely contain myself.

About halfway through the ride, though, my focus would
change. Instead of enjoying the remainder of the ride, I could
hardly wait for it to be over so I could rush back to the end of
the line and ride it again.

I rarely paid any attention to the second half. All I could
think about was how much fun it was going to be the next time
around. Or the third time. Or the fourth.

I'm sure I missed out on a lot of fun during the second half
of those rides. Those who design amusement parks don't put all
the thrills in the first half of a ride. They usually design them to
be an exciting experience from start to finish. In fact, the second half is often the best part of the ride. The fun is there to be

enjoyed. If we're not paying attention, there's no one to blame but ourselves.

Life can be like an amusement park ride. It can be a series of gently paced ups and downs like a merry-go-round, or it can be a roller coaster adventure from start to finish with lots of exhilarating highs and breathtaking lows. Wherever the ride takes us or how much we choose to enjoy it, one thing is for certain: There is no second go-around. We can't hop off this ride and run to the back of the line and do it again. We only get one ticket. When our ride in this world is over, that's it—for this portion of the adventure anyway.

If you're over forty, chances are you're at the halfway point of the ride. Barring accidents, many, if not most of us, will live to be seventy or eighty or beyond. That means we've got just as many years left to live as we've already lived. So we shouldn't rush through it. If we close our eyes during the second half of this ride, we might be missing out on what could very well be the very best part.

"The Lord bless you and keep you; the Lord
make his face shine upon you and be gracious to
you; the Lord turn his face toward you and
give you peace."
—Numbers 6:24–26 NIV

Cooking
With Hot Flashes

After thirty, a body has a mind of its own.
—Bette Midler

Contents

1

Cooking With Hot Flashes

'Tis not knowing much, but what is useful,
that makes a wise man.
—Thomas Fuller

I'm hot. Not the gorgeous, voluptuous kind of hot. I'm just hot.
My husband tells me I even sizzle. But that is not a compliment. It is simply a statement of fact. I am, at times, quite literally sizzling. So much so that I have been ordered to stay away from dry brush and dead Christmas trees until my body has finished going through this transitional period known as "the change."

The change. Middle age. Menopause. Skin that doesn't fit us anymore. That is just some of what this book is about. But before you men get the misconception that this is a missive intended solely for women, let me remind you that both sexes go through the change. Men just seem to have a lot more fun with it than women. A man wakes up one morning and instead of putting on his usual conservative suit and silk tie, he tosses them both aside, slips on his jeans and unbuttons his shirt to the middle of his chest, adds a couple of gold chains, and goes out and buys a new sports car. That's how the male side of the species faces the midlife transition. For them, it's called a "mid-life crisis," and it's practically a celebration. They begin acting younger, not older. They join health clubs, change their hairstyle, their clothes, their demeanor, and their lingo. They get a renewed zest for life. They're not like us. They've never been moved to the smoking section of a restaurant because they were still smoldering from a hot flash. They don't attend weddings just so they can hang around the ice sculpture. They don't sweat puddles every night, so deep they have to wear a life jacket to keep from drowning. The change is easy on them.

But for us women? We can rocket from a normal 98.6-degree body temperature to *volcano* in ten seconds or less. There are veteran firemen who haven't seen that kind of spontaneous combustion. I'm convinced the only reason any of us get invited to outdoor parties is to serve as the heat lamp.

Perhaps one of these days medical science will develop a thermostat patch for menopausal women that will automatically readjust our body temperature whenever it nears or reaches the boiling point. Who knows, researchers might already be working on this concept even as this book is hitting the bookshelves. I sincerely hope so because when it comes to hot flashes and other symptoms of menopause, we women have suffered far too long in silence!

Oh, all right, who am I kidding? It's never been in silence. If we menopausal women are anything, it's vocal. We know the words "Is it hot in here or is it me?" in twelve languages. We live to let others in on our misery.

"Are you sure Arctic Winter is the lowest setting on your air-conditioner?"

"So, how flexible is cryogenics? Can't I be frozen just until after menopause?"

"That's the third sofa my body has set on fire this week."

We've complained, yes, but until now, we have done little else. We've left it up to the medical community to come up with whatever new and innovative ways they could find to help us handle the uncomfortable, and even dangerous, symptoms of menopause. We haven't done anything significant ourselves to protect us from the symptoms (although flame-retardant pajamas have helped), alleviate our misery, or even find a positive side to menopause. We've never organized a Million Menopausal Woman March on Washington. (What over-forty woman could deal with that kind of claustrophobia?) We haven't spoken out on the floor of Congress. (We figure they've already seen enough uncontrollable crying from the minority party.) As far as I can tell, we haven't done much of anything to make this change of life not only more endurable for us, but perhaps even *financially beneficial.* That is, until now. That is, until *Cooking With Hot Flashes . . . and Other Ways to Make Middle Age Profitable.*

I don't mean to brag, but I believe this book, which is the first to introduce the concept of using hot flashes as an energy source, could quite possibly put me in the running for a Pulitzer or, considering the positive effect it could have on menopausal mood swings, perhaps even a Nobel Peace Prize.

As with many other life-changing discoveries, this hot-flash energy idea came to me quite by accident. One day while clutching a handful of groceries to my chest, I made my way through a crowded supermarket, stood in the checkout line, then continued to cradle the groceries in my arms as I walked home, all the while having one of the worst hot flashes of my life.

But as I was putting the food items away, I noticed something quite remarkable. I discovered that by keeping my groceries pressed against my upper body, my hot flash had apparently cooked a steak to medium and thawed out a bag of frozen peas!

That is what got me to thinking: *I could save a fortune on my gas bill if I just started using my hot flashes to cook with!*

People, this could be the answer to all our energy needs! Who knows? Maybe that's how fire was discovered in the first place. Maybe it wasn't a couple of cavemen rubbing two sticks together as our history books have taught us. Maybe it was a menopausal cave woman who got a hot flash, leaned against her thatched hut, and set it ablaze!

For years scientists have been missing the mark. They've been looking for the answer to the world's power needs in all the wrong places. Since there will never be a shortage of middle-aged women, this natural source of heat energy is virtually unlimited and thus far untapped. Forget building more nuclear power plants. Forget alcohol energy, wind energy, and natural gas energy. Hot-flash energy could be just the discovery to revolutionize the world. Why, just one baby boomer high school reunion could yield enough heat energy to light the entire city of Cincinnati! The possibilities are endless!

But remember, you read it here first. Not in *Newsweek*. Not in *Time*. Not in *Science News*. It was here. A major, world-changing discovery humbly announced within the pages of this book, without a lot of hoopla, without a lot of fanfare (although a couple of oscillating fans pointed in my direction sure would've helped).

Now that I have stepped forward and revealed my discovery to the public, I believe it is only a matter of time before we will be seeing this new source of energy running heavy machinery, automobiles, and even aircraft. The possibilities are limited only by our imagination, our ingenuity, and the intensity of our hot flashes.

Perhaps you are wondering, as I did, why someone has never tapped into this obvious source of energy before now. Excellent question. We women have complained about our hot flashes, comedians have joked about them, pharmaceutical companies have spent hundreds of thousands of dollars trying to bring products to the marketplace that will help alleviate our discomfort, and husbands have gasped at astronomical air-conditioning bills from keeping our houses at a cool and comfortable negative 21 degrees. But even with this much attention, to my knowledge, no one has ever suggested harnessing this natural and abundant source of energy and making it profitable for the world. Maybe we've overlooked it because it seemed too simplistic. Maybe gasoline and electric companies didn't want us discovering such a revolutionary alternative energy source, and their lobbying groups kept us from researching the idea. Maybe we were all just too stinkin' hot to spend that much time in a lab coat. Who knows? It could be any number of reasons.

But since no one else has stepped up to the plate, the duty has fallen to me. So while I await word on my patent application, I figure I might as well go ahead and talk about some of the other ways all of us, men and women alike, can make it through these years known as middle age. Who knows what other solutions to the world's problems are yet to be discovered by studying this passage into the second half of our lives—the time when our muscles might ache a little more, our skin and hair are sure to loosen just a bit, and our knees and opinions won't be bending as easily as they used to. This book is about survival. It's about adventure. It's about discovery. And it should have been about twelve bucks, unless you got it out of the sale bin. In which case, I thank you. It's so embarrassing to walk into a bookstore and find your book hanging out in one of those. So you have my sincere gratitude for rescuing another one.

I hope you enjoy the read, this light-hearted look at our journey into middle age and beyond.

If not, feel free to use it to fan yourself.

I don't deserve this award, but I have arthritis and I don't deserve that either.
—Jack Benny

2

Take Our Money ... Please

The only reason I made a commercial
for American Express was to pay
for my American Express bill.
—Peter Ustinov

I don't know about you, but I resent it when advertising companies target younger audiences over older ones. We're just as important, aren't we? We like to spend money, don't we? One look at an outlet mall will tell you, we are a shopping force to be reckoned with.

So why aren't more marketing companies targeting our age group? Why are there so many youth-oriented programs and advertisements on television today? Why are we being ignored? Don't companies realize they are missing a huge market?

Now granted, a visit to the local mall will show you there are a lot of teenagers hanging out there these days. But are they shopping? Are they spending money? No. They're "hanging." Contrary to what our skin might be doing, we members of the over-forty crowd don't "hang." We shop, and not just window shop either. We're serious buyers. When we pick up an item and turn it over to see the price, we often carry it right on over to the checkout counter and pay for it. Why? Because we know the energy involved with picking up items. We don't do it unless we're committed.

If you're still not convinced that middle-agers and seniors are the more dedicated shoppers, then ask yourself this question: *When is the last time you saw a seventeen-year-old pushing one of those little wheeled carts full of packages through a department store?*

I rest my case.

Teenagers don't push wheeled carts. They put whatever they buy in their backpacks or pockets. How much can pockets hold?

Barely anything. Even a backpack is limited. But a wheeled cart has plenty of space, and we are the kings and queens of the wheeled cart. Nothing holds a blanket, a box of Epsom salt, and a bag of prunes better than a wheeled cart. Sure, we may have rolled over a few toes in our rush to a Bluelight Special at Kmart, but the public needs to know that when we are on a mission for bargains, we take no prisoners.

We don't only patronize discount stores, shopping malls, and outlet stores either. We buy from catalogs, television shopping networks, and door-to-door salesmen who are one sale away from winning a trip to the Bahamas. It doesn't matter that we have never been to the Bahamas ourselves, we'll buy whatever we have to in order to help a total stranger get there.

We're trendsetters, too. Do you really think that teenagers

were the ones who started the baggy-pants craze? They weren't. Let me remind you that grandpas have been wearing baggy pants for years. But did clothing manufacturers ever jump on this idea and market the look to Grandpa's age group? Have you ever seen a Calvin Klein commercial with an eighty-year-old shirtless man, wearing pants two sizes too big and hiked up to his armpits, saying "Just be"?

I don't think so. But they took this look and aggressively marketed it to teenagers. Teenagers in their big, baggy pants aren't original. They're not trendsetters. They're just wannabe grandpas.

Another trend that teenagers get credit for starting, but they didn't, is all these wild hair colors. Have they forgotten who it was who started the blue hair trend? Grandmothers. But has one of these lovely ladies ever been offered her own show on MTV? Have they ever been featured on the cover of *Rolling Stone* or *Entertainment Weekly*? Do they get any credit for their hipness?

No. Like Grandpa, their style is copied with no credit given.

But by overlooking the middle-age and senior crowd, advertising executives are missing out on a huge market. Our demographic buys a lot more than just shoe inserts, corn pads, age-defying face creams, and support hose. We buy toys and computer games for our grandchildren, nieces, nephews, friends' children, and yes, even for ourselves sometimes. We buy clothes and household goods, computers and compact discs (even though the word disc makes us a little nervous). We buy high-ticket items, low-ticket items, and everything in between. Contrary to what you may think, limited budget doesn't mean broke. We'll spend, but we just want a good value for our money.

We buy furniture, clothes, makeup, purses, shoes, carpets, vacuum cleaners, ride-on lawn mowers, hot-water heaters, cars, and major appliances. You won't find all that on a teenager's shopping list.

We also pay for household repairs, patronize hair salons, restaurants (both fast-food and fine dining), and we go on trips (not just cruises or road trips in our Winnebagos; many of us still take business trips).

So why then aren't the marketing people targeting our demographic more often? Young professionals may make more money than us annually, but they've got $4.98 in their savings account. We may make less than they do, but we have substantially more in our savings accounts to spend. I myself am up to nine dollars now.

I suppose it will take a while to change the thinking of these advertising executives, so we'll have to be patient. In the meantime, we'll just have to continue doing what we've done all along: shop. Spend our money. And keep watching all those Calvin Klein commercials with their "hip" teenagers modeling those baggy britches, knowing all along that Grandpa could be doing a much better job.

*You can tell the ideals of a nation
by its advertisements.*
—Norman Douglas

3

Exercising Our Prerogative

*I burned sixty calories. That should take care
of a peanut I had in 1962.*
—Rita Rudner

They say our metabolism slows down during middle age. Mine
didn't just slow down. It pulled over and parked. No matter
what I do, I can't seem to get it to shift into gear and take to
the road again. It's perfectly content to sit there on the shoulder
of life's highway and watch the world go by. Meanwhile, every
morsel that I eat attaches itself to my frame and hangs on like a
barnacle on the Queen Mary.

The answer? Some say it's exercise. Regular exercise is supposed to increase the body's metabolism and help it burn off all
those extra calories that we happen to take in throughout our
day.

But I for one have never been very fond of exercise. I have
enough night sweats, why would I want to sweat during the
day, too?

Exercising with exercise equipment holds the least appeal for me. Sure, the TV ads make the rowing machines and various other equipment look easy. You don't see anyone huffing and puffing and begging for oxygen. The spokespeople simply do their workout, pat their cheeks and foreheads with a hand towel, and tell you how much it will cost (plus shipping and handling) to have one of their miracle machines in the privacy of your home.

Now, I might find working out on exercise equipment a little more tempting if there was more of an incentive than merely losing weight. If I'm going to work that hard on a machine, I want something worthwhile at the other end of all my stretching. In other words, I'd gladly do the Gazelle or the AB Slide if there was a box of Krispy Kremes just slightly out of my reach. I'd have no problem at all walking a treadmill if there was a hot fudge sundae staring back at me from the opposite end of the conveyor belt. Real incentives, that's what I need. Merely visualizing myself in a pair of size–8 jeans isn't enough anymore. I need tangible rewards, rewards I can see, feel, and cover with whipped cream and nuts.

Exercise videos and television programs don't motivate me either. I don't like all the yelling.

"Get off that sofa and get moving!" the trainer will bark.

Now, first of all, I'm not usually sitting on the sofa. I'm laid out on the recliner. There is a difference. And secondly, why can't she ask nicely? When you're already so out of shape that one sit-up takes half the afternoon, who wants a drill sergeant making you feel bad about it? The way I see it is, if someone wants me to twist and bend my body into contortions that have

never before been seen or imagined, there had better be a
"pretty please" attached.

I don't know about you, but I don't need any more guilt. I
already feel guilty enough every time I take my fork up to the
dessert bar at the buffet and skip the plate. (Okay, like nobody
else has ever thought of doing that?)

And anyway, it's not like I don't get any exercise at all. I
walk to my mailbox every day, and on some days I have had to
look all over the family room for the remote, and who knows
how many steps I take doing that? I do knee bends getting the
Fritos that I keep on the bottom shelf of the cupboard and
shoulder stretches reaching up for the Breyers in the top
freezer. I'd like to see someone come out with a video featuring
these kinds of exercises.

But I'm not completely convinced we should be burning all
these calories, anyway. How do we know it's a good thing? Has
anyone ever researched where all these burned calories are
going and what they might be doing to our environment? What
if burned calories are, in fact, what's messing up the ozone
layer? What if it isn't hair spray at all? What if one day we discover that calories are something we were supposed to keep
with us, not go sending off willy nilly into the atmosphere?

Until more research is done on exactly where all these spent
calories are going and how the loss of them is affecting our
world, I choose to limit my incineration of the little guys. It's
not that I'm lazy. I'm patriotic. Wait, no, it's more than patriot-
ism. This is a much higher calling. This has global significance.
This could be yet another world-changing idea. I shall clear
space in my office for my second Pulitzer. And I shall set an

example to all others by vowing to burn only a handful of calories every day. It's the very least I can do to save our world.

Whenever I feel like exercise I lie down
until the feeling passes.
—Robert M. Hutchins

4

I Left My Chin in Ol' Zimbabwe

I've had more parts lifted
than an abandoned Mercedes.
—Phyllis Diller

The latest marketing angle for plastic surgery is the combined surgery/safari trip. Have you heard about these? You go on a safari in some faraway land and get your face lifted at the same time. Imagine it—bagging some wild game and getting rid of a few under-eye bags at the same time. How convenient is that?

The theory behind mixing these two activities, I suppose, is so that the recovery will be discreet. Elephants don't care whether or not your stitches are showing, and who's a giraffe going to blab your face-lift secret to?

After the safari and operation, you simply return to your homeland looking twenty years younger and no one is the wiser.

Another activity that is growing in popularity is the Botox home party. From what I understand, you invite some of your closest friends over and a doctor explains the benefits of Botox, and then he or she will give Botox injections to whomever wants them and is deemed a good candidate for them. It's like a Tupperware party, only you and your guests are the ones trying to lock in your freshness.

Times have sure changed, haven't they? I remember the day when plastic surgery was something people only whispered about.

"Do you think she's had any work done?"

"Please, she's gone through more cuts than a Republican budget."

But these days, there are no whispers. The people themselves brag about what they've had done. It's like they consider themselves walking works of art.

"That's a Dr. Carter nose, isn't it? I recognize his style."

"Actually, it's a Doc Sheridan. He's a little more impressionistic than I'd like, but I suppose I'll eventually get used to both of my eyebrows being on the same side."

These days, celebrities, politicians, and even everyday people have no problem confessing their nips, tucks, reductions, and enhancements. They're proud of them.

A few celebrities, however, have proven that too much of a good thing can have undesirable results. I don't have to name names, because I think you have a good idea of whom I'm talking about. They've had so much plastic surgery, they don't look real anymore. They're like caricatures of themselves. It's sad, but at this point, I don't know if there's anything they can do about it. They've reached the point of no return. They can't be very happy about that either. But it's not all their fault. Where were their friends? Where was their family? Where was their doctor? Where was someone, anyone, who could have said to them, "Look, I love you, but your nose is starting to invert. You gotta stop, man"?

A plastic surgery intervention was desperately needed.

Don't get me wrong. I'm not against plastic surgery. But everything should be done in moderation. People shouldn't go through a dozen different noses before they find one they like. This isn't Silly Putty they're working with; it's flesh and bone and cartillage. If you've already had a successful experience with plastic surgery, I'm happy for you. All I'm saying is know when to stop. And if you've never had plastic surgery but are contemplating getting some work done, I would simply say to talk to your doctor and your family and do whatever you believe is best for you.

And if that involves going on a safari, then do it. Or if it means staying just the way you are, that's great, too. The important thing is to just be you.

Wrinkles should merely indicate
where the smiles have been.
—Mark Twain

5

They're Out to Rule the World

There was no respect for youth when I was young, and now that I am old, there is no respect for age—I missed it coming and going.
—J. B. Priestly

The kids are taking over. I'm not talking about all the doctors, policemen, politicians, and attorneys who seem to be getting younger and younger each year. I'm talking about children. Real children. More specifically, toddlers. They could be your nieces and nephews, your grandchildren, your neighbors' kids, or in some cases, even your own children. And sure, they seem innocent enough sitting there in their cribs or on the floor playing quietly with their toys, but it's all a ruse. They have an agenda, they're committed, and they've been outsmarting us for years. Everything they do is to advance their plan to take over the world, and it's high time someone blew their cover.

And so I shall.

This plan of theirs has been unfolding ever so subtly over the years. Even I didn't suspect anything was amiss at first. But I see it all quite plainly now.

First, I'm not sure how they did it, but somehow these little rug rats have managed to take over the control of our television sets. Instead of watching our favorite news programs or the History Channel, we find ourselves caving in to their desires and watching *SpongeBob* and *Jimmy Neutron* for hours on end. Granted, we do get involved in the programs and even catch ourselves laughing out loud sometimes, but has anyone played their theme songs backward to see if they're sending subliminal messages to the adult world?

"You will let me play ball in your house."

"You will take me to Chuck E. Cheese's."

"You will give me an advance on my inheritance."

"You will let me braid your hair in tiny little braids and paint your toenails fluorescent pink."

Who knows what kind of adult brainwashing is going on during these seemingly innocent children's shows?

The television was just Phase 1 of the master plan. Phase 2 apparently happened while many of us middle-agers and seniors were taking naps. These innocent-looking children somehow convinced pharmaceutical companies of the need for our medicine bottles to come with childproof caps. Caps, I might add, that only *children* can open. Now, on the surface, childproofing medicine bottles probably sounded like a great idea, and I do not doubt for a minute that the staff at the Federal Drug Administration had plenty of reputable data to convince the agency to jump on board with this seemingly beneficial plan. But the FDA should have been a tad more skeptical. They weren't looking into the future and seeing where this action was taking us as a society. Adults are now at the mercy of children!

"I need my heart medication, Joey," Grandpa says. *"Can you come over here and get this blasted thing open for me?"*

"Sure, Gramps, as soon as you reveal the password to your safety deposit box."

These children are the same ones who also hide our glasses, our car keys, our wallets, the *TV Guide,* and then merely giggle, clam up, or speak some kind of gibberish when we try to interrogate them about the missing items.

"Where are my keys, Bobby?"

"Ahgagoga."

"Come on, boy, tell Nana where you put them."

"Dimofogu."

Their resistance to these inquisitions would impress military experts worldwide. Both the FBI and the CIA have tried to decipher their secret code, but it's unbreakable.

We're headed for trouble, people.

And who is it that gets the power seat at the dinner table? The "high" chair? (See, even the name sounds commanding.) Who is responsible for that incessant pounding on the metal trays that would make even the toughest grandparent shout out every password to every account he's ever owned? These toddlers, that's who.

Remember the good ol' days when children used to be at the mercy of adults when it came to their mobility? They either rode in a stroller or we carried them. That, too, has changed.

These days, kids have their own battery-operated cars to putt around in. They're eighteen months old and already they know how to drive. What's worse, we're probably the ones they persuaded to buy these vehicles for them.

Which brings us to their incredible business sense. These youngsters are nothing short of financial geniuses. Think about it. They come to our houses selling candy for their schools and youth organizations, then they return on Halloween and take it all back! Has anyone done the math on this?

I'm telling you, world, their hostile takeover has been planned right under our noses and we've been too blinded by their cuteness to see it. They've been holding high-level security meetings in sandboxes all over the globe. Sure, it all looks like innocent play to us, but it isn't. It's their own version of Camp David. Why do you think there's always one child who holds that ear-piercing high-pitched scream? You think it's a tantrum? I used to think that, too. But no longer am I that naïve. The scream is a cover-up so we won't overhear them discussing their takeover plans.

These toddlers have their own cell phones, computers, playhouses, and miniature emergency vehicles. What do they need us big people for? They've got almost everything required to run the world on their own.

The most amazing thing about this is how these little ones have managed to get us to run their publicity campaigns for them, and we've been doing it *pro bono*.

"You wanna see some pictures of the most beautiful grandchild on earth?"

"You think she's beautiful, wait 'til you see my grandbaby!"

We're ready to play dueling grandchildren at the drop of a photo album.

"Look at those eyes!"

"Look at those dimples!"

"He's the smartest kid in the world!"

So, all things considered, maybe we're just getting what we deserve. These little ones have been outsmarting us for years, manipulating us with their cute smiles and endearing hugs, while we've merely sat by and allowed it all to happen.

But it's not too late. We must wake up and smell the apple juice in the sippee cup. The future of the world is at stake! No matter how cute they are, we cannot continue to roll over and let these kids take over. We can't bury our heads and pretend we don't know what they're up to. It's time we quit being weak! It's time we stood up and drew a line in their sandboxes! It's time we let them know once and for all who's in charge here! It's time we . . .

Sorry. This chapter was going to be a lot longer, but a two-year-old in my doctor's waiting room just took my glasses and won't give them back, so I can't see my laptop keys.

And so the conspiracy continues. . . .

True terror is to wake up one morning and discover that your high school class is running the country.
—Kurt Vonnegut

6

The Fountain of Youth Uncovered

*I am my age. I'm not making
any effort to change it.*
—Harrison Ford

I seriously doubt if there really is a fountain of youth, but I think I might have stumbled across what could very well be the next best thing.

One day while surfing the Internet, I came across a rather interesting tidbit of information. I read that a can of WD–40 spray can be useful in the treatment of arthritis. I had never heard that before, and quite frankly, I don't even know if the claim is true or not. The manufacturer might not even be aware that someone is making this claim. But according to the information I uncovered, all you do is rub a little of the popular lubricant onto the affected area, and before you know it, you're doing cartwheels down the hallway.

As I said, I have my doubts about whether this really works, but it did get me thinking. What else might be lurking in our garages that can help us get through the second half of our lives? Could it be that the fountain of youth has been hiding out there all these years, while we've been searching the world over for it? Could it be that Craftsman can do us more good than anti-aging creams? Could Home Depot be the secret location of Shangri-La?

Who knows? But I figured it was worth checking out. So I walked into my garage and took a look around to see what I could find.

The first item to catch my eye was our Weedwacker. Could that be the perfect tool for trimming those pesky ear and nose hairs? Traditionally, the Weedwacker has been used for bigger jobs, but if you let ear hair growth go unchecked for a few weeks, the Weedwacker might be just the thing to tackle an unruly hedge or two.

Sandpaper is another garage tool that might be able to help us look younger. Why should we continue to mess around with goopy masques and toning creams just trying to get rid of all our dead skin cells? Why not sandpaper them off instead? Sandpaper is cheaper and can reach depths in our pores we never thought possible. (For those more difficult places such as elbows and heels, the electric sander might be able to work miracles, but we should each check with our own doctor first.)

Many of us have tried virtually everything to get rid of cellulite, but we haven't tried putty! Putty might be just the thing to fill in all those potholes and smooth out our legs again. If that doesn't work, we could try that Pops-a-Dent device. You know, the one they advertise on television that pops the dents right out of your car's fenders. It seems to me if it can do that, maybe it can fix cellulite, too. In other words, pull the "sink" right out of the "sinkholes."

The last garage tool that I'm going to mention, although I'm sure there are plenty more, happens to be the most versatile one, too. Duct tape. For those of us who can't afford an expensive plastic surgeon, duct tape might very well be our answer. It's affordable, easily accessible, and convenient to use. You can tape back loose skin, reinforce falling body parts, and who knows what else? It comes in colors now, too, so whatever your skin tone, whether you have blond, brunette, red, or black hair, there's a color just right for you.

Or on second thought, maybe it would be better if we all just got out of our garages and stuck with products that have already been proven to minimize the signs of aging. Bob Vila is busy enough without all of us showing up at his garage wanting makeovers!

*There is a fountain of youth: it is your mind,
your talents, the creativity you bring to your
life and the lives of the people you love.
When you learn to tap this source,
you will truly have defeated age.*
—Sophia Loren

1

The Ultimate Word on Aging

When I told my doctor I couldn't afford an operation, he offered to touch-up my X-rays.
—Henry Youngman

With all the books being marketed today on the subject of aging, you wouldn't think that some of the best advice on this subject would come from one of the oldest books around—the Bible. That's right. Even the heroes of the faith had to deal with many of the same problems that we face today, and they even wrote about it.

Just take a look at what we can learn from this "over forty" crowd of the scriptures. (By the way, I'm using the version of the Bible that's considered by the majority of theologians to be the most authentic. Large print.)

So what does the Bible say about aging?

❀ **Sometimes even kings can't seem to get warm.**
When King David was old and well advanced in years, he could not keep warm even when they put covers over him.
—1 Kings 1:1

✿ **Exercising, even if it's just walking around in circles, can keep you healthy.**

Moses was a hundred and twenty years old when he died, yet his eyes were not weak nor his strength gone.

—Deuteronomy 34:7

✿ **To dye or not to dye.**

The glory of young men is their strength, gray hair the splendor of the old.

—Proverbs 20:29

✿ **Even bald can be beautiful.**

When a man has lost his hair and is bald, he is clean.

—Leviticus 13:40

✿ **You deserve to be heard.**

Moses was eighty years old and Aaron eighty-three when they spoke to Pharaoh.

—Exodus 7:7

✿ **. . . but don't ramble.**

Seated in a window was a young man named Eutychus, who was sinking into a deep sleep as Paul talked on and on. When he was sound asleep, he fell to the ground from the third story and was picked up dead.

—Acts 20:9

✿ **Don't get stuck in your ways.**

Better a poor but wise youth than an old but foolish king who no longer knows how to take warning.

—Ecclesiastes 4:13

❀ **The older you get, the more you deserve respect.**

Listen to your father, who gave you life, and do not despise your mother when she is old.

—Proverbs 23:22

❀ **Insomnia is curable.**

I will lie down and sleep in peace, for you alone, O LORD, make me dwell in safety.

—Psalm 4:8

❀ **God's not through with you yet.**

They will still bear fruit in old age, they will stay fresh and green . . .

—Psalm 92:14

❀ **You are not alone.**

Even to your old age and gray hairs I am he, I am he who will sustain you. I have made you and I will carry you; I will sustain you and I will rescue you.

—Isaiah 46:4

❀ **And you are not forgotten.**

Abraham was now old and well advanced in years, and the LORD had blessed him in every way.

—Genesis 24:1

❀ **Geritol's good, but God is better.**

He will renew your life and sustain you in your old age.

—Ruth 4:15

❀ **And never ever say never.**

After Noah was 500 years old, he became the father of Shem, Ham and Japheth.

—Genesis 5:32

My secret for staying young is good food, plenty of rest, and a makeup man with a spray gun.
—Bob Hope

8

Another Fine Mess

Try to relax and enjoy the crisis.
—Ashleigh Brilliant

I fully understand the importance of airport security. In these times in which we live, it has become an accepted part of life. So I didn't mind at all when I had to comply with some of these security measures when my rhinestone-sleeved sweater recently set off the alarm at a Missouri airport.

You know the routine. As soon as I walked through the security scanner, it started beeping. A guard politely asked me to step to the side, and of course I did. He asked me to stretch out both of my arms. I did that, too. He asked me to spread my legs. I did that as well. I went along with the routine even though I had a pretty good hunch as to what the problem might be.

"It's the rhinestones," I said as he waved his security wand down and around my right arm. "I'm sure it's the rhinestones."

The guard didn't seem very interested in my assessment of

the situation. He merely indicated that I should stay still and stay quiet while he continued.

There was no beeping on my right arm, so he moved on, waving the wand down and around my left arm. But there was no beeping with my left arm either. Next, he scanned my legs. Nothing. My shoulders. Nothing. My head, an even eerier silence. I waited for him to comment about that, but they're not allowed to joke around.

Then the silence was broken.

Beep, beep, beep, beep . . .

He had moved the wand in the vicinity of my lower back.

Aha. There was the problem. But what could it be? I asked myself. There wasn't anything in my lower back area that should be setting off the alarm.

He moved his wand up to my shoulder area. The beeping stopped. He waved it around my hip area. Nothing. Then he moved it back down to my lower back and around to the front of my stomach area, and . . .

Beep, beep, beep . . .

There was no question about it. He had found the problem area.

"It's here," he said emphatically. "There's something under here."

Of course there was something under there. It was my stomach. But it shouldn't have been triggering a security alarm. I don't eat *that* much iron. But I didn't say that, remembering the no-joking-around rule.

"What've you got under there?" he asked.

"Nothing," I said.

"Nothing?"

"There's nothing there," I said confidently.

"You wearing a belly ring?"

Right, I laughed to myself. AARP was running a special. But I didn't say that either.

"No. No belly ring," I assured him.

"Belt?"

"No."

"Metal plates?"

"I could probably use a few, but no."

All right, I didn't say that either. These kinds of situations are very difficult for humor writers. But I realized that it wasn't the time or the place, so I edited myself.

The guard wanded me again, just to double check, and once again everywhere was silent except for my lower torso.

Beep, beep, beep, beep, beep. The alarm was insistent. Something was there.

"I don't know what it could be," I insisted. And I honestly didn't. I had already mentally surveyed my body. There wasn't anything there that should have been causing all this commotion.

The guard felt around my waistline one more time.

"There's something here, ma'am. Feels like some sort of fanny pack. You got a fanny pack under there?" he pressed.

"No."

"Then what's under there?"

"Just my stomach," I repeated. If my stomach felt like a fanny pack to him, I was sure there was a better way for him to have worded that. But again, my lips were sealed.

Other guards were starting to move in closer now as backup.

"What's the problem?" one of them asked, sizing me up.

"Something keeps triggering my wand," he said.

A suspicious glance was exchanged between the guards, while my mind reviewed my body once more from head to toe. No belt. No metal plates. No belly ring. No fanny pack. There was nothing that should have been setting off any alarms. And yet it was.

Beep, beep, beep, beep.

Just as I was envisioning the nightly news featuring my picture, it suddenly dawned on me. In the hustle and bustle to get to the airport, the girdle that I don't always wear but had decided to wear that day because the skirt I was wearing seemed to scream for it had bunched itself up into a tiny roll that I had told myself I was going to fix once I got on the plane. Never figuring a girdle in any condition would trigger the alarm system, I had forgotten all about it.

But because it had bunched up into a roll, the metal stays must have appeared on the X ray to be two or three times thicker than a normal girdle and were now sounding all sorts of alarms.

I leaned over and discreetly whispered to the guard that I thought I knew what the problem might be. I explained the rolled-girdle theory, he felt the bulk again, then concurred with my assessment.

"It's just a girdle!" he explained to the other guards and also to the crowd of people who had now gathered, curiously staring at the group inspection of my midsection.

"It bunched up," he said, relieved that his duties were done and the crisis of the moment had been successfully averted.

I could hear a few snickers as I waited for the boarding process to begin, and I believe I heard the word "girdle" spoken in Spanish, French, and Japanese. A few school-age kids pointed, and I think I saw the pilots receiving a briefing before boarding the plane.

When I finally stepped onto the plane myself, I walked straight to the airplane lavatory and took off that trouble-causing body tourniquet. It wasn't easy, considering the small space I had to do it in. I accidentally rang the flight attendant three times and turned on the faucet with my right hip. But after tugging and pulling, pulling and tugging, I was free at last! It felt great. I could breathe again. And I could rest assured that I wouldn't be setting off any more airport alarms.

To tell you the truth, I don't even know why I was wearing that crazy thing in the first place. Considering what I had paid for my airline tickets, wasn't that enough of a squeeze?

> **In youth we run into difficulties.**
> **In old age difficulties run into us.**
> —Beverly Sills

9

Brain-Aerobics

*Ever wonder if illiterate people
get the full effect of alphabet soup?*
—John Mendosa

A recent medical report stated that the simple act of juggling helps to keep the middle-aged brain alert. So, I've been doing a lot of that lately. I've been juggling my mortgage, my car payment, my utilities, and my credit card payments. I haven't noticed any significant difference in my brain power, but my head does seem to be hurting a lot more.

This same report also said that getting plenty of sleep can rejuvenate the mind and improve reflex time. I don't think I believe that either. The other day I woke up from a wonderful nap just in time to see that I was about to drive right off the road. It still took my reflexes a good five or six seconds to kick in. Frankly, I don't see where that nap helped me very much at all.

Another activity that is reported to be good for our brains is working crossword puzzles. I'm not sure if it is the act of completing the puzzle, or if it's just all that hunting around for a pencil that helps to stimulate our brain waves.

One look at the spam in our e-mail in-boxes will tell you that there certainly is no shortage of products on the market that guarantee (and I use the term loosely) to improve our brainpower in middle age. The subject lines vary, but each company seems to be playing to this same basic desire. We want our brains to stay as young and healthy as possible for as long as possible.

Personally, I don't get caught up in all this hype because I'm pretty sure my brain is going to outlast my body. My body clearly has had more wear and tear on it than my brain. The reason for this is that over the years I've purposely endeavored to keep my brain in relatively new condition, only using it on special occasions.

When my mother was alive she used to say that certain foods were "brain foods." Hot oatmeal fell into this category. She may have been right. Oatmeal does make you feel smarter. Especially when you realize you just paid around a buck for a box of it, as opposed to four dollars for a box of cereal.

My mother never told me this, but I've wondered if cheesecake isn't brain food, too. Here's my theory. Many say that the best cheesecake is New York cheesecake. New York is home of the Metropolitan Museum of Art, Columbia University, Cornell University, and the New York City Opera.

See the connection?

Let's try "patty melt." A patty melt is made with sourdough bread. San Francisco is famous for sourdough. San Francisco is home to the San Francisco Law School and the de Young Art Museum.

Chicago-style pizza? Chicago has Northwestern University and the Chicago Arts District.

Baked Alaska? The University of Alaska Museum.

Tennessee Tea Cakes? Vanderbilt University.

The way I see it, oatmeal isn't the only food that is good for our brains. There are plenty of other desserts, entrees, and deep-fried appetizers that could very well increase your brain power. Boston Cream Pie (Boston University and Harvard Medical School), Texas chili (Texas A&M), California nacho cheese (Berkeley, USC, and UCLA), Kentucky Fried Chicken (University of Kentucky). I could go on, but I believe I've made my point.

So whether it's vitamins, brain exercises, or even my list of "brain foods," the important thing is that we do something every day to nourish and stimulate our minds.

Tonight I'm having Tiramisu and canolis. Obviously, I'm studying abroad.

You are the same today that you are going to be five years from now except for two things: the people with whom you associate and the books you read.
—Charles Jones

Ten Things You Don't Realize Until Middle Age

* Good posture was a good idea.
* When given a choice, downhill is the preferred direction.
* No matter how big you get, you never outgrow naps.
* The Weather Channel is great television.
* As long as your car's left-turn signal is keeping time with your car radio, there is no need to turn off either one.
* It doesn't matter how long you live, you will never go through all the hot-sauce packets you've been given at Taco Bell.
* Pants really do seem to fit better when they're pulled up to your armpits.
* Some mornings facial concealer should come with a roller.
* Chocolate isn't a food group. It's a whole diet plan.
* Sometimes pantyhose just aren't worth the fight.

11

It's Not Just the Economy That's Sagging

I am a fighter. Gravity is my enemy.
—Gertrude Schwartz

A few years ago, I moved to the South. So did my body. In fact, there are several parts of me that have relocated to the deep south.

I'm not sure why, but gravity seems heavier in middle age than it did when I was younger. And therein lies the problem. You may not believe this, but gravity has gained weight. I'm still working on how to go about proving this, but I'm convinced it's true. Just ask yourself, is it harder for you to get up from a sitting position these days? Is it harder for you to climb out of bed in the morning? Is it harder for you to hold your head and shoulders back? If the answer is "yes," don't be discouraged. It's not you. It's gravity. Gravity keeps gaining weight and we just can't go on lifting it up anymore.

Gravity's weight gain is the reason behind the little flesh avalanches my body has been having lately. I'm convinced of it. These are parts of me that have stood faithfully at their posts decade after decade. There wasn't a deserter among them. But now, these same parts have begun to give me the slip.

Take my eyebrows as just one example. Before hitting middle age, they used to sit firmly above my eyes. They were happy there. They didn't have any real complaints. They didn't shift to the right or to the left. They didn't slide down or move over. They stayed perfectly in place, right where God originally designed them to be. Not once did I have to give them a second thought.

But something happened to them once I hit middle age. They let go, surrendered; they hoisted the white flag. They had held on for as long as they could, then simply gave up. They served me well, but they have now gone AWOL. At the present moment, both of my eyebrows are drooping down so low in front of my eyes, I can pluck them without using a mirror. Whenever I work at my computer now, I have to tilt my head back just to keep them from slamming down on my keyboard. I can't write this way. I need to see what letters I'm tyzyping. (Sorry, that should have been "typing." See what I mean?)

But I can't put all the blame on my eyebrows. The little troopers have simply succumbed under the expanding weight of gravity.

A lot of me has given up and let go lately. In addition to my eyebrows, my cheeks have suffered substantial slippage, too, thanks to the added weight of the g-word. My cheeks used to have a firm grip on my facial bones, but not anymore. Now they're hanging down like the jowls of a Saint Bernard. Even the best glamour photo can't be touched up enough to hide something like that.

Every day I wonder what body part will become the latest casualty in this seemingly uncontrollable flesh avalanche. I'm dropping faster than the interest rates of 2003. I feel like a Mrs. Potato Head being rearranged by someone with a cruel sense of humor who's playing around with all the parts, putting them in places they've never been before and do not belong.

Without a doubt, gravity has had the biggest effect on my skin. To put it bluntly, my skin has been my downfall. Menopausal skin is like pantyhose that start out at your waist in the morning and work their way down to your ankles by noon. You end up looking like you're wearing slouch socks when you're not.

But there's not a lot we can do about any of this. Gravity is well past its middle age. If it's going to gain weight, this is the time that it would be happening. Still, it makes you wish that we would have been handed some sort of a warranty at our birth, something that would cover us in middle age when we begin suffering significant body-part movement. Our homes are covered for foundation slippage. Why not our bodies? When you think about it, it's not that far-fetched a concept. Both Betty Grable and Mary Hart had their legs insured for a million dollars. Others have insured different parts of their bodies, too. Why couldn't there be a Skin Slippage clause or a Falling Eyebrows Indemnity policy?

Another life-changing idea from just one middle-aged

author. I'm going to have to buy a bigger house just to display all the Nobels.

But I'm afraid until Lloyd's of London or State Farm or some other insurance company finds a way to make this kind of policy affordable for everyday people, it'll have to remain just another good idea. We'll have to deal with the damages caused by Flesh Falls all on our own, and try our best not to trip over our ankles.

Old age is like a plane flying through a storm.
Once you're aboard, there's nothing you can do.
—Golda Meir

The Sandman Cometh . . . But He Delayeth

Waking up in the morning would be a whole lot easier if it involved flopping into bed, burying my head into my pillow, and closing my eyes.
—Jeffery D. Trock

Maybe it's just me, but it seems that once we enter the middle-age years, we don't get or require as much sleep as we once did. One reason for this could be the fact that at our age there are a lot more fun things to do in bed. Now, I'm not talking about the obvious (shaking your spouse and telling him or her to "Roll over, you're snoring again"). I'm talking about all those *other* fun things to do.

For instance, when we were children, all we had to count before drifting off to sleep was a bunch of imaginary sheep jumping over a fence. How boring was that? But now that we're older, we can lie in bed and count floaters! (If you don't know what floaters are, they're those little black things that float across your field of vision every now and then, and they seem to get more prominent in middle age.) Once floaters have been deemed harmless by your opthalmologist, they can really be quite entertaining. Especially at bedtime. Simply lie back on your pillow and follow the path of one until it floats out of sight, then pick up on another one just as it enters your field of vision. Do this for a few minutes, and before you know it, you're snoozing like a baby. Or you're permanently cross-eyed.

Another fun thing to do in bed is what I call The Blanket Tuck. With this game, timing is everything. The tuck has to be perfectly timed to occur just prior to your spouse's rolling over. Being as discreet as possible, tuck the blanket under the side of your body closest to the outer edge of the bed. You want to make sure that it is a tight tuck, as tight as you can get it. Then, when your spouse tries to roll over, he or she will move, but the blanket won't. Imagine the playful giggles the two of you will share as you enjoy this little game together.

"Give me the covers!"

"You give me the covers!"

"Give me the covers!"

"You give me the covers!"

Why, you'll feel like newlyweds again.

Another fun activity to play in bed is Mattress Ice Skating. This involves simply moving your bare feet in a circular motion around your partner's icy toes and pretending you're skating. For extra enjoyment, try a few figure eights.

Reading is another activity to do in bed, but not just the warning label on your pillows. That's fun, too, but I'm talking books. My husband loves to read in bed, which I believe has been the reason for much of our closeness. He likes to read big, thick history books that tend to make his side of the bed sag. This causes me to roll over to his side of the bed and he thinks I'm being romantic.

I love to write in bed. Over the years, I've found that some of my best ideas come to me in the middle of the night. I also know that if I don't write them down, I'll forget them by morning. So I grab a pen and paper in the dark and scribble down all the important points of my idea. It could be an idea for a book, a screenplay, a song, or a sketch. Whatever happens to come into my mind, I'll jot it down.

In the morning I can't read a word of it. Before I became a writer, I had no idea that between the hours of 2 and 4 A.M., I'm bilingual.

I'm sure there are plenty of other fun things to do in bed during your middle-age years, but this should give you a few tips to start with. And just remember, if you really get bored, you can always go back to doing that other thing you used to do when you were a whole lot younger.

Sleep.

I usually take a two-hour nap from one to four.
—Yogi Berra

13

Not by a Hair on My Chinny Chin Chin

I refuse to think of them as chin hairs.
I think of them as stray eyebrows.
—Janette Barber

When we women hit middle age, we start wishing for something that will hide our wrinkles. A beard is the last thing on our minds.

What is it about menopause that makes the hair on our heads start letting go, while the hair on our faces seems to sprout overnight like Jack's beanstalk? Has anyone come up with a good explanation for this? We hear so much about mysterious crop circles popping up in wheat fields overnight; but to my knowledge, no one is investigating where all these chin hairs are coming from. Isn't their sudden nocturnal appearance every bit as puzzling? I can go to bed with a nice smooth chin, and by morning I look like I should be baaing. This is not normal.

These hairs are often not even the same color as the hair on the rest of our bodies, which makes them appear even more mysterious. But did you ever see an episode of *The X-Files* dedicated to the sudden materialization of chin hairs? Has *Unsolved Mysteries* ever covered this unexplained phenomenon? Or *60 Minutes* aired an exposé?

To my knowledge, the answer is no. So once again, I'm taking it to the public myself. Put the crop circle mystery on hold. Bigfoot and the Loch Ness Monster are going to have to wait. We middle-agers have been left to twirl our chin hair long enough while pondering this conundrum. We want answers and we want them now. Where is Morley Safer when we need him? Agent Fox Mulder, report back for duty. Robert Stack, look into this problem for the good of your country. We demand to know what possible reason there could be for this spontaneous chin-hair growth on menopausal women. Is it so our grandchildren will have something to hang on to when they climb into our laps? Is it so we'll be able to tell which way the wind is blowing on any given day? Is it to save us a fortune on dental floss? What possible purpose could there be for this enigma?

We have been patient long enough. We have tried handling these mystery hairs on our own. We've shaved or plucked them, but it still doesn't deter them in the least. They simply grow back, and when they do, it's with a vengeance. The new hair is darker and more coarse, and sometimes it will even bring a buddy hair along with it.

We must have answers now. But then again, maybe it's better that we don't know. Some mysteries are better left alone.

When solving problems, dig at the roots instead of just hacking at the leaves.
—Anthony J. D'Angelo

14

Bumper Stickers for Middle-Agers

- ✿ I snore, therefore deal with it.
- ✿ Friends don't let friends drive napping.
- ✿ If you can read this, thank your bifocals.
- ✿ Let me repeat myself. And also, let me repeat myself.
- ✿ I ♥ my air-conditioner.
- ✿ Driver carries no money. He can't remember where he left it. He doesn't even know he's driving.
- ✿ The light at the end of the tunnel is your optometrist.
- ✿ Got Supp-Hose?
- ✿ I brake for leg cramps.
- ✿ Honk if you have all your original body parts.

15

Speak Now or Forever Hold Your Peace

The rumors of my death are greatly exaggerated.
—Mark Twain

Nine days after a 6.6 earthquake hit Bam, Iran, rescue workers managed to pull a ninety-seven-year-old woman from the rubble—alive, uninjured, and apparently, quite thirsty. According to reports, the elderly lady credited God with her amazing miracle of survival, then she asked for a cup of tea. When rescue workers brought it to her, she thanked them, then mustered up just enough energy to complain that it was too hot.

Obviously, somewhere along the way to her ninety-seventh birthday, this incredible woman had learned the importance of speaking up. Not only had she survived the massive earthquake, but she had survived ninety-seven years on this earth. She knew that alone entitled her to a few things, and one of them was to have her tea at whatever temperature she so desired. Good for her!

No matter how old you happen to be right now, you, too, have earned the right to speak up. Life gives you that right. Babies know that. They come into the world and immediately they start letting us know what they want.

"Wah!" ("I want my milk!")

"Wah!" ("I want a cookie!")

"Wah!" ("I want those $100 sneakers!")

And so it goes.

Somewhere between birth and middle age, however, some of us forget about the importance of letting our needs (or even our wants) be known. That's not to say that we should act like spoiled children. But if we've allowed the pendulum to swing too far away from our needs because we didn't want to rock the boat, or we've tried our best not to get in anyone's way, maybe it's time to take a lesson from a ninety-seven-year-old woman in Iran and speak up.

It's not easy, though. Especially if you're used to being non-confrontational.

"My foot? Yes, as a matter of fact your car did just roll over it, but don't worry. I'm sure the feeling will return eventually."

"I'm sorry. How thoughtless of me to try to order my food while you are standing in line behind me talking on the cell phone. I hope I didn't disturb your call."

Many of us have been performing the role of doormat for so long, it's become a very comfortable role. What we're forgetting, however, is the simple fact that each of us was made for a reason. We have a purpose. A mission. And to achieve that mission, from time to time we're going to have to speak up. If we constantly allow our voice to be silenced, then our mission will be routed.

A friend of mine used to tell me that when I reached a certain age, I would find it easier to speak up for myself. She said that it was just something that seems to kick in after forty. She was right. Maybe it's because we finally realize in the second half of our lives that our peace of mind is just as important as anyone else's peace of mind. As is our happiness. And as is our truth.

Still, the choice is ours. We can live our lives, or we can let others, circumstances, and fear limit us.

The fact that you're still around today is no accident. Recall the first major illness or accident that you had as a child. If you had lived a hundred years ago, you probably would not have survived it. Medicine has made so many advances over the last hundred years that many of the things that used to take someone's life back then require nothing more than a prescription today.

But you weren't alive back then, you're alive now. And so far you have survived everything that life has brought your way. Clearly, you have a purpose. So speak what's on your heart. Share your ideas, your opinions, and your suggestions for improving the world. Don't let others intimidate you out of standing up for what you believe. Whether you're 44, 64, or 84, you're a survivor. Don't hide away in your house, just watching year after year after year slip by. Do something. Be active. There's a reason that you're still here. Live like it.

We are the hero of our own story.
—Mary McCarthy

16

I Am Not Hungry, I Am Not Hungry, I Am Not Hungry

Never eat more than you can lift.
—Miss Piggy

I'm on the metric diet. It's a great diet plan. You just buy a scale that measures your weight in metric. You can eat whatever you want and never break 100.

Extra weight and middle age just seem to go together, don't they? For whatever reason, we wake up one morning and discover we're retaining more water than Atlantis. We can't fit into most of our clothes, and we figure there is only one thing to do—go on a diet, right?

If you watch television, listen to the radio, read magazines and junk mail, you would get the impression that we are obsessed with dieting. Each year it seems some new fitness guru comes out with a new way for us to lose weight (and for him or her to become a millionaire). There's the no-carb diet, the low-carb diet, the low-fat diet, the high-carb/low-fat diet, the no-sugar diet, the interrogation diet (you don't eat anything, but are still accused of it), and of course, the shame diet (a personal trainer follows you along the buffet line muttering insults under his breath).

"You're not really going to eat that, are you?"

"Fried corn on the cob? Where's that on your diet plan?"

"This is your third plate, you know. I don't care if it is a saucer, it still counts!"

So what's the best diet, the one that will help you lose the most weight and get your personal trainer or other weight-loss cheerleaders off your back?

Good question. No matter how many promises they make, it all comes down to this: the best diet is the one that works best for you. Weight Watchers, Jenny Craig, South Beach, and Atkins all offer plenty of amazing testimonials. But if those diet plans don't work for your body, what good are they to you? We're all different. The perfect diet for you might be the worst diet for me, and vice versa. So we experiment. We try this one and that one and that other one until we finally find a diet plan that will give us the results we want.

But why does losing weight have to be so hard anyway? The answer is simple. Science is once again missing the obvious solution. Science should be working to find a way to put the most calories in the food products that we like the least, and the least calories in the food products that we like the best. If they would figure out a way to do this, our problems would be solved. Imagine the dialogue.

"Brussels sprouts? They look good, but I'd better not. Gotta watch the ol' waistline, you know."

"No cauliflower for you, young man, until you finish all that Cinnabon!"

"You've had enough carrots, sweetie. They're going to ruin your dinner. If you must eat something, eat some brownies."

Now I ask you, doesn't that make a lot more sense? Why should we continue to force ourselves to eat the right foods when all we have to do is make the food we hate the enemy and turn what we love into health food. We need to take the calories out of that banana split and put them into cabbage where they belong. Why should we hold our noses every time we eat broccoli? We all know that broccoli is good for us, but come on, it's a flower.

All we would need to do is take the nutrients and low calorie count of broccoli and switch it with, say, a funnel cake. Who among us would complain about that? Imagine funnel cakes being touted as the latest breakthrough in healthy eating, with dieticians telling us to have at least three servings of it a day. Imagine seeing the heart-friendly symbol next to it on the menu. It brings a tear to your eye, doesn't it?

My sincere hope is that someone reading this book will be moved to dedicate his or her life to this revolutionary dietary research. Perhaps I'm speaking to you, or to one of your children or grandchildren. Whoever it is, if you would do this for your world, you would be doing us all a great service. One of these days we could be hearing about the Sara Lee Diet Plan, the Ben and Jerry's Weight Loss System, and the "Krispy Kreme

10 Days to a Brand-New You" Challenge. You know who you are. I hereby leave it in your hands.

*The second day of a diet
is always easier than the first.
By the second day, you're off it.*
—Jackie Gleason

17

The Raven-ing

Once upon a diet dreary,
I lay famished, weak, and weary,
hunger pangs too fast and numerous
for my stomach to ignore.
Bathroom scale, it was just mocking.
Still, I would have eaten caulking,
if somebody wasn't knocking,
knocking at my condo door.
"O be Pizza Hut!" I muttered,
knocking at my condo door.
"Double Cheese, I'm praying for!"
I was on the Atkins Diet
'til a breadstick caused a riot.
On to Weight Watchers to try it,
hoping that I could eat more.
But they had a rule they followed—
a whole ham could not be swallowed.
So in self-pity I wallowed,

licking crumbs up off my floor.
Then I heard more of that knocking,
tapping, rapping at my door,
and wondered who it could be for.
Oh, I've dreamed of eating Twinkies,
licking filling off my pinkies.
Scrambled eggs and sausage linkies.
Little Debbie cakes galore!
Dreamed of sourdough from 'Frisco,
every snack sold by Nabisco,
chocolate bars and even Crisco.
Could I last a second more?
I was starved down to my core!

    Drat this diet evermore!
It is water I'm retaining,
that's the reason for my gaining.
And don't think that I'm complaining,
I just need to eat some more!
I love fat, I won't deny it.
Food is better when you fry it!
See a Snickers and I buy it,
then I keep on wanting more!

    Drat this diet ever more!
So I turned the knob and then I
opened up the door, but when I
saw the one who wanted in, I
had to shut the door again.
'Twas my trainer looking for me,
to work out, she would implore me.
How I wish she'd just ignore me!
But I was late for my weigh-in.

258

"Look at all the weight you've packed on!
All the burgers you have macked on!
All the Ding Dongs you have snacked on!"
She never screamed like that before.
With the accusations flying,
I assured her I was trying.
I was starving, maybe dying,
But she heard me out no more.
Made me promise I would diet,
then told me to just be quiet.
Exercise? I was to try it,
so I did what she implored.
I stepped back and took position.
I would stop her inquisition.
Did a leg lift in submission,
as I'd kick her out the door!
    Drat this diet evermore!
Now I'm back to eating Twinkies,
licking filling off my pinkies.
scrambled eggs and sausage linkies,
Little Debbie cakes galore.
I don't need no weight loss planning.
Workout tapes I will be banning.
In the space I'll end up spanning,
I'll be happy to my core!
    And I'll be hungry *nevermore*!

18

The Super Senior Bowl

You guys line up alphabetically by height.
—Bill Peterson,
Florida State football coach

If there isn't one already, someone needs to start a seniors' football league.

There's a Senior Tour in golf and it seems to be doing rather well, so why not advance the concept and have one in football? The baby boomer generation would be avid fans. It would be our chance to see all our favorite players who have long since retired.

A few rules of the game would have to be changed, of course.

For one thing, the center wouldn't be required to bend over for the snap. It might take too long for him to get back up, and that clock is ticking. Even the word "snap" might need to be changed since it could cause the team doctor to rush unnecessarily onto the field with a splint.

Instead of assigning arbitrary numbers to all the players, I would suggest they simply put their ages on the jerseys. That way, we could follow the game a little more easily and have a greater understanding of the plays.

"Number 72 hikes the ball to 60 who passes it to number 80. What a throw! He hasn't passed anything like that since that kidney stone in '83. And yes! The pass is good! 80 takes the ball and runs . . . er, walks . . . er, is being carried to the 32-yard line. But not before being tackled by 78 and the rest of the opposing team. Ladies and gentlemen, take a look at that pileup! Have you ever seen anything like that before? All the players are down and a stretcher is being brought onto the field even as we speak. But who's it for? 78? 80? All of them? . . . Wait a minute, wait a minute. It appears . . . yes, yes, someone is already on the stretcher! I don't believe it! The stretcher is carrying the replacement linebacker! Now, that's something you don't see every day, a player being carried onto the field. But number 92 is not just any player, folks. He's the oldest player in Senior Football League history. Who can forget that game when he broke the record for most yardage? One hundred and twelve yards! (Sixty-eight yards to the end zone and 44 more to the rest room!)"

Of course, you can't have a seniors' league without cheerleaders.

"I'm tellin' ya, folks, in all my years of covering professional sports, I've never seen cheerleaders move like that! You'd think those oxygen tanks would slow them down, but these gals are out there giving it everything they've got! And even though that one gal still hasn't gotten up from those splits she did during the first quarter, this is one impressive pep squad! And sure, we all remember that one awkward moment when they threw one of the gals up in the air, and before she came down, they had forgotten what they had done with her. But did they quit? Did they give up? Did they catch her? No! But they didn't let that

stop them. They hung in there and kept on cheering. These gals have spirit! Why, just listen to them cheer.

"*2–4–6–8, what disc can we herniate? All of them! All of them! Yea!*"

Yes, from the team to the cheerleaders to the traditional pouring of the Geritol over the coach's head, a seniors' football league would be great fun to watch. And I haven't even talked about the wave yet.

"*Here it comes.*"

"*Here what comes?*"

"*The wave. Get ready!*"

"*Okay, but who am I waving to?*"

"*Nobody.*"

"*Then why do you want me to wave?*"

"*It's what you do at football games.*"

"*We're at a football game?*"

"*Never mind. It's over.*"

"*Who won?*"

"*Not the game. The wave is over.*"

"*Just as well. I'm not waving at anyone unless you tell me who it is I'm waving to!*"

All right, so maybe the concept needs a little work. But I still think it's worth a try. Why, I can hear the vendors now. "Get your granola! Get your soy! Get your prune danish!"

> **We're going to turn this team
> around 360 degrees.**
> —Jason Kidd

19

Classic Tunes Updated for Aging Baby Boomers

- Hank Williams—"Your Skippin' Heart" (formerly "Your Cheatin' Heart")
- Glen Campbell—"By the Time I Get My Teeth In" (formerly "By the Time I Get to Phoenix")
- Otis Redding—"Sittin' at the Doctor's All Day" (formerly "Dock of the Bay")
- The Platters—"Sweat Gets in My Eyes" (formerly "Smoke Gets in Your Eyes")
- Paul Anka—"Put Ben-Gay on My Shoulder" (formerly "Put Your Head on My Shoulder")
- Aretha Franklin—"R-U-N-A-A-R-P?" (formerly "R-E-S-P-E-C-T")

- ✿ The Supremes—"Where Did My Mind Go?" (formerly "Where Did Our Love Go?")
- ✿ Elvis Presley—"Blue Suede Orthotics" (formerly "Blue Suede Shoes")
- ✿ The Tokens—"Can't Get to Sleep Tonight" (formerly "The Lion Sleeps Tonight")
- ✿ Elvis Presley—"That's All Right, Grandma" (formerly "That's All Right, Mama")
- ✿ Gene Pitney—"It Hurts to Be This Old" (formerly "It Hurts to Be in Love")
- ✿ Neil Sedaka—"Standing Up Is Hard to Do" (formerly "Breaking Up Is Hard to Do")
- ✿ Bobby Vee—"Take Good Care of My Knee Joints" (formerly "Take Good Care of My Baby")
- ✿ Marvin Gaye—"I Heard It Through My Beltone" (formerly "I Heard It Through the Grapevine")
- ✿ Perry Como—"Catch a Falling Friend" (formerly "Catch a Falling Star")
- ✿ Elvis Presley—"All Hooked Up" (formerly "All Shook Up")
- ✿ The Supremes—"You Can't Hurry Me" (formerly "You Can't Hurry Love")
- ✿ Ricky Nelson—"There Goes My Figure" (formerly "There Goes My Baby")
- ✿ Martha & The Vandellas—"Hot Flash" (formerly "Heat Wave")
- ✿ Roy Rogers—"Yellow Toes of Texas" (formerly "Yellow Rose of Texas")
- ✿ The Comets—"Nap Around the Clock" (formerly "Rock Around the Clock")

20

High-Fiving Thighs

What you eat standing up doesn't count.
—Beth Barnes

My inner thighs never used to be this close. In all the years that I've been hanging around them, the right one has stayed to the right side of my body, and the left one has stayed to the left. This has been the understanding between them, and they've respected each other's space. They've been cooperative and dutiful. Whenever I walked, one didn't trespass on the other's territory, and they didn't slap each other in some high-fiving thigh way. They simply stayed at their post, content, satisfied, and separate.

Since hitting menopause (and, all right I confess, more than my share of all-you-can-eat buffets and southern "meat and threes"), all that has changed. My thighs have gotten a lot friendlier with each other. They overlap a good two or three inches and whip against each other every time I take a step. It's like I've grown my own mud flaps.

No one really knows about this but me. For the most part, all of this thigh trespassing takes place under my clothing, and most people have no hint that anything out of the ordinary is happening. But it is. Sometimes the friction is enough to heat the wrinkles right out of my jeans. And it can be noisy, too. Sometimes people turn their heads as I walk by and comment,

"Did you hear that?"

"Yeah, what was it?"

"It sounded like two cats fighting on a leather sofa."

Like other changes in middle age, these thigh appendages seem to have appeared with no warning. One day I fit into my jeans perfectly fine, and the next day I'm needing to line them with Vaseline just to get them past my knees. Perhaps this is why so many middle-agers and seniors have insomnia. Considering all the bodily changes that keep happening during the night, we're afraid to go to sleep!

They say Pilates is good for toning and shaping the upper thighs, so I'm seriously thinking about giving it a try (interpreted, that means I've bought the tape but haven't opened it yet).

In the meantime, I guess I have no other choice but to put up with all the fighting my thighs are doing with every step I take.

"Hey, get back over on your own side!"

"Oh, yeah? Who's gonna make me?"

"This is my territory!"

"No, it's not. I was here first!"

"Were not!"

"Were too!"

"Were not!"
It's sad, isn't it? And they used to get along so well.

I don't jog, if I die I want to be sick.
—Abe Lemons

21

Going Through the Changes

Change is inevitable—
except from a vending machine.
—Robert C. Gallagher

They say wisdom comes with age. And in a lot of ways that's true. We've had a lot of time to think about how we can improve the world if only given the chance. They may not all be great ideas, but some could be pure genius. But who asks us? We're walking around with all this wisdom, and no one is coming up to us and inquiring as to how we'd run things. I haven't received any calls from the president, have you? No one from Congress has called either. The governor hasn't even stopped by for a chat and a burger while we discuss the affairs of the state.

The phone company hasn't sent anyone to my house to see if there's any way to improve their service to me. And no one from CBS, NBC, ABC, or FOX has called my house to see if their programming is to my liking. No one's asking me if I have any better ideas about how to run the world. I do, and I'm sure you do, too. But all our input is being forced to stay put. It's their loss, of course.

The first change that I would make would be with the calendar. I've long felt that some months deserve more days while other months could be greatly improved if their allotment was cut back just a little. Take April, for example. The way I see it, April really only needs fifteen days. After tax day, April is basically over. We don't want to think about April anymore. We're ready to put it all behind us and move on to May. Why pretend we're enjoying the second half of April? We're miserable and April knows it. Let's be honest with ourselves and move on.

On the other hand, December is a fun month and should be extended. Especially the period of time between Christmas and New Year's Eve. Who among us couldn't use another week to handle all the gift returns, out-of-town relatives, and the writing of our New Year's resolutions? We would take the days that we took from April and add them all to December.

February is long overdue for some extra days as well. February has been shortchanged for years and I don't think anyone really knows why. What kind of trouble can a month get into anyway? What could February possibly have done to deserve such treatment? February is the "love" month. It's been bringing us warm and fuzzy feelings for a long time now, but how do we repay it? We make it a junior month, a second-stringer, a mini-page on the calendar of life. It gives us romance and we give it inferiority in return. Oh, every four years we feel guilty enough to throw an extra day its way for leap year, but even with that, it only brings February's count up to twenty-nine days, which is still shorter than all the other months. February is not stupid. It knows what's been going on. February's been a real trooper, and it's high time we rewarded that kind of dedication to duty. The new calendar that I propose would be an attempt to make up for all the years of calendar abuse and grant February another four weeks. February would go from being the shortest month to being the longest. It would be a sort of "Take that!" to those day hogs like January, March, May, and July. Not to mention August, October, and December. It would finally be February's time to shine.

June is a month for weddings and could, I'm sure, use a few more weekends just to accommodate them all. I wouldn't give June any more workdays, though, because traditionally June is a vacation month. Who wants more workdays in a vacation month?

As for November, for all intents and purposes, it's over after Thanksgiving. True, there are all the after-Thanksgiving sales, but their focus is really Christmas and they rightfully belong in the month of December.

Another thing that I would change is television. In my opinion, television still skews too young. That's why you'll never see *Geriatric Survivor: Last Senior Standing,* or *My Big, Fat, Obnoxious Retirement Party.* The ironic thing, though, is we're the ones who are probably watching the most television. My husband watches the Weather Channel like it's a mini-series.

"Can we turn it now? It's been four days and nothing's changed."

"All right, one more Local on the 8s and I hand over the remote."

He watches the History Channel, Discovery Channel, Animal Planet, and whatever looks good on the networks and other cable stations. I watch the twenty-four-hour news programs, *Everybody Loves Raymond* reruns, and some of the new reality shows. I also watch the Home and Garden Network, and we always try to watch *Meet the Press*. Like teenagers, we flip through the channels with our remote controls, looking for something interesting to watch. With only a hundred stations to choose from, that's not always easy.

We like some of the new season's programs, and we don't care for others. We like some of the made-for-TV movies, and we don't care for others. We like some of the late-night talk shows, and we don't care for others. We have our own tastes, to be sure, but give us quality shows and I think you'd be surprised at how many of us middle-agers would watch them.

Another thing that I would change about the world are all the perfume and cologne samples that advertisers keep putting in magazines. You know the ones I'm talking about, those little inserts where you simply peel back the protective strip and get a whiff of whatever aroma they happen to be advertising. If you have allergies like me, one pass through the magazine can leave you sneezing for hours. So I would like to make a suggestion: Instead of perfume and cologne samples, why don't they give us something we could really use? Scratch-and-taste samples of some of their featured recipes? *Bon Appétit* magazine could really be "bon appétit." You could lick yourself a four-course meal by page 28.

I don't know if any of my suggestions will be taken seriously or not, but that's all right. I am speaking up, and that's the important thing.

A fanatic is one who can't change his mind and won't change the subject.
—Winston Churchill

22

Suggested Movies for Middle-Agers

* Hey, Dude, Where's My Teeth?
* Legally Gray
* Florida's Most Wanted
* Gangs of Palm Beach
* Cold Feet Manor
* Near-Total Recall
* Man in the Iron Lung
* Sleepless in Every City
* Catch You If I Can
* The Rock (And the Rest of My Kidney Stones)

23

When I'm an Old Lady

When our youngest son was an adolescent, my husband had him write a note and sign it, stating that my husband could live in his garage when he was old. My husband grew up living in a one-car garage, so it was one of those, "Just give me a garage and I'll be happy" sort of discussions that led to the note. It was really just a joke, but my husband had it framed and proudly shows it off to guests. I don't have a note yet. I'll have to get one though, because living with my children, getting on their nerves, embarrassing them, and being demanding is the one thing to look forward to in old age. It pays them back for those 2 A.M. feedings, the temper tantrums, the spilled milk, and everything else!

I'm not sure who wrote the following, but it says it all.

When I'm an Old Lady

When I'm an old lady, I'll live with each kid,
And bring so much happiness . . . just as they did.
I want to pay back all the joy they've provided,

Returning each deed. Oh, they'll be so excited!
When I'm an old lady and live with my kids.
I'll write on the walls with reds, whites, and blues,
And bounce on the furniture, wearing my shoes.
I'll drink from the carton and then leave it out.
I'll stuff all the toilets and oh, how they'll shout!
When I'm an old lady and live with my kids.
When they're on the phone and just out of reach,
I'll get into things like sugar and bleach.
Oh, they'll snap their fingers and then shake their head,
And when that is done I'll hide under the bed!
When I'm an old lady and live with my kids.
When they cook dinner and call me to eat,
I'll not eat my green beans or salad or meat.
I'll gag on my okra, spill milk on the table,
And when they get angry I'll run . . . if I'm able!
When I'm an old lady and live with my kids.
I'll sit close to the TV, through the channels I'll click,
I'll cross both eyes just to see if they stick.
I'll take off my socks and throw one away,
And play in the mud 'til the end of the day!
When I'm an old lady and live with my kids.
And later in bed, I'll lay back and sigh;
I'll thank God in prayer and then close my eyes.
My kids will look down with a smile slowly creeping,
And say with a groan, "She's so sweet when she's sleeping!"
When I'm an old lady and live with my kids.

Author Unknown

24

Striking It Rich

*I used to sell furniture for a living.
The trouble was, it was my own.*
—Les Dawson

If you've made it to middle age, chances are you've seen your share of ups and downs in your financial standing. It doesn't matter if you invested in real estate, the stock market, gold bars, or collectibles, they've all had their share of fluctuations.

When we were newlyweds, my husband and I bought land in the desert. It was our retirement investment. The salesman convinced us to buy the parcel with the tease that it would be worth some hundred thousand dollars in ten years or so.

It's been three decades now and it's not worth much more than what we paid for it, not even counting the interest. The problem is some years ago the government deemed the area a sanctuary for a rare gnat. (I'll wait a moment while you reread that last sentence.) Now that you know there is nothing wrong with your eyes, merely our investment instincts, I'll continue.

Our investment property has become a sort of gnat refugee camp, and so far there's been nothing that we can do about it. We haven't been able to build any permanent structure on the land because it might disturb the natural environment for the gnat. We can sell the property, but we wouldn't get very much for it. Gnats don't carry a lot of cash and humans prefer getting a little more return on their investments. So there it sits, gathering tumbleweeds and fast-food trash, and I assume, more gnats.

That's not the only investment that hasn't panned out for us. We invested in art, too. Our pieces haven't gone up in value as much as we'd like, except for the one on velvet. I think that's because the artist hand-signed it down by Elvis's right leg.

We also used to have some antique crystal and depression glass that my husband had inherited from his mother. The Northridge, California, earthquake took care of any monetary value of those. I salvaged the sentimental value, though, by gathering up some of the pieces to put into a mosaic someday.

And therein lies my point. Nothing is guaranteed for us in life. We can make a fortune in the stock market and lose it all the next week. Real estate can boom and bust, and we can boom and bust right along with it. Collectibles are only worth what someone is willing to pay for them. One year they could command a fortune, the next year we can't give them away.

The true value of a possession, the unchangeable value, will always be the sentimental value. It isn't the house that's worth so much, it's the memories you made in it. It's the Christmases you spent sitting around the fireplace while you watched *It's A Wonderful Life* or *A Christmas Story* on television. It's all those nights the family spent playing board games around the table.

Or the late-night talks you had with your children, sitting on the edge of their beds. No matter what our real-estate appraiser says, it's the memories that determine the real value of a home.

By the same token, the only truly valuable works of art in our possession are the paintings and sculptures created by our children or grandchildren, the ones that are so proudly displayed on our refrigerator doors. They may not be hung in the Getty Museum or in the Metropolitan Museum of Art, but their value is priceless for they are truly irreplaceable.

When we look at our possessions in this way, it won't matter if the value of our home goes up or down, if the stock market soars or plunges, or if our collectibles collect worth or not, for we'll know that we are wealthy in the things that really matter.

> **You cannot have everything.**
> **I mean, where would you put it?**
> —Steven Wright

25

Broadway for Middle-Agers

- ✿ Annie, Get Your Girdle
- ✿ Gramma Mia!
- ✿ After the Fall . . . And I Can't Get Up
- ✿ I Love You, You're Perfect, Now . . . What Was I Talking About?
- ✿ A Raisin in the Mirror
- ✿ Beauty and the Plastic Surgeon
- ✿ Bunion King
- ✿ I'm Miserables
- ✿ West Side Bursitis
- ✿ Owe Rent
- ✿ Much Ado About Cholesterol
- ✿ Hello, Doctor!

26

All Puffed Up

A woman is as old as she looks before breakfast.
—Ed Howe

Middle age has made me puffy. I never used to be puffy. Puffy wasn't a look I was going for, and as far as I know, puffiness has never been featured on the cover of women's magazines as the latest beauty secret. You won't read articles titled "Ten Sure Ways to Puff Up by Summer" or "Where Celebrities Go to Puff." But for some reason, puffiness of varying degrees seems to show up in middle age unannounced, unexpected, and most definitely unwelcomed.

Before I go on, I should clarify one thing. The puffiness that I am referring to is not the same puffiness that I and others like me tend to get after three trips to the buffet counter. Buffet-induced puffiness at least brings with it the memory of fried chicken, potatoes, gravy, and pecan pie to help us cope. Middle-aged puffiness offers no such memories. Its stealth arrival is usually in the middle of the night. The puffee (person doomed to puff) has no idea that it is coming. She simply goes to bed one night looking perfectly normal, and by morning, she's the Michelin Man.

I say "she," but it happens to men, too, and men have the added danger of the necktie. This is of grave concern because the necktie can develop noose-like qualities as the puffage increases. A noose is not a good fashion look.

Aside from the swelling neck area, under-eye swelling is another concern. Often called "bags," these little pockets of puff can make one appear older than he or she actually is. I don't know if it's true, but I read somewhere that applying a dab of Preparation H under each eye is supposed to help. But two words of caution. First, I would check with your doctor before dabbing any medication under your eyes. And second, be careful not to mix up the tube of hemorrhoid cream with your tube of foot cream. Hemorrhoid cream tends to promote shrinkage, and I'm not positive, but this could be why some older people keep getting shorter.

Another part of the body that is prone to puffiness is the cheek area. This seems to be the area where I have my biggest problem. My cheeks have puffed up so much that squirrels have been known to follow me home just to see where I hide my stash of nuts.

My hands can get puffy, too. So much so that even though I know it's there, I haven't seen my wedding ring in over four months.

And if you tend to be as sedentary as I am, your legs can really puff up, especially as the day wears on. I can put on a pair of baggy jeans in the morning, and by mid-afternoon, I need the Jaws of Life to get me free from them. And let me tell you, there's nothing more embarrassing than having to be cut from denim. At least with a real accident, there's an emergency vehicle on stand-by and people are hovering over you, assuring you that everything's going to be all right. But trust me, no one cares about someone getting rescued from a pair of Wranglers.

"Is she going to be all right?"

"It's her own fault. Denim can only stretch so much."

The most serious puffage, however, occurs in the feet and ankles area. Too many of us don't get up and get our blood circulating like we used to. We spend our day either sitting at our computers, behind the steering wheel of our car, at the dinner table, or on the sofa in front of our television sets without so much as a twitch of a toe.

Regular movement is the best way to keep the puff at bay. That, and whenever possible, keep your feet elevated. (This is a little difficult to do while driving, unless you have cruise control. Even so, you might get a ticket if your feet are blocking the windshield.)

Another helpful tip in combating the puff problem is our choice of apparel. For me, turtlenecks are a big no-no. It has been my experience that turtlenecks will merely exaggerate puffiness. I wore a turtleneck for our family portrait last year and my cheeks appeared to block out two family members who were standing behind me. Like my wedding ring, I knew they were there, but no one could see them.

Choice of jewelry is another consideration. Depending on the level of water retention one happens to be experiencing at the moment, choker necklaces can be considered a form of slow suicide. Hence, the name "choker." Longer necklaces are far more flattering and will permit you to continue to indulge in that activity that has become a favorite among so many of us—breathing.

So whether right now you're a pre-puff, mid-puff, or post-puff, just remember it's not your fault. This kind of puffing has nothing to do with eating and everything to do with middle age. No matter how bloated you feel, just know that you are every bit as pretty or handsome as you ever were. And though the event happened years ago, I myself have taken some solace in those immortal words that were overheard at the dedication ceremony of the Hoover Dam.

"She's a beaut, boys, and boy can she hold the water!"

Happiness can exist only in acceptance.
—Denis De Rougamont

27

Reversal of Misfortune

Sometimes I lie awake at night, and I ask, "Where have I gone wrong?" Then a voice says to me, "This is going to take more than one night."
—Charlie Brown

Have you ever considered keeping a journal of all the mistakes you've made in life? If you're like most of us, it would take more than one journal. Maybe four or five. Or perhaps dozens.

What if you kept another journal to document every time someone has hurt you? That could fill up dozens, too. And how about another journal for all the times you were betrayed, the false accusations you had to endure, and every discouraging remark that was ever spoken to you?

After a while, you would have an awful lot of journals filled with an awful lot of negative memories, wouldn't you? But other than getting all that pain off your chest, what good would they really do?

Maybe there's a better use for all that paper. Instead of

writing about every mistake you've ever made, why not write about all the lessons you've learned from those mistakes? Write down how you've grown from your hurts and failures. Write how it felt to be falsely accused of something, or overlooked for a promotion, or kicked when you were down, and how that experience gave you a little more empathy for others who might have suffered the same pain. Now those would make some interesting reading, wouldn't they?

Unfortunately, we cannot prevent life from bringing us to some pretty painful places. They're not our first destination choices by any means, but nevertheless, they're written down on our ticket and sometimes there's not a lot we can do about the itinerary. It's like flying from California to New York and you have to make one or two stopovers along the way—you didn't ask for those stops, that's just how the ticket came.

Life's little side trips can be like that. We may not have asked for them, and we certainly don't have to enjoy them. But they don't have to affect our final destination. We can continue on our journey, perhaps a little wiser, perhaps a little more determined, but not deterred in the least. Whatever memories and lessons we choose to take away from each of our stops is up to us.

The secret to a happy life is not perfection. It is contentment, and contentment isn't something that can be ordered from QVC or bought and sold on eBay. You can't borrow it from your neighbor or send away for it through a catalog. Contentment is something we have to want, work for, and once we get, do everything we can to keep it.

Contentment doesn't mean that everything has, is, or will go smoothly in your life. It simply means that whatever is happening, you're not going to stress over it. You've given the matter to God to handle (he's better qualified to take care of it anyway), and you're free to live at peace.

So quit dwelling on whatever negatives have come your way. No one has done this thing called "life" without running into a little turbulence along the way. Life is about lessons learned, judgments improved, forgiveness rendered, trust renewed, hurts healed, behaviors changed, boundaries defined, and successes enjoyed even after multiple failures.

Why do you think people say such nice things at funerals? Because their loved ones had no flaws? Hardly. We all have flaws. Individuals are admired at the end of their life not because of their perfection, but because of their perseverance. They may have endured plenty of setbacks, failures, and hurts, but with them came plenty of opportunities for them to shine. And to be content.

Many people die at twenty-five and aren't buried until they are seventy-five.
—Max Frisch

28

The Rise and Fall of Cellulite

*Laziness is nothing more than
the habit of resting before you get tired.*
—Jules Renard

My husband's uncle, Rev. Anthony dePompa, who is in his nineties, has been doing water aerobics every week for years. Water aerobics are good because they allow you to exercise with less risk of injury. I think I'm going to sign up. I figure that even if I don't get into shape, staying in the water that long would at least give me an excuse for my wrinkles.

There are other reasons why I like the idea of exercising in water. I can blame my extra weight on the optical distortion of the water. I can splash water on my back and shoulders and make it look like I've been sweating. And a pool has got to smell a whole lot better than a gym!

If I never get around to joining a water aerobics class, however, I'm fairly certain I'm still getting a good workout just going about my daily routine. If I had a pedometer, I would know how many miles I walk in a twenty-four-hour period. It has got to be pretty impressive. From the moment I get up in the morning, I'm burning the calories. It's like I'm on my own personal marathon. I walk from the bed to the kitchen to make a couple of Eggos, then walk over to the computer desk to do a single knee bend into my chair, then I do an hour or so of finger exercises on my keyboard before walking to the pantry for a snack.

After that, it's off to the mailbox to check on the mail, then to the refrigerator for a sandwich, and back to the computer for another knee bend and more finger exercises. Then I walk back to the cupboard for a bag of Fritos, giving my arm muscles a good workout just trying to open it. After walking around the family room looking for the remote, I do another knee bend onto the sofa and more finger exercises changing the channels. After another hour or so, I do a sit-up, then get on my feet again and walk to the freezer for some weightlifting (a pint of Ben and Jerry's in each hand), then walk back to the computer for more finger exercises between the keyboard and lifting spoonfuls of Chunky Monkey and Chocolate Chip Cookie Dough to my mouth. Then it's back to the pantry for some chips, and . . . Whew. I'm exhausted just thinking about it!

As you can see, even if I never get around to joining an aerobics class, I think I'm still covered. Besides, I also try to fit in my agitator workout every day. It's my own workout plan that I'm seriously thinking about marketing. The agitator workout is where I sit on my washing machine during the spin cycle and just let it shake the weight off of me. It works a little like the old vibrating belts, only you don't have to stand. The seat's not all that comfortable, but it's a good workout. And whenever it gets an uneven load, I can really feel the burn (especially if I'm using the "Hot-Warm" cycle).

Speaking of vibrating belts, I know I already told the story of my vibrating belt experience in my book *Didn't My Skin Used to Fit?*, so I won't repeat myself here. But suffice it to say that in my own opinion, my new agitator workout is much safer. So be watching for my new workout video to be released.

(All right, I confess. The above tease was just a shameless plug for my other book, so I will go ahead and share the story here, too. It merits being repeated anyway.)

You see, it was like this. I had some cellulite in my arms and legs and wasn't too thrilled about it. I had heard that a vibrating belt might help, so one day I decided to give it a try. I vibrated my legs, hips, and arms, envisioning all the cellulite being shaken from my body and my memory. It felt great.

When I was done, the cellulite of course was still there, but I figured it was just a matter of time before it would all begin to smooth out and I could return to my BC self (before cellulite).

It turned out to be just a matter of *one* night. When I got up that next morning and looked at myself in the mirror, I could not find any upper-arm cellulite. I could not find any upper-arm cellulite because *all of my upper-arm fat had somehow slid down to my elbows!* There were two huge cavities in each of my arms, and my elbows were bulging like Popeye's! I wanted to cry. I wanted to laugh.

I wanted to cry and laugh. I couldn't believe the image staring back at me in the mirror. The ironic thing was I had done it all to myself in an effort to *improve* my body. It was akin to choking to death on a vitamin, or perhaps drowning while attempting a push-up in a water aerobics class.

I made an appointment with my doctor who examined me, then called a partner of his into the office to take a look.

"How'd you say you did this again?" he asked.

I told him, and they both just stared at me in amazement. There wasn't anything they could do. So I quit wearing short sleeves and tried my best to hide my Popeye arms.

I thought I was going to have to live like that for the rest of my life, but after two years I awoke one morning, glanced at myself in the mirror, and noticed something interesting. My upper-arm fat that had slid down to my elbows had somehow made the return trip. Just as mysteriously as it had fallen, it had risen to duty once again, as though nothing had ever happened.

Now, granted, this was just *my* experience. You could try a vibrating belt and have perfectly fine results. But I think I'm going to stick with my agitator workout program. The only danger I see with that is falling off the machine. And if that happens, there is usually a full basket of laundry nearby that I can aim for.

We all get heavier as we get older because there's a lot more information in our heads.
—Vlade Divac,
NBA basketball player

29

Until

*You are as young as your faith,
as old as your doubt,
as young as your self-confidence,
as old as your fear,
as young as your hope,
as old as your despair.*
—Paul H. Duhn

Now that we've entered into the second half of our lives, what advice do we have for others on the best way to cope? Attitude.

It's all about attitude.

- Be positive *until* your circumstances improve.
- Be generous *until* you aren't even aware of your sacrifices.
- Be curious *until* there is nothing left to learn.
- Be unconditionally loving *until* you no longer need to be loved unconditionally.
- Be courageous *until* there is nothing left to stand up for.

❀ Be content *until* you need nothing more than what you already have.

❀ Be available *until* you hardly notice the inconvenience.

❀ Be joyful *until* the sadness is healed.

❀ Be forgiving *until* you need no forgiveness from anyone, anywhere, anytime.

❀ Be thankful *until* you run out of things to be thankful for.

A positive attitude may not solve all your problems, but it will annoy enough people to make it worth the effort.
—Herm Albright

30

Picture This

Beauty is in the eye of the beholder; but it may be necessary, from time to time, to give a stupid, or misinformed beholder, a black eye.
—Miss Piggy

Pictures. One snap of the camera and they've captured a moment, a memory, and sometimes every wrinkle and dark circle on our faces. There are, of course, lighting and makeup tricks that can help, as well as special lenses that a photographer can use. But everyday folks don't always know about these. Movie stars do. That's why you'll often see magazine covers featuring a sixty-year-old legend who barely looks forty. It's not so much a matter of her ageless beauty being captured on film as it's a matter of a very creative makeup artist and photographer.

The worst pictures for me are the outdoor shots. Have you ever had someone snap a close-up of you while you're squinting into full sunlight? Your face can end up looking like a page out of a Rand McNally map. Downtown Cincinnati, to be exact. Every street, or rather, every line and wrinkle shows up. Even the cul-de-sacs.

Some of the best pictures I've seen of others have been taken at glamour photo studios. Have you been to one of these places? Before posing for your photographs, the staff gives you a complete makeover. They do your hair and makeup, then let you select an outfit from their collection of glamour clothing, or if you'd prefer you can bring your own change of clothes.

One year, I took my mother to have glamour photos taken and we surprised the family with the photographs at Christmas. My mother was a beautiful woman, even without any makeup. But after the professional makeover, she looked amazing. Which brings up another point. If AARP doesn't already sponsor one, I think they should sponsor a beauty contest for middle-agers and above. There certainly wouldn't be any shortage of contestants. Sophia Loren, Diane Keaton, Connie Stevens, Meryl Streep, Oprah Winfrey. Do any of these celebrities look like little old ladies to you? And that's not even counting all the non-celebrities who could compete.

So let the snapping begin. Make your appointment with that professional photographer. Book an afternoon at a glamour studio. Or take your own. Say cheese and start capturing those Kodak moments of your life. Pictures are how you and your family and friends get to relive their favorite times with you. Pictures capture birthdays, vacations, reunions, parties, graduations, family weddings, and every other event of your life. They're your mind's memories preserved forever on photo paper.

Then, once you have them, don't just pack them in a box and hide them away in the attic or closet, never to be enjoyed again. Take them out and show them off. Pass on their stories to the next generation. Relive those moments. That's what pictures are all about. They're history. Your history. They let future generations know you were here. And they remind everyone just how beautiful you are . . . No matter how many birthdays you've celebrated.

As a white candle
In a holy place,
So is the beauty
Of an aged face.
—Joseph Campbell

31

Geritol Gangsters

*I had to stop driving my car for a while . . .
the tires got dizzy.*
—Steven Wright

I once got a ticket for going 35 miles per hour in a 25-mile-per-hour zone. What can I say? I'm a rebel.

But that's the kind of tickets we middle-agers get. You won't see us standing before a judge trying to explain why we were drag racing down Main Street or why we crammed ten people into a Volkswagen and drove to a rock concert on Friday night. First of all, we prefer matinees, and our idea of racing is beating everyone else to the bread station at the cafeteria.

The kind of driving infractions we commit aren't the kind that get a lot of coverage on *Cops*. We get nabbed for double parking at the walk-in medical clinic. We get written up for jaywalking in front of Wal-Mart. And yes, we get ticketed for going 35 miles per hour in a 25-mile-per-hour zone.

No matter how baggy our pants might be, it's plain to see

that we are not a very tough bunch. We don't look tough, we don't act tough, and we certainly don't talk tough.

"Yo, Earl."

"Whazup, doggie?"

"I think it's supposed to be 'dawg.'"

"Dawg?"

"Yeah. It's 'Whazup, Dawg?'"

"Sorry, housey. My boo boo."

"You mean, 'Sorry, homey. My bad.'"

"Right on. So, what's the haps, Paps?"

"I'm just kickin' it."

"Leg spasms again?"

"Yeah, but I'm just chillin'."

"Circulation problems?"

"Word."

"I hear ya, doggie."

"Dawg."

"Whatever."

Not exactly "gangsta rap," is it? But most of us accept the fact that we're not that hip anymore. Lingo, styles, music, rules, everything keeps changing so fast, we couldn't keep up with all the trends anyway. What's in today is old school tomorrow. Then just wait a decade or two, and it'll start all over again.

There's something to be said for old school, though. Old-school comedy means comedy you can enjoy and not feel embarrassed about. Old-school prices means gasoline you don't need to take out a second mortgage on your home just to purchase. Old-school politics means qualified people running for office without feeding the public's insatiable thirst for scandal, and old-school home prices mean $100,000 will buy more than a park bench.

No, our generation may not be considered cool anymore. We may not say "dawg" or "my bad" or any other hip expressions (or whatever was hip as of this printing). You may not spot us speeding down the freeway in the fast lane. More often than not, we'll be ones in the slow lane just driving along, enjoying the scenery (we use less of that overpriced gasoline that way). We'll be voting for the man or woman we think is best qualified to run the country, no matter how much the media bashes him or her. We'll be supporting entertainment we think is worthwhile, and we'll be staying home more often than most in order to enjoy the house we've been making a lifetime of payments on. And most importantly, we'll be doing it all while wearing comfortable shoes.

All things considered, maybe we are the "cool" ones after all.

The best part of aging in this business is losing that obsession about work and being able to spend a little more time with family.
—Clint Eastwood

32

Laugh Lines

One of the major problems in the world today is that we've lost our sense of humor.
—Leo Buscaglia

You won't see their faces on the walls of post offices around the country. Their profiles won't be featured on *America's Most Wanted*. You won't even read an exposé about them in your town newspaper. But they're threatening our way of life, and somebody needs to stop them.

Who are they? People with no sense of humor.

They're not in the majority, thank goodness, but there are enough of them around to make the rest of us feel more than a little uncomfortable.

These humorless people are easy to spot. They're the ones sitting at that Jerry Seinfeld show, arms crossed, daring him to make them laugh. They're hanging out at Blockbuster or Hollywood Video, badmouthing all the comedies.

"I hated that movie. Don't rent it. I didn't laugh once."

They may go by different aliases—"Grouch," "Grumpy," "Ol' Stick in the Mud," "Wet Blanket"—but we know who they are and they have one mission in life—to bring the rest of us down.

Laughter is healthy. It has the power to make you forget your problems, even if only temporarily. A hearty laugh can even burn thirty-five calories! How's that for a diet plan? Do without white bread if you want; I'd rather laugh.

Personally, I love to laugh. It's one of my favorite emotions. I'd much rather be in the company of people who love to laugh than people who love to complain.

There are different humor tastes, of course. Some of us like comedy that's a little more sophisticated; others enjoy slapstick. Some like blue-collar humor and jokes about everyday family life; others prefer topical material about what's happening in the news, like the comedy of Jay Leno or David Letterman. Some like physical comedy; others like to hear funny stories, such as the ones told by Bill Cosby and Garrison Keillor. There are those of us who like to get our daily dose of funny by reading the comics in our daily newspaper, while the rest of us prefer getting our daily laughs from our co-workers, friends, and family.

But even with all that laughter going on around us, there are still some folks who just don't get it. They think life is far too serious to laugh about. For whatever reason, they refuse to give themselves permission to laugh.

"I'm too dignified."

"I'm too tired."

"I'm too stressed."

"I'm too old."

So many excuses, so little joy.

But Ward Cleaver was right when he said, "You're never too old to do goofy stuff." A good sense of humor isn't something we outgrow. From the very beginning of our journey to the final chapter, laughter is a necessary part of life. It's like breathing. We have to do it to survive.

So be on the lookout for the humorless. You'll recognize them by the clouds over their heads and the scowls on their faces. Don't let their negative attitudes and sour comments spoil your own zest for life. Protect your joy at all costs.

You can, of course, try reminding these people of the health benefits of laughter and how a cheerful face can take a good ten years off their appearance and even help with their diet plan. But I'd use caution before sneaking up behind them and tickling them, unless you can run really, really fast.

Does God have a sense of humor?
He must have if He created us.
—Jackie Gleason

33

Ten Commandments for Aging

❀ Thou shalt not raise up thy pants unto the uttermost parts of thy armpits.

❀ Thou shalt not look at thy face in a magnifying mirror, for thy heart's sake.

❀ Thou shalt not curse the name of thy dietary plan.

❀ Remember the place where thou hast left thy car keys, glasses, and other possessions, or buy tracking devices.

❀ Honor the rules of spandex that the circulation in thy legs may be long on this earth.

❀ Thou shalt not steal the age of thy neighbor.

❀ Thou shalt not commit to baby-sit more than six grandchildren under the age of three at one time, lest thou become a babbling loon.

❀ Thou shalt wear comfortable shoes so that thou wouldst not have a harvest of bunions and corns.

❀ Thou shalt not bear false witness with thy comb over.

✿ Thou shalt not covet thy neighbor's taco, or hot and spicy sausage, or any other food items that thou knowest will war against the innermost regions of thy body.

34

Will Work for Respect

If you don't want to work, you have to work
to earn enough money so that
you won't have to work.
—Ogden Nash

In some industries, there appears to be a prejudice against hiring middle-agers. Employers seem to want to hire only those who have an entire career life to give to the company.

But in today's ever-changing, fast-paced, 401(k)-transferring world, workers don't necessarily have the company loyalty they once did. If another, better offer comes along, they're gone. So career-building arguments no longer seem valid.

Middle-agers, on the other hand, have a lot to offer corporate and industrial America. Instead of easing them out of the work force, employers should be trying to hire as many of them as possible. They have experience, they have knowledge, and they have discipline. But because they also might have gray hair, wrinkles, and a pre–1960 birthday, they're all too often shut out of the employment process.

But for all you potential employers out there, here are just a few advantages awaiting you when you hire someone over forty.

Advantages to Hiring Middle-Agers

- ✿ We won't address you as "Yo, bossman."
- ✿ We won't leave skateboard marks on the walls of the building.
- ✿ We won't call in sick because our new tattoo is infected.
- ✿ You can send us to Milwaukee for a training conference, and we can find it on the map.
- ✿ We're old enough to know that we don't know everything.
- ✿ We'll show more respect for a boss thirty years our junior than some employees show to a boss thirty years their senior.
- ✿ At staff meetings, we'll say "Yes, sir" or "Yes, ma'am," instead of "I'm down with that."
- ✿ We won't use the company phone to call Australia just because we think the accent's cool.
- ✿ We won't argue with you over whether or not we should remove our tongue ring, eyebrow ring, and various other body-piercing jewelry. Outside of the staples from our gall bladder surgery, we're not into having metal accessories stuck in our skin.
- ✿ We would never say to a customer on the phone, "I woke up from my nap for this?"

Opportunity is missed by most people because it comes dressed in overalls and looks like work.
—Thomas Edison

314

35

The Comb-Over Conspiracy

The most expensive haircut I ever had cost ten pounds. And nine went on the search fee.
—William Hague, England

They're just wrong. I don't believe God ever intended for man to grow his hair as long as possible on one side of his head just to flip it over and wrap it around the other side. This was not in the original design. There is no scripture in Genesis that says, "And God fashioned Adam's comb over and saw that it was good." The comb over is something that man came up with all on his own. Sort of like the Edsel.

But man was wrong.

Now, before I go on, if you are reading this and you happen to have a comb over, you need to know that it is not your fault. Society has told you that it's okay to play this little hair trick on the public. It has told you that no one will notice that your bangs are merely your back hair being combed forward. But society has been leading you on.

Don't get me wrong. You have a right to grow and comb your hair in whatever direction you care to. All I'm saying is don't be disillusioned into thinking that the public isn't aware. We've seen enough bad comb overs to be quite skilled in following a hair to its root, regardless of how far away that root might be.

I've often wondered who came up with the comb-over concept in the first place. Did this person walk in from a windstorm with his hair blown in a dozen different directions, look at himself in the mirror, and say, "It's a miracle! My bald spot's gone!"?

Even with its drawbacks, though, the comb over seems to have a few advantages over the toupee. I knew a man who bought a top-of-the-line toupee and wore it everywhere he went—to the beach, in the shower, golfing. He even played baseball in it. It looked so good, you wouldn't have known he was wearing one had it not been for that one game when he slid into second base and his toupee went on to third. (The incident gave a new meaning to letting the wind blow through your hair. It also made it difficult to score the game because he was called out on second base, but his hair was clearly safe on third.)

As real as they can look, toupees can still fly off, slip off, or slide off when you least expect them to. You can even accidentally put one on backward, like one friend hurriedly did when I surprised him with a hospital visit. I kept telling him to turn around and face me, but then realized he already was.

Hair transplants are another alternative to the comb over. This is where the doctor will take hair from another part of your body and surgically implant it on the top of your head. Some transplants look amazingly natural, while others can leave you looking as if you have little electrodes coming out of your scalp.

Maybe our forefathers had the right idea. George Washington, Thomas Jefferson, and Benjamin Franklin all knew perfectly well how to handle their hair-loss problems: they just threw on a powdered wig.

So maybe that's another good option. Of course, a powdered wig would make some heads turn at the golf course. But considering the shade they'd offer, and the padded protection against stray balls, they might not be such a bad idea.

I love bald men. Just because you've lost your fuzz don't mean you ain't a peach.
—Dolly Parton

36

Pistol-Packing Gramma

On my first day in New York a guy asked me if I knew where Central Park was. When I told him I didn't he said, "Do you mind if I mug you here?"
—Paul Merton

According to reports, the number of seniors buying guns has doubled in recent years. I had no idea that bran had such a serious side effect.

All right, so maybe it isn't the bran. Maybe it's just the times in which we live. It seems every night our news is filled with stories of sniper shootings, carjackings, muggings, and other violent crimes. Seniors, like many of us, might not be feeling all that safe anymore. So a certain percentage of them are beginning to pack heat.

Now, before you start choosing sides on this issue, know this—this chapter isn't a debate over whether or not everyday citizens should have guns. It's merely an observation of the fact that some older members of our society are beginning to feel the need to fight back.

I recall a newspaper report some years ago of a grandmother who purse-whipped a would-be mugger until he finally took off running. No doubt there are plenty of other cases on the police files where an older person has stood up to an assailant. I'm sure the police would say doing that isn't a very good idea in most situations, but apparently some simply reached a point where enough was enough.

Part of the problem is the growing attitude that it's every man for himself. Certainly, we have the Good Samaritan laws for life-threatening emergencies, but people are still hesitant to get involved in other people's problems these days.

I stood in the middle of a very busy street one night in Southern California with a stalled car, and not one person stopped to help me push it out of the way. They sent their encouragement by way of their car horns (and a few other gestures) as they drove past. I had caused a major traffic jam and was prolonging their drive home. My problem had become their problem and they were none too happy about it.

But no one offered to help.

I finally had to leave my car, walk to a gas station, and call home. Two of my sons arrived a short time later and pushed the car out of the street. By then, the traffic jam stretched for miles. I was tired, frustrated, and cold. But I was finally out of everyone's way.

In days gone by, there wasn't a need for the Good Samaritan law. People just instinctively helped.

But these are different times. Today good deeds are sometimes punished. The world is a dangerous place, and helping out a perfect stranger or in some cases, even an acquaintance, can be pretty risky. So maybe it's not so surprising that more and more of the older generation have begun to arm themselves. Again, I'm not saying whether or not I think this is wise. I'm just saying that for whatever reason, it's happening.

Middle-agers, on the other hand, don't seem to be getting caught up in this trend as much as seniors. I don't know if this means they're anti-gun or if it's just because in menopause, packing more heat is definitely not something you want to do.

We live in an age when pizza gets to your home before the police.
—Jeff Marder

37

Pleasin' the World

I don't know the key to success, but the key to failure is to try to please everyone.
—Bill Cosby

If you've learned anything by the time you reach middle age, chances are you've learned this—you can't please everyone.

Mail carriers have certainly learned this.

"The mail's late again. Can't he ever get it here on time?"

"Did he have to bring me all these bills? Couldn't he have just skipped my house today?"

Police officers know it, too.

"Officer, come quick! There's someone trying to break in my house!"

"Doesn't that cop have anything better to do than to give me a ticket?"

And pastors have also learned it.

"Your preaching's too long."

"Your preaching's too short."

"You never visit."

"You're too intrusive."

No matter what you do, no matter how sincere your motive, somebody isn't going to be happy. Teachers know it. Parents know it. Counselors know it. Interior decorators know it. Hair stylists know it. Politicians know it. Artists know it. And just about everyone else knows it. You can't please everybody.

But we sure try, don't we?

"You can't see the movie over my head? I'm sorry. I'll lie down here on the floor. Is that better?"

"Did I mind waiting for twenty minutes while you answered your other call? Of course not. Maybe you can do a load of laundry, too, while I hold."

The older we get, the more we come to realize that no matter how much of a people pleaser we happen to be, some people have made up their mind not to be pleased. If they are looking to find something to criticize us for, they will most assuredly find it. But by the same token, if they want to find something worth complimenting and encouraging us about, they can find that, too. It just depends on what they're looking for.

So what do you do? Change yourself to accomodate everyone else's tastes, standards, and desires? You be yourself. Not anyone else, just you, the man or woman you were created to be. Certainly, you'll want to strive to be the best you that you can be. But never let anyone's negative comments determine your identity. You are you. No one else can fill that role. And no one else but you has been given the part.

It's sad that it takes so many of us half a lifetime to figure out that being who we are is a pretty good person to be.

When I give a lecture, I accept that people look at their watches, but what I do not tolerate is when they look at it and raise it to their ear to find out if it stopped.
—Marcel Achard

38

Excuse Us

✿ Excuse us if we drive too slowly in front of you. We're taking our time and enjoying the scenery. Have you looked at it lately?

✿ Excuse us if we offer our help when you don't need it. It's not because we think you can't do something, it's because we'd like to see if we still can.

✿ Excuse us if we talk too much about our ailments. We'd love to talk about other things, but no one asks us those questions anymore.

✿ Excuse us if we don't walk fast enough in front of you at airports, malls, and grocery stores. In our heads we are running (and we're leaving you in our dust).

✿ Excuse us if we prefer to watch old movies and comedies. We're from a generation where the good guys won and the comedy wasn't blue. And we liked it better that way.

✿ Excuse us if we want to be spoken to with respect. We were taught to respect our elders, and we have been looking forward to finally being treated that way ourselves. It's been a long time coming. So do us a favor and let us enjoy it.

✿ Excuse us if we ask you to call a little more often. Hearing your voice, even for only a minute, makes our day.

✿ Excuse us if we don't understand body piercing. We're not out of it. We just get enough piercing from our weekly B–12 shots or insulin injections and can't understand why anyone would want to voluntarily get stuck with needles.

✿ Excuse us if it takes us a little extra time to rise from a sitting position. If our knees are weak, it's from a lifetime of hard work. In our day, we admired that in a person.

✿ Excuse us if we forget to wipe our mouths. There's a good chance someone wiped yours plenty of times when you were little.

✿ Excuse us if when you visit, we don't seem to want to let you go. We know we'll have to, we just like to stretch out the moment as long as possible.

✿ Excuse us if we ask for a hug. It reminds us how much we're loved and that's better than the newest miracle drug on the market.

39

First Impressions

*I don't plan to grow old gracefully. I plan to have
face-lifts until my ears meet.*
—Rita Rudner

Have you ever crawled out of bed in the morning, looked in a
mirror, and wondered how someone managed to transplant
your knee skin to your cheeks during the night without waking
you up? Okay, it's not really your knee skin, but for some
unknown reason I can wake up in the morning and my face
will have taken on every fold, crease, and pucker of my bed-
ding. I can't tell you how many times I have awakened with the
impression of a crocheted pillowcase pressed deep into my
cheeks. And I don't even own a crocheted pillowcase.

Part of the blame for this lies with the loss of elasticity in
our skin over the years. When we were young, a relative could
pinch our cheeks and, even though we might not have enjoyed
it, the little piles of flesh would return to their natural position
within seconds, no harm done. But pinch a middle-aged cheek

and it's a different matter altogether. When pinched, middle-aged skin can stay all bunched up, looking not unlike a relief map of the Appalachian Mountain ridge.

Lack of moisture also plays a significant role. Many of us middle-agers suffer from dry skin. Not just regular parched skin. Sahara desert kind of dry, parched skin. The kind of skin that needs its moisturizer spray gunned on. Drinking eight glasses of liquid a day is supposed to help hydrate the skin, as is a good skin moisturizing system. This is especially important if you want to avoid those embarrassing situations like diving into a swimming pool and soaking up all the water like a giant sponge.

In addition to a regular hydration regimen, plenty of products and procedures available today promise to help. There are antioxidant creams, exfoliation processes, and of course, face food. Face food is simply what it says, food for the face. Instead of going into the mouth, these food products are made to go directly on your face. There are lemon and orange masques, peach and mango facial creams, mint and avocado peels, cucumber eye patches, and cherry and peppermint lotions. They're supposed to be good for your skin, but I'm not sure I agree with the whole concept. If I have to be on a diet, why should my face be eating better than I am? Why should I deny my body a slice of pie at Marie Callender's while my face is eating a mango peel?

I do want to take care of my skin, though, so I suppose I'll need to do something. God may be the lifter of our head, but when it comes to our facial skin we're on our own.

I'm so old they've cancelled my blood type.
—Bob Hope

40

Dream a Little Dream

A man is not old until regrets
take the place of dreams.
—John Barrymore

We cannot possibly get to this point of our lives without having fulfilled a few dreams, forgotten about some, and still be hanging on to a few others.

Perhaps in our youth we had aspirations of becoming a rock star. But now, the only rock we talk about is the one they removed from our gall bladder. Maybe we dreamed of becoming a Wall Street broker, but never made it out of our hometown, much less all the way to New York.

So what happened? How did we get off track?

The answer is simple—life.

Funny how life has a way of forcing us to reassess our dreams, adjust our sails, and chart out new courses. Perhaps that business degree we were working toward had to be postponed because we lost our job and were forced to drop out of college. Or that art school scholarship had to be forfeited because we needed a job to help support our aging father. Our dreams may have been to become a police officer, an attorney, a minister, or any number of other career choices. But we had to abandon them. Perhaps we made the right decision for the wrong reasons, the wrong decision for the right reasons, or maybe it was apathy that snuffed out our dreams. Or it could be that we were too afraid of the risk and played it safe.

God has designed a life plan for each one of us. It was custom-fitted to our talents and personality, and it usually involves a step of faith. But that step, the first one, is always up to us, because along with his plan, he has also given us the freedom of choice. We can decide to pursue our dreams and be satisfied in the attempt, or we can simply exist, accepting life as it comes and never quite live up to our potential. We can pursue the best, or we can settle for less. It's our decision.

If you've done the latter, if you've settled, the good news is, it's not too late. There are plenty of middle-aged and senior adults who did some of their greatest work and made their biggest impact on society during the second half of their lives— Mother Teresa, Grandma Moses, Colonel Sanders, Ronald Reagan, Winston Churchill, Franklin D. Roosevelt, just to name a few. As Yogi Berra said, "It ain't over 'til it's over."

There is nothing sadder than an unfulfilled life. Someone who is well past the halfway point of life, convinced that they missed out on their true calling. Dreams don't come with expiration dates. Take advantage of the years that lie ahead of you and do what you were created to do, whatever that happens to be. Whether it's in education, politics, science, medicine, arts, or any other field, the world needs what you still have to offer.

I was sixty-six years old. I still had to make a living. I looked at my social security check of $105 and decided to use that to try to franchise my chicken recipe. Folks had always liked my chicken.
—Colonel Harland Sanders

41

Ten Things I Knew I Would Never Forget Even in Middle Age

1.
2.
3.
4.
5.
6.
7.
8.
9.
10.

   (Okay. Never mind.)

42

For He Was a Jolly Good Fellow

I arise in the morning torn between a desire to improve the world and a desire to enjoy the world. This makes it hard to plan the day.
—E. B. White

One of the cleverest comedy sketches I ever saw was on the old *Tonight Show* with Johnny Carson. Johnny was delivering a eulogy for the creator of the thesaurus. Instead of saying just one word to describe the different aspects of the funeral or the deceased, he went through a long list of synonyms. *"He's away, no longer here, gone to a better place, departed, checked out, belly up, pushing up daisies, kicked the bucket . . ."*

That's not the dialogue verbatim, but you get the picture. It was a very funny idea for a sketch.

Real funeral tributes, however, are usually far from funny. Sometimes they're far from truthful, too.

"He was the most wonderful man I ever knew. He was like a brother to me."

In reality, the deceased hadn't heard from the speaker in over twenty years.

"I don't know what I'm going to do without her. She was my life."

The truth is, when she was alive, the speaker never had a kind word to say about her.

Eulogies, no matter how glowing and eloquent, don't do much good if they're full of sentiments the departed never knew during life. How much better it would be if the speech we write out for someone's funeral were words we had already spoken to him while he was alive.

Life gets hectic. We need to go here, we need to be there, we have to start this, we have to finish that. Deadlines are hovering over our heads, faxes are coming in, cell phones are going off, and computer screens are freezing up on us. We're stressed, overcommitted, booked up, stretched out, and tired. How in the world do we fit in personal relationships? There simply is no time.

Or is there?

Somehow we seem to find the time and the way to rearrange our calendars, put our business matters on hold, and practically move heaven and earth to be there for a loved one's memorial service.

Maybe we could try just a little harder to rearrange our calendars for a luncheon with our friends, or a day in the park with our spouse, or that visit to our children or, in some cases, grandchildren.

None of us knows how much time we have left. We can hope it'll be another fifty years. But there are no guarantees for any of us. As much as we don't like to think about it, we're all going to have to face the end of the party someday. As a comedy writer, I've often wondered if I'll go in some bizarre way. Perhaps my husband will have to tell our friends and loved ones,

"We told her not to use the computer while in the bathtub, but she just mumbled something about a deadline, plugged it in, and deleted herself. We tried to save her as a text file, but we got there too late."

However it happens, or whenever it happens, is not up to us. The only thing we do have power over is to make sure we are making a difference in someone's life each and every day.

Maybe not everyone's life. That would be impossible. But someone's life. And the best place to start is with those who mean the most to us.

They say such nice things about people at their funerals that it makes me sad that I'm going to miss mine by just a few days.
—Garrison Keillor

43

I Hear Ya

You have to endure what you can't change.
—Marie de France

Does anyone know what it is about earlobes that makes them start to sag after middle age? Even people who have never worn earrings find their lobes suddenly hanging a little closer to their shoulders. I myself have had to quit wearing shoulder pads for this very reason. My earlobes kept rubbing against the pads, and I was afraid the friction might cause the foam in them to spontaneously combust.

As far as I know, there is nothing we can do about this earlobe problem short of surgery. We can't go on an earlobe diet, and to my knowledge, there aren't any earlobe workout videos on the market.

The size of the actual ear seems to change over the years, too. For reasons unbeknownst to most middle-agers, ears seem to go on a sudden growth spurt after passing age fifty, in some cases growing to incredible proportions. Not large enough where involuntary flight was involved, but enough for the average person to note the difference.

Big earlobes don't seem to be as big a problem for women. We can double pierce our ears and fold the lobe upward, pinning back some of the spare flesh. It doesn't look that great, but at least it gets the lobe up off the shoulder pad, reducing the potential for fire.

But what can men do? Other than growing sideburns and a full beard to hide them, or wearing a turtleneck and tucking their lobes under the collar, they don't have much of a choice.

In addition to the fire hazard, elongated lobes can be dangerous in other ways, too. In windstorms, they can get to flapping too much in the crosscurrent and before you know it, you've slapped yourself unconscious. And women need to use caution with curling irons. Some have been known to accidentally curl their lobes with their hair, and aside from the third-degree burns, earlobes really don't look that great in a flip.

So if you've been watching your earlobes growing bigger and bigger year after year, try following the above precautions. They just might save your life. And if you really hate your earlobes, just think about all the shade they provide in the summer.

Know what's weird? Day by day, nothing seems to change, but pretty soon . . . everything's different.
—Calvin from *Calvin and Hobbes*

44

Outgrowing Fun

When I was born I was so surprised
I didn't talk for a year and a half.
—Gracie Allen

I have two birthdays. For eighteen years, I celebrated September 2 as my birthday. I figured since my mom was there, she had to have known when I was born.

But apparently there was some confusion. According to my birth certificate, which I sent away for when I turned eighteen, I was born on September 1, not 2. I could understand the discrepancy if my birth had taken place around midnight, but according to the certificate I arrived much earlier in the day on the first.

Still, I can't blame my mom for the mix-up. I was the last of five children, so I'm sure by then she was pretty tired. The fact that she knew it was the month of September is probably good enough. Besides, now I get to celebrate both the first and the second, so it works out kind of nice; especially if someone forgets to call, they get a second chance.

Birthdays are important. They're the anniversary of the day when we first came into this world, took a single gasp of air, and screamed at the top of our lungs to let everyone within ear-shot know that we were here and it was time to party!

As we grew, most of us continued having a great time. We didn't worry about the grocery bill while sitting there in our high chair eating chocolate cupcakes and asking for more. We didn't think twice about the state of the economy as we played with our toys or colored in our coloring books. The rising cost of gasoline and car insurance never even entered our minds as we rode our tricycle around the patio or dared to take that first ride on a two-wheeler.

Then came school. This was an adjustment. We had to start balancing fun with work. There were tests and homework and science projects and books to read before we could even think about doing anything fun.

Our first job reinforced this thought, too. We were learning the concept of earning money to pay for whatever fun we were having. We were also discovering that someone else had been footing the bill for our fun all our life. Now it was our turn to step up to the plate and start paying our own way.

Marriage brought us even more responsibilities, more bills, and longer hours at work. We still tried to make time for fun, but it wasn't as easy now. How could we spend an evening just laughing and having fun when there were so many other, more important things to do?

The birth of our children brought some of that carefree fun back into our lives. But often as an onlooker. We could watch our kids playing with their toys or riding their two-wheelers, but we were too busy writing checks for our monthly credit card payments. We knew we'd have more fun later, but right then all we really wanted to do was get a good night's sleep.

And so, here we are. Our kids are grown. The toys (our own and our children's) are all packed away, or we sold them at a garage sale. We have a lot more time on our hands for fun, but unfortunately, by now too many of us have lost our sense of humor. The weight of all the years of responsibilities, bills, disappointments, hurts, and troubles has pressed down on us for so long, we don't remember what it was like to enjoy life.

When we were young, no one had to tell us to have fun. We just did it, remember? We could play with a string for hours, skip a rock along a stream, fly kites, swing on a swing at the park, tell jokes, write funny notes to a friend, build something out of nothing, watch our favorite TV shows. Whatever we did, we made it fun. We enjoyed it to the fullest. Sometimes we even had more fun with the box a toy came in than we did with the toy itself.

So how do we find that spirit of fun again? We simply let it out. It's been inside us all along.

> *God writes a lot of comedy . . . the trouble is,*
> *he's stuck with so many bad actors who*
> *don't know how to play funny.*
> —Garrison Keillor

45

Ten Things to Do the Day You Retire

1. Conduct a memorial service for your alarm clock.
2. Have another memorial service ten minutes later for the snooze alarm.
3. Clean out your desk and find every item that you had reported lost over the last twenty years.
4. Turn in your company key. (Now that you found it and four copies in your desk drawer.)
5. Plant hydrangeas in your lunch pail.
6. Build a business card bonfire and roast marshmallows.
7. Write your boss a letter telling him how much he or she has meant to you over the years.
8. Tear up the above letter, and write another one that you can actually give him or her.

9. Review your financial situation, determining how long you can stay retired before you have to go out and look for another job.
10. Look for another job.

46

Another Way to Look at It

You know, somebody actually complimented me on my driving today. They left a little note on the windscreen, it said "Parking Fine."
—Tommy Cooper

What if age spots were considered beauty marks and wrinkles were something you asked a plastic surgeon to add, instead of take away? Imagine a world where every birthday was looked forward to with as much excitement and anticipation as your twenty-first. What if rocking chairs were as hip as Harleys and baggy skin was chic? What if we were able to turn society's opinion of the over-forty crowd around to where middle-agers were looked upon with envy?

"Oooh, she just got her first liver spot. It's not fair! She always gets everything before I do!"

"Look at her over there, flaunting her cellulite. I bet it's not even real."

"I'm going to the Tan and Wilt. You know how I like to get a head start on my wrinkled look before summer gets here."

"What's wrong with me? I'm in my thirties and gravity hasn't set in yet. I feel like a freak!"

Don't think it will ever happen? Look at how the public's attitude toward cigarette smoking has changed. Remember when non-smoking sections used to be two broken-down booths in the back of restaurants? Then it grew to half the restaurant, then the whole restaurant, and now in some states, there's a no-smoking policy in all public places.

So how do we go about changing the public's perception of the over-forty crowd? One thing we can do is convince more national magazines to feature pretty middle-aged women and well-toned middle-aged men on their covers. In their interviews, middle-aged entertainers can refer to their liver spots as beauty marks and talk about their hot flashes with the same enthusiasm as they would a trip to Cannes.

We can book great-looking representatives of our age group on all the talk shows, and show before-and-after pictures featuring the blandness of perfect skin next to the amazing character of aging skin.

When you get down to it, what's so great about smooth, taut skin anyway? Wrinkles tell stories. What stories does a twenty-year-old face have to tell? It may be pretty, but there is no history, no back story. I, on the other hand, have an entire novel written on my face. On some mornings, it's a trilogy.

So let's all do our part. Let's make the world wish they were one of us. We've got what they really want down deep inside. We've just got to let them know it.

Beautiful young people are accidents of nature, but beautiful old people are works of art.
—Eleanor Roosevelt

47

Advantages to Aging

❀ You can use PoliGrip to repair broken knickknacks.

❀ You can fall asleep during an hour-and-a-half sermon and people will assume you're praying.

❀ You can drive the median on the highway and avoid the traffic.

❀ You get to take advantage of those senior discounts.

❀ People hold the doors open for you, which usually gets you in line in front of them.

❀ You can answer your grandchildren's history questions with firsthand accounts of your childhood.

❀ People let you be cranky.

❀ You can turn up the television set louder than your grandson's stereo.

❀ Three sit-ups count as exercise.

❀ You can walk down the street talking to yourself, with or without a headset.

48

Bookkeeping 101

Have you had a kindness shown? Pass it on;
'twas not given for thee alone, Pass it on;
Let it travel down the years,
Let it wipe another's tears,
Till in Heaven the deed appears, Pass it on.
—Henry Burton

It's important for us to keep good records of our debts. I'm not talking about debts to Visa, MasterCard, or others who not-so-freely gave to you, then charged outrageous interest rates while you've paid them back over a mere twenty or thirty years. Those debts are easy to keep track of and hard to escape.

I'm talking about emotional debts, kindness debts, friend-ship debts, and the huge debt we owe those who have fought and continue to fight for the freedoms we all enjoy. We owe a debt to our parents, who sacrificed so we can have what they never had; to our teachers who spent extra time with us helping us realize our own potential; and of course, to our faithful friends who were there for us when we needed them most. That's why *It's A Wonderful Life* is such an inspirational movie. George Bailey's friends remembered their debts. They remembered how much they owed George for his past kindnesses. They owed him their loyalty. They owed him their faith in his goodness. They didn't walk out when he needed them most. The people of Bedford Falls kept good record of their debts.

Too many of us don't keep good books. We forget the favors paid to us, the kindnesses shown to us, the good advice given us, and the love bestowed on us. We forget a lot.

I'll be the first to admit that I'm in debt up to my eyeballs with people. I owe my personal freedoms to every uniformed man or woman, soldier, police officer, and other peacekeepers who have ever fought for our country or put their own safety at risk so I can sleep peacefully at night.

I owe another enormous debt to my parents, who worked tirelessly to make sure there was food on the table and a roof over our heads. I'm the youngest of five children, and while my parents certainly had their challenges, and we weren't rich by any stretch of the imagination, I cannot ever remember going to bed hungry or cold.

I'm also in debt to my friends who have stood by me in good times and difficult times, who've been rocks of encouragement, saying just the right things at just the right times. I wouldn't want to think what my life would be like without them.

I owe my children a huge debt, too, for blessing me more than they'll ever know simply by being in my life. Through them, I've learned to trust God, believe in his perfect timing, and understand his loving fatherly qualities. Knowing how we want the best for our children helps us understand how God wants the best for us.

I owe a debt to those who have in any way encouraged me in my writing—so many family members, pastors, editors, friends, English teachers, and especially the person who wrote to me saying that he found one of my articles in a trashcan, liked it, and wondered if I had written any books. (I wrote back telling him that I had and which trashcans he might find some of them in, too.) Writing has always been my passion, and thanks to so many, and especially you who are buying the books, it has become my livelihood.

I owe a debt to every person who has ever made me laugh. Professional comedians such as Jackie Gleason, Bob Hope, Jerry Lewis, Steve Martin, Jerry Seinfeld, Dick Van Dyke, the entire cast of *Everybody Loves Raymond,* and so many others. And the non-professionals, just everyday people who have shared laughs over lunches, business meetings, parties, or who simply sent a note or a funny thought to make me smile.

I even owe a debt to those whom I've encountered through-out my life who haven't been so kind, perhaps even downright nasty. We've all had people like this cross our path, but they can teach us a great deal, too. If nothing else, they can show us how *not* to treat others.

So, yes, I am in debt. I am up to my eyeballs in debt. And the debt just keeps growing. Every day I become indebted to someone else who has graced my life with their kind words or encouragement.

I hope, too, that I'm listed in other people's records for

whatever kindnesses I've shown to them. That's what life is all about—remembering our debts. Remembering those who have helped us, sacrificed for us, inspired us, and loved us for who we are. Life is a combination of laughter and tears, good times and not-so-good times, encouragers and discouragers, for they have all made us who we are.

We all have bad days, we all have disappointments, we all have to deal with unkind people, but if we are honest with ourselves, truly honest, we would have to admit that there are a lot more people on the positive side of our balance sheets than on the negative side. The problem is we just forget to make the entries.

When it comes to life, be an accurate bookkeeper.

> *By the time you're eighty years old*
> *you've learned everything.*
> *You only have to remember it.*
> —George Burns

49

Caretakers

There's so much pollution in the air now
that if it weren't for our lungs
there'd be no place to put it all.
—Robert Orben

What if the world were a library book that we had to check out at our birth, then turn back in just before our death? How much do you think we'd be fined for the condition in which we're returning it?

Don't get me wrong. I'm sure the majority of us don't want to purposely hurt the earth. We want to protect its beauty and even improve it so those who follow after us will enjoy the fruits of our progress. But progress, good as it is, comes at a price.

Automobiles have made getting to work much easier, but they have also been a major contributor to pollution.

The telephone made it possible for us to communicate with loved ones and business associates all over the world. But now with cell phones in such abundance, we find ourselves listening to everyone's private conversations wherever we go. (Aren't you amazed at how many people will sit at McDonald's or Burger King and discuss company takeovers, unsatisfactory employees, and other delicate business affairs within earshot of everyone around them? We're going to have fast-food workers going from "You want fries with that?" to running multi-million dollar companies thanks to the education they're receiving from eavesdropping on CEOs for free.)

The Internet, which enables us to reach almost any company or person in the world, was another terrific idea. But the Internet also enables almost any company or person in the world to reach us with an endless bombardment of spam. And don't forget about the identity thefts.

Another idea that someone of our generation came up with is credit cards. Think of the convenience! Think of the opportunity! Think of the 22 percent interest! It has been estimated that the average credit card debt now carried by American families is around $9,000. Sure, credit cards seemed like a good idea when they first came out, but things have gotten out of hand when they're sending two-year-olds those "Congratulations, you're already approved!" letters. I'm sorry, but two-year-olds don't need an American Express or a MasterCard. One Visa card is enough.

Television was from our generation, too. We can now get the news as soon as it happens. The downside? We can now get the news as soon as it happens. Sometimes even before it's verified for authenticity. They also give us every sordid detail of news stories that aren't even adult friendly, much less child friendly. What all this information, speculation, innuendo, and sometimes even fabrication is doing to us as a society is yet to be fully determined. We'll find out, I suppose, when we check in our "library book" at the end of our watch.

The advances we've made in medical research have given us antibiotics to combat all sorts of diseases. Unfortunately, because of our own misuse of them, we now have smarter viruses that are mutating and becoming less susceptible to our "miracle drugs."

Our advances in DNA studies have given us amazing crime-solving abilities and fast-tracked us on the path toward cures for many life-threatening diseases. But it has also given us the moral dilemma of cloning.

Progress. It comes at a price.

So how will our "library book" be handed back in? Will it be tattered and ripped and stained from our not having taken very good care of it? Or will we be turning in a book that we've not only enjoyed every page of, but one that's in even better condition than when it was first handed to us? The answer is up to us.

> *I'm moving to Mars next week,*
> *so if you have any boxes . . .*
> —Steven Wright

50

Sending My Regrets

**Someday we'll look back on this moment
and plow into a parked car.**
—Evan Davis

We all have them. Those memories that make us shudder.

Those times when we think, *What in the world was I thinking?*

Those days when we mentally beat ourselves up over why we didn't do this or did do that. You know, all those could'ves, should'ves, and would'ves of life. They're called regrets, and who among us doesn't have some?

I regret that perm I got when I was a teenager. But at least this year the curl finally relaxed.

I regret not having the foresight to have invested in IBM.

I regret not having taken a picture of my Popeye arms after my upper-arm fat avalanche. (But I do at least have medical documentation.)

Other regrets, though, are a little harder for us to live with.

Regret that we didn't spend enough time with that loved one before he passed. Regret that we didn't stand up for a friend when she needed our support. Regret that we didn't do enough, give enough, go enough, or be enough.

We certainly can't erase our past regrets, but we can do something about minimizing any future ones. If you believe that one day you're going to regret not having spent enough time with your children, spouse, parents, friends, or any other loved one, then start spending more time with them now.

If you're going to regret not having thanked someone for something they did for you, even if it was years ago, thank them now.

If you're going to regret not having used your talents more, start using them now.

If you're going to regret not having saved more of your money, then start saving more now.

If you're going to regret not having seen more of the world, then start traveling now. Even if you can't afford to travel to faraway places, take in some weekend trips. There are plenty of places of interest to visit right here at home.

If you're going to regret not having spoken up for someone who couldn't speak up for herself, then speak up now.

If you're going to regret not having chosen to do the right thing more often, then start choosing to do the right thing now.

Regrets. You'll only have as many as you allow yourself to have.

> **_You can't keep blaming yourself._**
> **_Just blame yourself once, and move on._**
> —Homer Simpson

51

Top Twenty Things That You Might Have Been Looking For When You Couldn't Remember What It Was You Were Looking For

1. checkbook
2. sweater
3. glasses
4. paper
5. pen
6. wallet
7. magazine
8. address book

9. tape
10. cell phone
11. medicine
12. towel
13. candy
14. purse
15. calculator
16. shoes
17. paper clip
18. husband
19. pet
20. the right house

52

Survivor

**The hardest years in life are
those between ten and seventy.**
—Helen Hayes

No matter how much you wish you didn't have to accept it, no one gets through this life without realizing one very basic truth—the journey isn't perfect. We can wish for it to be perfect, we can hope and pray that it will be perfect, we can live in denial thinking it is perfect. But despite all our good efforts, it is more likely that we'll have a lot of failures and successes, hurts and healings, plans and adjustments, fulfilled dreams and forgotten ones.

So what do we do? How do we survive this thing called life? We learn to partake of the four basic attitudes every day.

Appreciate
Adjust
Persevere
Celebrate

Each day of your life should have a healthy serving from every one of these groups.

Appreciate. This is where many of us struggle the most. When things go wrong, it's easy to allow the current crisis to partially or completely block the good in our life from our field of vision. We focus on our trials and forget our treasures. We see our problems and ignore our pearls. But to truly appreciate life, we have to look at the whole picture.

Adjust. Life is about making adjustments. Rewriting the script of our lives as we live it. It's about changes—some planned, others unexpectedly thrust upon us. Sometimes life goes in the exact opposite direction of what we wanted. We may have had dreams of our son going to West Point, but he decided he'd rather work at Wiener Hut (he thinks their hats are "way cooler"). The daughter we groomed to enter the medical field entered rehab instead. The child we hoped to send to Yale is now living in a commune outside of Phoenix. What happened? Simple. A parent's dreams met a child's choices.

If we did our best, all we can do is hope and pray, leave the outcome in God's hands, and . . .

Persevere. Why? Because we have to. And not just for ourselves. We persevere for those around us. When we make it through a problem, others look for a little residual hope to help them make it through their problem, too.

And because we persevere, we can . . .

Celebrate. We're alive and that is more than enough reason to party! We survived all the times when we didn't know where our next meal was coming from. We survived that night when we didn't think our son or daughter was going to make it through their latest crisis. We survived that day when the world was filled with uncertainty and none of us, not even our leaders, knew what was going to happen next. We survived that job loss, that surgery, that car accident, that earthquake, that hurricane, that tornado, that stock-market adjustment. We've survived it all. And chances are we'll survive a lot more before this ride is over.

So remember the four life groups—appreciate, adjust, persevere, and celebrate. Are you getting enough of each of these in your daily diet?

The answer to old age is to keep one's mind busy and to go on with one's life as if it were interminable. I always admired Chekhov for building a new house when he was dying of tuberculosis.
—Leon Edel

53

What Was That?

Little Johnny asked his grandma how old she was. Grandma answered, "Thirty-nine and holding." Johnny thought for a moment, and then said, "And how old would you be if you let go?"
—Anonymous

Have you ever had something flash across your field of vision, but since you weren't really paying attention, you didn't get a good look at what it was?

"Hey, what was that?" you might have said to whomever was standing by you at the time, hoping they caught a better glimpse of it than you did. All you know is something went whooshing by, but as to what it was, you don't have a clue.

If we're not careful, that's what we'll be saying about our lives someday.

"What was that?" we'll ask. "Did you see what just flew by? I didn't get a good look at it, but I think it might have been my life."

We've all been reminded umpteen times how fleeting life is, but how much do we really believe it? We certainly didn't believe it in our teens. We were in too much of a hurry to graduate high school or get to our twenty-first birthday to think about the downside of rushing through our years.

In our twenties and thirties we were too busy pursuing our careers, building our families, and going after our dreams to notice how quickly the calendar pages were being turned. We kept up that frantic pace until we finally passed the middle-age marker, and now time is passing so quickly, we're begging someone to help us put on the brakes. Or better yet, shift to reverse.

But life doesn't work that way. It only has one gear, and that's forward. How quickly or how slowly we move ahead in that gear is up to us.

It's not easy, though. We get caught up in the daily struggles of our existence—financial worries, traffic jams, crowded malls, rude waiters, pushy neighbors, manipulative people, insensitive bosses—all the things that can and do consume much more of our time than we realize or want. Before we know it, we've wasted a week dwelling on this problem, two weeks worrying about that problem, or even a year or more nursing an old wound. If we're not careful, the people and problems that deserve the least amount of our time end up taking the most of our time. Time that, no matter how hard we try, we are never going to get back.

Let me ask you, are you making the kind of memories you want to have at the end of your life? Do you hold up those car payment receipts with the same enthusiasm as you would hold a photo of you and your family vacationing in Nantucket? Is the picture of you sitting at your computer as exciting as one would be of you landing a big catch off the Florida coast? Are you happy with the way you are spending your time?

"You don't understand. I've got my SUV payment, my credit card bills, the mortgage, my cable bill. Someday I'll take a vacation, but I just can't do it this year."

But next year rolls around and you can't afford to take one then either. And the next year. And the next. Before you know it, more of your life has just whooshed by and you have nothing more to show for it.

Maybe it's time we all revisited our day planners. Maybe it's time we finally admitted to ourselves that the days and weeks we're spending now on whatever we're spending them on won't be coming back. Maybe it's time we treated our spouses and our children, our parents and our friends as more valuable commodities than stocks, bank accounts, or social standing.

Yesterday is what it was. All we have is today and tomorrow. From birth to middle age to our senior years, it's up to us to live our lives to the fullest, to not give others the power to decide how happy, how satisfied, or how fulfilled we're going to feel. Too many of us aren't living the life we want to live because we're living someone else's dreams, or we're chained to debt, or we've committed to things that our heart just isn't in, and now we feel trapped, or we've allowed others to steal our joy.

So take a moment and ask yourself, what is it that is most important to you? Is whatever it is high on your priority list right now, or does your priority list need a rewrite?

It's up to each one of us to live every day, every hour, every minute of our lives so that when we get to the end, we won't have to say "What was that? Did you see what just flew by? I didn't get a good look at it, but I think it was my life."

Each day comes bearing its own gifts.
Untie the ribbons.
—Ruth Ann Schabacker

Growing Your Own Turtleneck...

and other benefits of aging

To my loving aunts Sibyl, Clara, and Wilma, who have stayed forever young, who have never lost their sense of fun, and who have proved that true beauty only grows through the years.

Contents

It's Only Right

It does not require a majority to prevail,
but rather an irate, tireless minority keen to set
brush fires in people's minds.
—Samuel Adams

It's time. Actually, it's long overdue. They already have them for parents with young children. They have them for expectant mothers, too. They have them for physically challenged men and women. While all of this is good and necessary and certainly helpful, I for one think that it's high time grocery stores and malls started designating a few parking spaces for another segment of the population—menopausal women.

Menopausal women could use a little consideration, too, you know. Do you men and young people have any idea what driving around a parking lot looking for an available parking space does to a menopausal woman? Even the streets of Los Angeles haven't seen that kind of road rage. I once watched a middle-aged woman hit-and-run three grocery carts, sideswipe a newspaper stand, and nearly crash into a shelf of propane tanks just trying to beat an SUV to an open parking space. Even with all that effort, she still lost the race and stopped right there in the middle of the parking lot and had a good cry. My heart went out to her, but I still didn't move my SUV. In a parking lot situation, it's every menopausal woman for herself!

Before grocery store managers designate these spaces for us, there are a few things they should keep in mind. First of all, a menopausal parking space will need to be extra wide. You know how claustrophobic we hot-flashing women can get in close quarters. We need plenty of room to breathe and move, even if it is outdoors. There's nothing worse than pulling into a parking space and realizing the Volvo next to you has parked so close to the line that you have to climb out of your window and over your hood to exit your car. I would, therefore, suggest the size of these special menopausal spaces be about twice the size of a regular parking space. An RV- or tour-bus-parking size would be just about right. If it can fit a Winnebago, it'll fit a middle-aged hot-flashing woman in a Honda Accord.

Another nice touch that store managers could do would be to circle the spaces with giant fans or misting machines. What menopausal woman wouldn't be moved to tears if she were to open her door and be greeted with gale force winds or a refreshing mist on her way into the store? (I'm getting all weepy just thinking about it.)

But if grocery store managers really want to draw the menopausal crowd to their stores (and let's face it, we baby boomers are quite the shopping force), why not go all out and put our parking spaces *inside* the store, say in the frozen-food aisle. Menopausal women would drive for miles to get to park their car in there and have that blast of frozen-food air hit them the minute they open their car door. Forget double coupons! Forget free tickets to Disneyland! Forget giveaways and contests! Give us arctic air and we'll be loyal customers for life! And really, when you think about it, is getting to park our cars in the frozen-food aisle that much to ask, especially when you consider all the store managers who are already letting children drive those little kiddie carts around in their stores? I guarantee you we'd hit fewer customers with our cars than the kids do with theirs.

Being able to park our cars right in the store would also save us time and energy loading the groceries into the trunk or the back of our SUVs. All we would have to do is drive our car up to the check-out counter, pay the bill, put the bagged groceries directly into our car, and then drive away.

But designated parking spaces at grocery stores is only the beginning. I would also like to suggest that officials at the Department of Transportation begin looking into the possibility of adding a special "menopause lane" to all our interstate highways. I realize this could get pricey and on the surface might appear to involve some tax hikes to pay for it, but hear me out. It's a known fact that menopausal women sometimes have difficulty making decisions, am I right? Wait, maybe I shouldn't say that. Aw, why not? It's my book. No, wait. It's a generalization and . . . Oh, never mind, I'm going to leave it in because it's true. We do have trouble making decisions. A separate menopause lane would help us with this indecisiveness because there would be an off-ramp every five hundred feet or so to accommodate last-minute exit decisions of the menopausal woman. The resulting decrease in car accidents due to multiple and unsafe lane change attempts should defray the cost of adding such a lane. And think of the gasoline savings. Here in the South if you miss your off-ramp, you sometimes have to drive an extra ten or fifteen miles before you can get off the highway and reverse your direction. That's a lot of unnecessary fuel we menopausal drivers are wasting just because we can't make up our minds in time to exit when we're supposed to. So in actuality, a menopause lane would be saving the country both money and precious fuel. If we as a nation are truly seeking to lessen our dependence on foreign oil, adding several extra off-ramps would be one way to help us achieve this goal. So a tax hike wouldn't even be needed because the menopause lane would pay for itself over time.

And there are even more benefits to a menopause lane. You know how we menopausal women tend to be forgetful? How many times has one of us driven in the fast lane from, say, San Diego to San Francisco with our left-turn signal blinking the entire way? Well, if we were restricted to driving in our own menopause lane, that sort of behavior wouldn't bother any of the other drivers. No one would think twice about our turn signal staying on for one hundred, two hundred, even five hundred miles. They would simply see what lane we were driving in, nod their heads sympathetically, and say under their breath, "Ah, the menopause lane. Of course." The same thing goes if we happen to be zooming along with a can of soda or our purse sitting on the roof of our car.

Other drivers might notice it, but instead of pointing and laughing, like they do now, they would once again notice what lane we are driving in and cut us some slack.

The signage for these lanes would be important. Aside from the Menopause Lane signs, I propose that the only other signs allowed in our special lane would be: Wind Gusts Next Five Miles. What hot-flash suffering fifty-year-old woman wouldn't love five miles of wind gusts? All Turn Off Air-Conditioning Next Five Miles signs, however, like the ones they post before steep inclines, would be strictly prohibited. Forcing a menopausal woman to turn off the air-conditioning in her car for any distance should be considered life endangerment and tossed out of the vehicular code in all states anyway.

The menopause lane should also be exempt from speed limit signs. Speed limit signs only confuse us. How many menopausal women have been pulled over by a patrol officer simply because they had inadvertently gotten the highway number and the speed limit signs mixed up? For you young people or men reading this, I can assure you that this is easier to do than you might realize. You see, when a menopausal woman glances at a highway number sign, all she sees is the number and can easily assume that it's referring to the speed limit. When you're in the middle of a hot flash, you're not always thinking clearly. I've inadvertently mixed up highway number signs and speed limit signs myself on many occasions. It doesn't matter much if you're on Interstate 40, but you should see how quickly people get out of your way on the 210!

But why stop with parking spaces and extra lanes? Banks would also do well to offer their customers a separate menopause banking line. Let them keep one roped-off line for their regular customers, but over by the air-conditioning ducts they could rope off another line for all of us menopausal customers. This line would have its own special teller, too—one who has been specially trained in menopause management. Let's face it, menopause customers need special consideration when it comes to banking. We sometimes forget whether check #485 was written for our house payment of $1294.00 or to the paper boy for $12.94. It's a minor mix-up, but believe me, it can really mess up your accounting. By helping us with problems like this, bank managers would also be helping the community. How many times does a non-menopausal customer get stuck in line behind an estrogen-deprived woman who is sobbing uncontrollably and holding up the line because her checks arrived in the mail with the wrong cartoon character printed on them? Other customers don't understand these emotional outbursts. To them the woman's outburst seems irrational, so they get impatient with her. But menopausal customers understand. In a menopause line she would receive the empathy and patience she needs. In fact, everyone in the menopause line would probably be crying along with her.

Banks should offer us our own menopause credit cards, too. These would look a lot like a regular credit card, except they would come with a warning to salesclerks: *Menopausal customer. Confront about over-credit-line limits at your own risk.*

And for gold accounts, the card would come with its own mini-fan attached to it.

Churches could do their part, too, by offering a custom menopause hymnal for their middle-aged parishioners. Many of the hymnals that are on the market right now were compiled by men. Men don't always understand the needs of the menopausal church woman. Menopausal women might not feel all that comfortable singing songs like "All Consuming Fire" and "Roll On, O Billow of Fire." While these are classic and inspiring hymns, we're already hot enough. We'd much rather be singing songs like "There Shall Be Showers of Blessing," "Send Down The Rain, Cool Water," and "This, Too, Shall Pass."

And don't even get me started on department store dressing rooms. Menopausal women have wanted and deserved their own mirrorless, low-lit dressing rooms for years. But have department store managers listened to us? No. In fact, most of them have done the exact opposite. With each new swimsuit season it seems they add even more mirrors and brighter lights to these cubicles of terror. I went in one the other day that was so brightly lit it made me feel like I was changing clothes in the middle of a nighttime highway construction site. Come to think of it, I probably could have used some of the heavy equipment to help me get that swimsuit on!

The bottom line is this: Today's menopausal woman should be receiving far more attention and consideration than she is currently getting. We're human beings, too, with needs and feelings. Yes, we have hot flashes that make us spontaneously combust on a regular basis, and our night sweats can turn us into a water show, sprouting fountains of liquid in all directions in a matter of minutes, nearly drowning our house pets and any small children who happen to walk by. But none of that is our fault. It's not our fault if we have the natural ability to turn into a heat lamp at any given moment, capable of warming a 20' × 20' patio in four minutes flat. It's not our fault if we cry because Grape-Nuts just went on sale. It's not our fault if we care about the cartoon character that's on our checks. There are strange things happening inside our bodies that we have absolutely no control over.

So instead of judging us for all of these changes, why not offer us some support? Why not become politically active on our behalf? Why not join with us in our cause and help us at long last get our due? Write a letter to the Department of Transportation and suggest that a menopause lane be added to all the highways of this nation. Speak with your local banker about adding a separate line for their menopausal customers. Take our mission out of the shadows and force the world to quit ignoring our needs. Help us to organize our Million Menopausal Women March all the way to the White House and to the front steps of Congress. I realize that Washington, D.C., can get humid, and the thought of all of us crowded together marching as one through the streets in that hot, muggy air is what is keeping most of us from committing, but it's time to grab a sweatband and just go. It's time we menopausal women became a force to be reckoned with. It's time we formed our own club, like the red hat ladies, only sweatier.

And maybe it's finally time to elect a hot-flashing, night-sweating menopausal woman as president! What enemy in their right mind would take on an estrogen-deprived woman that close to the red phone? Talk about a homeland security plan!

The possibilities are endless. All it will take is for us to organize. But then again, on second thought, let's just stay at home in front of a fan.

I am extraordinarily patient, provided I get my own way in the end.
—Margaret Thatcher

Midnight at the Oasis

What I dream of is an art of balance, of purity and serenity devoid of troubling or depressing subject matter—a soothing, calming influence on the mind, rather like a good armchair which provides relaxation from physical fatigue.
—Henri Matisse

The first chapter dealt with middle-aged women. Now it's the man's turn.

Men, are you aware that there is a recliner chair on the market right now called the Oasis? This super plush, over-stuffed chair is being hailed as the ultimate recliner. With a span of forty-one inches from arm to arm, there is also a built-in remote control, a cup holder for one soda, and a thermoelectric cooler that holds up to six more cans! And that's not all. There is also an in-chair telephone, a six-point massager and heat system (for when you don't want to get up to turn down the air-conditioning), and for all of you sports fans, the chair is even available in your favorite team colors.

As good as this chair is, I still I think I could have designed an even better recliner. My idea of the perfect recliner would be one that has its own trash compactor large enough to handle pizza boxes and giant bags of stale popcorn. It would also have a super-powered garden hose complete with water hookup so you could just open the door and water your yard without ever leaving your seat. Or maybe I should go one better and make the chair a combination recliner/riding lawn mower. At half time, guys could press a button and ride out into the yard and mow some of the lawn before the game starts up again.

My chair would also have an indoor rotisserie/grill so men could cook dinner from the comforts of their chair. And since there would already be the water hookup for the garden hose, I could even add a shower head attachment to go along with it, and maybe a mirror so men could shower and shave and not miss a single play in the game. A computer with broadband connection would be a nice addition, too, as well as a FedEx drop box, in case he needed to mail anything. And like the overhead compartment on an airplane, the chair would have a compartment for storing extra pillows and blankets, too. And there would be a miniature refrigerator big enough to hold six-foot-long submarine sandwiches.

Another plus for many husbands would be for the chair to have rear- and side-view mirrors so they can see when their wife is entering the room with her honey-do list. This way, the men can pretend to be napping.

And finally, the chair would have a lightning rod, just in

case a severe thunderstorm ever rolls through; it would not so much deflect the electricity from a bolt of lightning as channel the natural energy to jump-start the tanning bed attachment.

Now *that* is a chair!

Sound too good to be true? Who knows, maybe someday La-Z-Boy or some other manufacturer will come out with a recliner like that. If they do, I have a feeling it'll be on every man's Christmas wish list. That is, until the recliner/fishing boat comes along. Or the recliner/twin-engine airplane. Or the . . . well, it's obvious the possibilities are endless.

Laziness is nothing more than the habit of resting before you get tired.
—Jules Renard

The Five People You Meet in a Buffet Line

Give me liberty or . . . OOOooo . . . A jelly donut!
—Homer Simpson

There is a book that has been receiving all sorts of critical acclaim. It's called *The Five People You Meet in Heaven,* and it has spent months on *The New York Times* Best-Seller list. They even made a television movie out of it. Now, while I'm sure it is a wonderful book, I can't help but wonder about all the notable people who aren't in the book—the people we don't hear much about. Like, what about the five people you meet, say, in a buffet line? Has anyone ever written a book about them? No. So once again the task has fallen to me. I may not be able to fill an entire book about these five noble souls, but the least I can do is dedicate a chapter to them.

Before I begin describing them to you, though, I must

confess that I myself am a buffet person. I happen to love buffets. I fully understand the urge to eat that third plate of food even after you've already unbuttoned, unbuckled, and halfway unzipped everything that can possibly be unbuttoned, unbuckled, and unzipped on your person. I understand the quest to get every penny of your seven dollars and ninety-nine cents' worth. Not everyone understands this compulsion, but I do. And I can certainly identify with the overwhelming need to scoop fourteen different casseroles onto your plate and enough dinner rolls for a party of eight. It's an unseen force that drives us to do these sorts of things. It is not an option, and I understand this.

Like all buffet people, I, too, have pondered the mysteries of the pudding trays, wondering how those stray peas found their way in there. I have survived tong fights with other customers over the last chicken drumstick. And I have on numerous occasions eaten crab salad that is spelled with a *k*, never once asking the question, "So what kind of fish is this *really*?"

Yes, I am a buffet person down to my very core, and I am proud of it. I am a dedicated and experienced partaker of the mac and cheese. I have been one with the corn fritter. I have piled my food so high as to interfere with the operation of the ceiling fans. I have scooped and dipped and grabbed and reached with the best of them. And on those rare occasions when I've had to stop at only my second plate of food (or roughly 40,000 calories), I have even endured ridicule by other, even more dedicated buffet people who have mercilously jeered me with cutting, hurtful labels like "buffet wimp" and "plate-o-phobe."

I say all of this so that you will know my point of reference. This is not a case of an outsider looking in. These are the words of someone who has held on to her fork until the waitstaff has had to unwrap her clutched fingers from around it. I am a buffet connoisseur, an all-you-can-eat maven, a dedicated defender of the potato and taco bar. In other words, I know whereof I speak.

Now for those of you who have never been to Branson, Missouri; Pigeon Forge, Tennessee; or basically anywhere in the South, and have yet to experience the world of the buffet, a brief definition of the buffet would be in order before we proceed any further. For one thing, buffets are different from cafeterias. At a cafeteria, you pay for each individual item on your tray. That can get expensive. You take a dish of corn, a scoop of mashed potatoes and gravy, a couple of chicken wings, and a slice of apple pie, and before you know it, your meal has cost you $27.98. You could have eaten steak and lobster for that amount of money, and not had to carry your own tray to the table.

For this reason, I feel that the buffet is better than a cafeteria. The rules of the buffet are quite simply that you are free to eat whatever you can possibly consume for one low price. It's all yours for the taking. Eat as much or as little as you want and there will never be any surprises when you get the bill. You know exactly what you're going to pay before you scoop out your first helping of fried okra.

Buffets are also different from meat-and-threes. Meat-and-threes are big here in the South, too. A meat-and-three is just that—one meat item and three vegetable choices for one low price. Some meat-and-threes offer a smaller version, the meat-and-two, for those of us on a diet. (For the diet plate, they only ladle one cup of gravy over your mashed potatoes instead of two.)

For my money, I feel the buffet is the best value. Why settle for only three sides when a buffet gives you your choice of twenty-six? Sometimes it's even more. And believe me, seeing all the different and creative ways they can use a pasta noodle is worth the price of admission.

Buffets are getting so popular right now that some unusual places are beginning to offer them—places like gas stations. I know that sounds odd, but it's true. Just drive along any interstate in the South, and you're sure to see a gas station advertising an all-you-can-eat buffet. Now, I'm not endorsing these buffets, nor am I warning you against them. I'm simply letting you know they are there. But I do have to say that getting gas where you get gas does sound a bit unnatural to me.

Wherever you find a buffet, though, one thing is certain—you're sure to meet the following five people.

First, there's *Muu Muu Mama*. Anyone who has ever been to a buffet has seen Muu Muu Mama. She is serious about her buffet experience. The muu muu she's wearing may or may not match her house slippers, but whatever you do, don't get in Muu Muu Mama's way. She is one determined soul and has elbowed her way past the best of them. You are a mere mortal and no match for such speed and agility. Just as you reach for the corn-bread dressing, quick as a flash she beats you to it. Reach for some steamed carrots, and she's already got her hand on the spoon. Go for the turnip greens, and she appears out of nowhere and scoops some onto her plate first. She has the reflexes of a Wild West gunfighter and the cunning of a stealth fighter pilot. She'll beat you every time. And she's the master of disguise. She may look like a size eighteen under all of that flowing material, but Muu Muu Mama weighs in at less than a hundred pounds. She just wears the muu muu so that when she leaves, she can sneak out thirty pounds of muffins for later.

Next, there's *Finger-Licking Freddie*. Watching Finger-Licking Freddie is like watching a ballet. As he dishes out his food, it's *The Nutcracker Meets Emeril* or *Swan Lake Meets Uncle Ben*. First he scoops some potatoes and gravy onto his plate, then gracefully raises his arm upward to lick his fingers. Without missing a beat, he steps lightly down the aisle and dishes up some salad. Some of the ranch dressing happens to drip down the side of his plate, but not to worry. Finger-Licking Freddie simply slides his finger along the rim, then gracefully licks his fingers again. He makes a quarter turn and moves on to the meat station. Some au jus drips onto his palm. He licks it up, does a turn to grab a roll, and sneaks a lick of the freshly melted butter on top of it. He scoops and licks so much that by the time he makes it to the last food station, he's already consumed eighteen hundred calories! But anyone who has been watching him is ready to applaud. Every move has been the epitome of grace and style and perfectly timed to the music playing over the intercom.

It's every bit as entertaining as any ballet you'll ever see. And I'm pretty sure the overalls are a lot easier on the circulation than ballet tights.

Chicken Wing Darla is the lady who will eat an entire tray of chicken wings, sucking every molecule of meat out of each one, stacking the ravaged bones onto her plate like a pile of greasy firewood. When you consider she's only working with four teeth, it's quite a feat. Frankly, I try to leave a little bit of meat on my chicken bones just out of respect. I figure if the animal laid down his life for my lunch, the least I can do is leave him a little dignity . . . and gristle.

Buffet Charley has hit every buffet east of the Mississippi, and you can tell. Like the state stickers that my parents used to stick to the windows of our station wagon to show people everywhere we'd been, Buffet Charley has the same idea, only he does it with gravy stains.

"See that one there? That's the sausage gravy I had down in Florida. And that one over there? That's the turkey and giblet gravy I had in Kansas. And that one right there, well, that's the country white gravy and mashed potatoes I had out west in Texas." He samples gravy like a wine expert tastes wine, taking a mouthful and swishing it around in his mouth. *"Ah, good texture. Full bodied and rich. No lumps. I would say it was made on Tuesday. Ah, yes, Tuesday, a very good day."*

Juggling Jimmy is the last of the five. Juggling Jimmy is easy to spot because of all the plates he juggles as he makes his way around the food stations. When you first see him, you're impressed because you think he's getting food for his wife and kids. *How sweet,* you think to yourself, *and so consid-*

396

erate. You might even chastise your own husband with a kick under the table or a dinner roll to the head, *"Why don't you ever do that for me, Harry?!"*

But as your eyes follow Juggling Jimmy, now with four plates and several dessert cups, all the way back to his seat, you notice that this guy is eating alone. Every single one of those plates are for him. Now you have to eat those words you said to your husband, but you're already so full you don't think you can squeeze in another bite, much less nine words and punctuation. But you do it because you have no choice. The truth is inescapable. Juggling Jimmy, like all the others, just enjoys getting his money's worth. He enjoys it so much, in fact, that he often times his arrival to be toward the end of the lunch buffet and just before they switch over to the dinner menu. He'll eat lunch, then sit around visiting with the other customers until the dinner buffet is put out. Then he'll get up and start with four plates all over again. He figures he's beating the system by getting two meals for the price of one, and no one is the wiser. People like Juggling Jimmy and Muu Muu Mama make you wonder how buffets can make any profit at all. But then, I suppose there are plenty of finicky adolescents who only take gelatin and crackers and their parents still have to pay $7.99 for them. So maybe it all evens out.

And there you have it—The Five People You Meet in a Buffet Line. There are other buffet people, of course. CEOs and plumbers, doctors and gardeners, business owners and retirees—all good people, every one. People who like to get a good value for their money, and maybe some extra muffins on the side. Muu Muu Mama and Juggling Jimmy are technically breaking the buffet rules, of course, but most of the time the FBI is too busy to crack down on them.

There is one thing that I do have to say about buffet people in general, though. After having traveled from buffet to buffet all across this great land of ours, I have discovered that buffet people are some of the friendliest people you'll ever find. They're also some of the most polite. Sometimes they'll even let you cut in line in front of them. Especially if you happen to have the last available chicken leg on your plate. Then, when you glance away from your plate just long enough to get a scoop of carrots . . . well, let's just say, all's fair in love, war, and buffet lines.

My doctor told me to stop having intimate dinners for four.
Unless there are three other people.
—Orson Welles

Last Breaths and Country Music

The trouble with real life is that there's no danger music.
—Jim Carrey from *The Cable Guy*

Maybe the Cable Guy had it right. How much easier would life be for all of us if every time we started to do something that would end with dire consequences, danger music would begin to play, warning us of impending doom, just like it happens in the movies? Wouldn't it be much nicer if we knew what not to do, whom to stay away from, and when to duck?

It would help us, too, if we could have romantic music playing at all the right times. Husbands and wives wouldn't have to guess what kind of mood each other was in; the music would tell them. Even if her husband was passed out on the sofa, a wife would know by the beautiful music that's playing in the background that love is in the air, despite all the snoring.

My husband and I live in the Nashville area, the home of country music. I love most kinds of music, but I especially enjoy country music. You can't beat songs like "Dropkick Me, Jesus, Through the Goal Posts of Life" and "You're the Reason Our Kids Are So Ugly." I grew up with a father who played a lot of country and gospel music in our home. But country music, and even gospel, has evolved over the years, keeping up with the times and gathering a whole new generation of fans along the way.

There is one thing that I've always wondered about, especially when it comes to certain country ballads and cowboy songs. There seems to be a good number of these old songs that were written about dying, and according to the lyrics, these songs were written by the very one who was doing the dying. Does that sound strange to anyone else besides me? They're nice songs, don't get me wrong, but they do make you wonder how it is that these songs ever got written in the first place. Songwriting is hard enough to do when you're healthy and sitting at your computer or in a recording studio. But to write a song after you've just had a bullet go through you, now that takes amazing concentration, skill, and fortitude.

Let's look at the words of one old cowboy song called "The Dying Outlaw."

Come gather around me, my comrades and friends,
For the sun it is setting on life's short day;
For I'm wounded to die and there's nothing to do,
But wait 'til my life ebbs away.

Now, right there is my point. Here is this mortally wounded cowboy outlaw, lying in the dust breathing what could possibly be his last breath, but instead of asking for someone to go fetch the doc, or even a Band-Aid, he's penning a song lyric. I don't know if he's writing it in the dust, or if he dragged himself over to his horse and grabbed a pad of paper and a pencil out of his satchel. All I know is this poor bleeding cowboy gathered up all the strength he had left and said, "I may have lead in me, but I've got a song in me, too! Stand back and watch me create! By the way, does anyone know what rhymes with bullet?"

The poor guy isn't even going to be around to spend the royalty checks if the song is a hit, but he's not giving any thought to money or even himself. He's simply thinking of future generations of cowboy music lovers, and he's penning his final thoughts as he breathes his last few breaths. Obviously, he's a deadline writer. Music companies would have loved him.

"When do you think you'll have the song finished?"

"Well, I'll probably be dead by one, so say, noonish?"

Poor guy. If only he had realized his talent and passion for songwriting earlier, his life might have taken a different turn. He could have been wonderfully successful in the music industry and turned his back on his life of crime. Music might have even ended up saving his life—after all, deadlines do have a tendency to keep one going.

"We'd really like another verse. Can you hang on a little bit longer?"

"I dunno. I'm getting pretty weak. I'll try to get one more

verse out of me, but there's no way I can write a bridge, too."

From ballads to pop to rock to country to gospel, the whole world loves a good song. Some songs soothe us, others make us feel romantic. Some energize us, others make us feel sad and melancholy, while still others can make us feel like we're on top of the world.

For us middle-agers and beyond, songs can do something else, too. They can take us back to a simpler time, back to a point in our life before we had lived so much of it. A song can transport us back through time to our high school graduation, our wedding day, or any other special time in our lives. They can rekindle the passion in our marriage, the love for our fellow man, and even our feelings for our very first dog. Tell me, who among us can listen to "Old Shep" and not tear up?

Songs can also get us moving again. It's hard to listen to a song with a good beat and not feel like tapping your toes or clapping along. And if you've never tried doing housework or yardwork to music, you ought to give it a try. You'll be surprised at how much faster you move and how much more you get done.

Songs can fill our loneliness, too, and be our company. We don't feel quite so alone when there's music playing in our homes.

So whether it's love songs, ballads, inspiration songs, rock and roll, gospel, or the dying-cowboy ballad, the important thing is to be sure we're all getting plenty of music throughout our day. Like they say, music is the soul of life.

It's easy to play any musical instrument: all you have to do is touch the right key at the right time and the instrument will play itself.
—J. S. Bach

We B Bussin'

For my part, I travel not to go anywhere,
but to go. I travel for travel's sake.
The great affair is to move.
—Robert Louis Stevenson

With each year that passes, the idea of going on one of those bus tours sounds more and more inviting. You know the ones I'm talking about. They go to different tourist attractions like Washington, D.C., Orlando, the Smoky Mountains, Branson, and many other wonderful places. The most tempting part of these trips is the fact that you can just sit back and leave the driving to someone else. How nice is that? Sure, every once in a while a bus driver will fall asleep at the wheel and end up making his own off-ramp and landing in a ditch, but to my husband and me, even that seems like a small price to pay for not having to deal with rush-hour traffic in unfamiliar towns. Besides, who am I to complain? I've had my own fair share of automobile mishaps. While I've never fallen asleep at the wheel (napping at red lights doesn't count), I do have a tendency to back into objects, like cars, lampposts, trash cans, lawn mowers, and other assorted temporary and permanent objects. I figure that if I were still dragging around on my rear bumper everything that I have ever backed into, I would have a two-mile-long procession behind me.

Besides not having to drive in strange towns, there are other advantages to taking a tour bus. For one thing, if a tour bus driver gets lost, he or she won't hesitate to stop and ask for directions, or at the very least consult a map. Tour bus drivers know they're on a time schedule and that it's their responsibility to find out precisely where they are and how to get where they need to go. They won't drive around aimlessly for hours on end, telling themselves and their passengers that the right road is "just around the corner."

If a husband, on the other hand, happens to get lost, you will visit four extra states before he'll even think about stopping and asking for directions. *"I don't need no stinkin' map!"* he'll say as you pass the same street for the eighteenth time. The only thing he uses a map for is to keep the sun off the dash or to swat some mosquitoes.

Another advantage to taking a tour bus trip is that most buses have rest rooms on board. You don't have to beg, threaten, or hold the driver hostage to get him to make a rest room stop. All you have to do is get up and walk to the on-board facilities, which I'm happy to say don't usually have all the graffiti that some gas station rest rooms can have. What would one of these bus passengers write, anyway? "AARP RULES"?

What is it about husbands that they hate to pull over to a gas station for these pit stops? Were they scared by a gas station attendant in their formative years? Or are they afraid they'll be made fun of by all those other male drivers they passed along the road? To a man, there's nothing worse than making great time, passing car after car, motor home after motor home, eighteen wheeler after eighteen wheeler, only to find yourself stuck behind those very same vehicles once you get back on the road after your stop. The ridicule and embarrassment for this kind of loss of time and distance is far too much of a blow to a man's driving ego. It can cause a man to pull over and move to the backseat, curl up in the fetal position and whimper like a baby for the next hundred miles. It's a sad sight and it could very well be the whole reason why husbands won't stop. It's not that they don't love us and want to take care of our needs, it's just that they know all too well where it can lead. They also know that it will cause them to come in last in the secret road race among men, and they're not about to forfeit their chances of winning the coveted trophy. No one ever sees this trophy, of course. They have to keep it hidden, otherwise we'll catch on to them and the contest will be over.

And so, a bus tour is sounding better and better to me. Or maybe someday I'll even get a job driving one. I hear in Branson they've got tour buses that can double as boats and be driven straight into the lake. That sounds like fun, and since I've already been doing that for years with my own car, I might as well get paid for it.

> *My husband would go to the ends of the earth for me. But if he'd just stop and ask directions, he wouldn't have to.*
> —Martha Bolton

6

Ideal Destinations for the Menopausal Traveler

* Cool, California
* Briny Breezes, Florida
* Energy, Illinois
* Relief, Kentucky
* Pep, Texas
* Sweatman, Mississippi
* Waterproof, Louisiana
* Burning Well, Pennsylvania
* Dripping Springs, Texas
* Thermal, California
* Tightsqueeze, Virginia
* Wide Awake, Colorado
* Why, Arizona

Death by Fashion

*Be not the first by whom the new are tried,
nor yet the last to lay the old aside.*
—Alexander Pope

I almost killed myself once. I didn't try jumping off a bridge or throwing myself in front of a speeding bus or anything like that. No, the way I almost did myself in was with a pair of tights. I wasn't depressed. I was just trying to be fashionable. And since it was winter, I was also trying to keep warm. But the tights were about two sizes too small (or I was two sizes too big), and by the end of the day, they had cut off my circulation so much that the room was spinning and I was starting to see glimpses of a tunnel of light.

I didn't actually want to die. It was just that I had purchased a pair of Petite tights by mistake, and I was trying to avoid the embarrassment of having to take them back to the store and ask for a larger size. So I went ahead and wore them anyway.

But squeezing my Tall size body into a Petite size pair of tights is a little like pouring a gallon of milk into a sippee cup:

No matter how carefully you pour, there's going to be plenty of overflow.

Tights aren't the only life-threatening item of clothing that I have encountered over my lifetime. I once had a pair of jeans whose zipper would periodically slide southward with no warning whatsoever, taking a souvenir clump of my skin along with it. Since I prefer all of my clumps of flesh to stay together, I decided to toss out the jeans.

But the most dangerous article of clothing ever designed has got to be the turtleneck. Not the flesh kind of turtleneck that inspired the title of this book. I'm talking about the real kind of turtleneck. Turtleneck as in "turtleneck sweater." If you ask me, the turtleneck should come with a warning. "The attempted removal of this product could be hazardous to your health . . . and dignity."

Let me explain. It was a day like any other day—I was shopping. Sweaters were on sale at this particular department store, and since winter was coming, I wanted to get a new one. I found a sweater I liked, a pretty red turtleneck, but they didn't have it in my size. The only one they had was two sizes too small, but since it was rather bulky, I convinced myself that I could still fit into it. And I did. Sort of. It took quite a bit of struggling, but there in the privacy of my dressing room, I somehow managed to get it on. It looked pretty good, too. So good, in fact, that I decided I was going to purchase it.

As soon as I started to take it off, though, things took a definite turn for the worse. Have you ever tried removing a two-sizes-too-small turtleneck sweater from your body? If you're still alive and reading this book, you probably haven't. For twenty minutes I struggled with that thing, only to get more and more tangled up in the process. I now know what a string of Christmas tree lights must feel like when you're trying to unravel them. I was withdrawing and inserting my arms and head into various holes, none of them the right one. I even ended up with one of my arms in the sleeve of another sweater that was hanging in the dressing room. If you ask me, the designer who first came up with the concept of the turtleneck sweater must have worked at Bellevue in the straitjacket department. For the life of me, I couldn't find my way out of that sweater! I looked like Houdini in an escape gone bad, and I was starting to hyperventilate with each twist and tug. I thought about calling the store security officer to help, but I didn't know how they handled their cases of "Turtleneck Assault."

Trying to maintain as much dignity as possible, I continued to wiggle and wrestle with the garment, but I was getting more and more entangled in the process. I stumbled out of the dressing room, still in the turtleneck of doom, and tried my best to flag down a store clerk, which was pretty easy to do considering the sleeves of the sweater were now dangling above my head, and when I moved back and forth in a rapid motion, they flapped in the breeze like a wind sock.

A clerk did finally come to my aid and helped me out of my predicament. She seemed to take it all in stride, too, which makes me wonder if this sort of thing happens to a lot of people when they try on turtlenecks.

I thanked her for releasing me from my entrapment, then

asked where the much safer cardigans were. She pointed to the next section over, but before I could walk over there, she made me sign a paper vowing to never trespass in the Petite section again. Since I had already signed a similar paper in the hosiery department, I willingly reached for the pen and signed it. I had been shamed enough—what was a little more humiliation? And anyway, staying out of the Petite section was for my own health and safety. As nice as it is to see a smaller size tag on an item of clothing that I happen to be wearing, I certainly don't want to require the Jaws of Life to be removed from it.

Clothing attacks such as the above are our own fault. In both instances I had tried on items that were not my correct size. But there are some situations where the fashion designers are at fault. How many times have they brought designs to the runways that were potentially lethal? Remember those blouses with long, flowing sleeves that came into fashion a few years ago? I bought several of them just to be in style, but I soon discovered that there was one little problem. Every time I cooked, they tended to catch on fire. My smoke alarm gets enough of a workout between my cooking and my hot flashes, so I don't need my blouses igniting and adding to the drama. I also didn't like how the sleeves tended to hang down past my jacket sleeves. I would try tucking them back up into the sleeve, but they would inevitably work their way out again and I would end up with what looked like propellers at the ends of each of my arms. I didn't care about the embarrassment. I was just afraid that I could take off in a gust of wind and no one would know it was the blouse's fault. For my own safety, and because I hate to fly, I had to give the blouses away.

Men have had to deal with dangerous fashions over the years, too. I wonder if anyone has ever done a survey to find out how many men have passed out from accidentally tying their necktie too tight? And bow ties? How safe can they be? Especially if you show up at a biker rally wearing one.

And whose idea was it to use straight pins to keep men's shirts folded neatly in their packages? I wonder how much blood has been spilled on the battleground of dressing rooms all over the world over this strange practice?

Dangerous fashions aren't anything new, though. The problem goes way back in our history. Ever heard of the hoopskirt? It's hard to believe that during the mid–1880s some designer was actually paid money for inventing this undergarment. Who knows how many women were knocked unconscious simply by trying to sit down in a hoopskirt. There aren't any records of injuries, but that's probably because the incidents were listed as "a severe attack of the vapors," when in reality it was hoopskirt assault. And where did the inventor of the hoopskirt come up with the idea anyway? While playing around with a couple of hoops one day, did he just throw some fabric over them and say to himself, *"Hmmm . . . now here's a style that will make a woman's lower half look even larger. Women are going to love this!"*?

Back then, there was also the corset. Now what kind of cruel mind was behind that insane fashion item? Corsets were such a tight squeeze on a lady that all sorts of body parts were being pushed into places where they didn't belong.

"Dahling, I can't help but notice that you have a hole in the vicinity of your throat. Did you have some sort of surgical procedure done?"

"Oh, goodness no, Abigail. That's just my belly button."

I'm glad someone finally wised up and we don't have to wear things like hoopskirts and corsets today. Can you imagine how long it would take to unfasten a corset at a buffet?

The Roaring '20s had its share of dangerous fashion, too. There was all that fringe and beads; and as if that new look wasn't dangerous enough, someone decided to make up the Charleston dance. I wonder how many women accidentally beat themselves to death doing the Charleston in those beaded dresses during that era?

What is wrong with us? Why do we consistently pay these fashion designers our hard-earned money only to have them come up with styles that have the potential to harm us? And who are these people, anyway? It used to be that most of the top fashion designers could be found living in Paris or New York. But I don't think that's the case anymore. If you ask me, they're all working at Goodwill now. That's right, Goodwill Industries. Maybe they're not on the payroll, but they're hanging out there, I'm sure of it. Think about it. Every time you go through your closet and finally give away all of your outdated clothing, what's the next hot style to hit the market? That's right—the very style you just gave away. So it stands to reason that someone on the inside track at Goodwill is going through these donations and bringing these fashions back into style as soon as you drop them off. The timing is far too perfect for it to be a mere coincidence.

You can try waiting out the designers, but it usually doesn't work. I know this from personal experience. I've held out year after year, passing on the donation for just a little bit longer, giving this shirt, those pants, that skirt one more season to see if the style was going to come back on its own, but it didn't. At least not until I actually took the outdated clothes off their hangers, placed them in a bag, and drove them over to a Goodwill donation center. Not until then did those looks ever start showing up on store mannequins again.

You can check out my theory for yourself, but I believe you'll find my thinking is right on. If anyone goes through their attic and gives away an old hoopskirt and corset, we're all in trouble.

The novelties of one generation are only the resuscitated fashions of the generation before last.
—George Bernard Shaw

Is There a Doctor in the House?

Never go to a doctor whose office plants have died.
—Erma Bombeck

Thanks to recent advances in medical technology, as well as an effort to keep expenses down for the patient, more and more surgical procedures are now being performed in doctors' offices instead of in a hospital.

Now, anything that will reduce the soaring cost of medical care is probably a good thing, but caution is still recommended. I recently read an article that said in some states, health boards are not required to regulate doctors' offices as vigorously as they would a hospital setting. If this is true, should something go wrong during the procedure, a patient's well-being could be jeopardized if the doctor's staff are not adequately trained or prepared, or if the office lacks the necessary equipment to handle the crisis.

While most doctors probably do their best to meet the government's standards, I'm sure there are some doctors' offices where caution would be highly suggested. Because of this, I thought it might be a good idea to issue the following warning as a public service:

Do not allow your doctor to operate on you in his office if . . .

- ❁ any of the surgical tools have the words "The Home Depot" printed on them.
- ❁ he has to clear off his copy machine to make an operating table.
- ❁ his procedure room has a drive-thru.
- ❁ his anesthesiologist is holding a hammer.
- ❁ his oxygen mask says "Property of American Airlines."
- ❁ anywhere on his medical license you see the words "For entertainment value only."
- ❁ everyone in his waiting room is a malpractice attorney.
- ❁ his EKG machine has only two knobs and the words "Etch A Sketch."
- ❁ his defibrillator is a fork and an electric outlet.
- ❁ you hear the word "oops" more than three times—and he's just trying to cut through the surgical supplies packaging.

It's good to save money, especially in the increasingly costly field of medical care. But it's up to us to make sure that the care we are receiving is the best care available. Take time to ask whether or not your doctor's office is properly prepared should an emergency arise during any in-office surgical procedure. After all, your body is the only one you're going to get. It's just one to a customer, and it has to last you a long time, so take the best care of it you can.

Medical Definitions for the Middle-Aged Patient and Beyond

As you move through the middle-age years and beyond, it's a good idea to keep up with the latest medical terms. Should your doctor refer to any of the following on your medical report, you want to be in the know. The following list is provided for this purpose:

Fibrillation— not confessing to your doctor about the four chili dogs you had just before the chest pain began

Anti-inflammatory— not wanting to argue with your doctor over a billing error

Bronchospasm— leg cramps after a day of horseback riding with your grandchildren

Atrophy—	what you win in the Baby Boomer Bowling League
Microcirculation—	not meeting many people at the retirement home Christmas party
Serological—	eating sensible cereal
Carbohydrate—	drinking bottled water in your car
Thermoregulation—	asking your spouse to get you a second blanket
Arrhythmogenic—	the urge to dance in a sterile environment
Gastralgia—	that nauseous feeling you get when looking at the price of gasoline
Benign—	a possible winning number in a game of bingo at the seniors' center
Lower GI—	a low-ranking member of the military
CAT Scan—	looking for the jazz station on your radio

They had me on the operating table all day.
They looked into my stomach, my gall bladder,
they examined everything inside of me.
Know what they decided? I need glasses.
—Joe E. Lewis

10

New Prescription Medicines for Middle-Aged Patients*

Fanthropan: Provides immediate relief from menopausal hot flashes. Open box, discard medication, then wave the "Possible Side Effects" insert in front of face until hot flash subsides.

Silencithor: Insert one pill into each ear one hour prior to grandchild's birthday party. Provides temporary deafness for up to three hours for one dozen four-year-olds. Silencithor PM is double the size and strength. When inserted into ears it can block out spousal snoring of up to twenty-one decibels.

Lazichor: Take one dosage every morning for eight-hour relief from wife's honey-do nagging. Induces temporary but instant comalike state. Works best if taken in recliner in front of television set.

Golficillin: One tablet taken one hour prior to tee time provides invisibility for up to ten minutes, which for most adult male patients is just enough time to make it out of the house with your golf clubs.

Memorazine: For memory enhancement. Take one every morning to remember what other pills you're supposed to be taking. Will also work to enhance memory for when you walk into a room but can't remember why you walked into the room in the first place.

Summersporin: Two drops in each eye will temporarily dim vision for up to two hours per dosage during swimsuit shopping season. Works best if administered ten minutes before entering dressing room.

*Check with your doctor to see if these new medications are right for you.

11

What Are They Doing Now?

Retirement at sixty-five is ridiculous.
When I was sixty-five I still had pimples.
—George Burns

Retirement doesn't mean you're dead. It just means you don't have to look alive unless you want to. You can sleep until noon, then laze around on the sofa the rest of the day if you so choose. You can stay in your robe and slippers until supper. Or even next summer. You don't have to shave your face or your legs (whichever applies) for weeks. Maybe even months. Men can look like ZZ Top if they want to and women can grow bangs on their knees if they so choose. It's their choice. Retirement means you are master of your own ship and hair follicles. You can chart an independent course.

As a retiree, whatever you do and wherever you go is strictly up to you. No matter how many people you've worked for in your lifetime, you are your own boss now—

theoretically speaking, of course. You may still have your spouse to answer to, and perhaps a couple of precocious two-year-old grandchildren. But as far as having to get up in the morning and report to work, that's a thing of the past. You can toss out your alarm clock and never have to answer your beeper or work cell phone again.

Ah, yes, retirement is wonderful. The freedom, the peace, the quiet, the sleeping in, the naps, the independence . . . that is, until you take that first post-retirement job. And many retirees do exactly that. Research tells us that it's healthy to stay busy and to keep one's mind active after retirement.

Second careers are also the perfect opportunity for you to try something different and learn new skills. If you retired from a high-stress job, you might prefer spending your middle-aged years working in a far more relaxed atmosphere. If you spent twenty or thirty years working in a, how shall we say it, *boring* industry, then you might be ready for a little more excitement this time around.

After my husband retired from the Los Angeles Police Department (three times, to be exact—I believe he holds the record), and after working for a period of time as Security Manager for one of the major television studios, he didn't want any job where high levels of stress were involved. He had seen enough tense situations to last him a lifetime.

So his dream job became operating the train at Knott's Berry Farm. Not that there is anything wrong with being a train conductor at an amusement park. I'm sure it's a job that requires a good amount of skill. Dodging park guests has to be tricky, especially when they are crossing the tracks with an armful of giant stuffed animals and balloons blocking their line of vision.

I think the main reason my husband wanted to be an amusement park train conductor is that he thought it would be cool to pull the cord and sound the whistle. I offered to have a cord and whistle installed in our SUV, one that he could pull whenever he drove up our driveway, but he didn't seem to think it would be the same. (So apparently, it wasn't only the whistle. It must have been the uniform, too.)

Whatever his reasoning, his dream job never came to fruition. We moved to Tennessee and commuting to Buena Park, California, wasn't really an option.

In Tennessee, though, he ended up taking a job at the Opryland Hotel. It wasn't operating a train, but it was close. It was operating the boats that take the tourists down a canal that runs through the hotel. The uniforms were khaki, and not as cool in his opinion as a train conductor's uniform, but all in all he did enjoy that job. He was glad he didn't have to carry a gun (goldfish don't get all that violent), and there weren't any muggings to have to deal with on that canal either. That's probably because a mugger would have had to snatch the purse or wallet, dive overboard, then swim through a treacherous two feet of raging—okay, rippling water to make his escape, and do it all while listening to "Achy Breaky Heart" over the speaker system. Apparently no mugger wanted to put their lives in that much jeopardy. Besides, any assailant would have been quickly overtaken by busloads of vacationing tourists, and we all know how quickly they can turn into vigilantes when someone threatens their enjoyment of a lobby boat ride.

Even without the danger and prestige of the train conductor job, the Opryland job still ended up going to my husband's head. He began making me and our children address him as "Admiral," and all night long he would make us listen to his tales of harrowing adventures while commanding his "fleet of ships."

But as beautiful as the setting was (and the Opryland Hotel is amazing), even he needed a little more excitement than a lobby boat ride. So he began thinking about reentering the security field.

He is now Chief of Security of an art museum, which is not only a peaceful and beautiful place to work, but it also makes better use of his police and security skills. Finally, a perfect fit.

Finding that ideal second career isn't always an easy thing to do. Unfortunately, society is too often geared toward younger and younger workers. But that rationale doesn't make much sense to me. Why would a company overlook the already proven qualities that a seasoned middle-ager can bring to the table? Twenty-year-olds just don't have the same experience and sound judgment of an older worker. Middle-agers aren't going to use the company Internet for video games or demand special parking for their skateboards. But too often companies don't see these obvious advantages, and they overlook quality for youth, time and time again.

I'm sure we all know highly skilled individuals who have been looking for that perfect second career for years, but with no luck. From retired teachers to retired entertainers to retired CEOs, there's a wealth of knowledge and talent out there in middle-aged land sitting dormant. It's a shame to continue to let the skills and experience of so many individuals go unused simply because they've passed the halfway mark of life. The business world needs to get busy and tap into this well of dormant but still very impressive talent and knowledge. Wal-Mart greeters, as good of a job as that might very well be, shouldn't be the only choice for these dedicated and capable workers. Age and experience is a plus, not a negative. Employers could reap the benefits of some other employer's years of training and save themselves money and problems in the long run.

If you're one of the ones who is currently looking for a second career, I would encourage you to not give up. Don't buy into the notion that your skills are no longer marketable. There are plenty of people who have made their greatest impact on society during the second half of their lives—Colonel Sanders, Grandma Moses, Ronald Reagan, Jimmy Carter, just to name a few. Just keep looking. That perfect opportunity is bound to come along one day. It did for my husband. He loves where he works now. It's the perfect fit he had been looking for after nearly three decades of police work. And don't think for a minute that his position at an art museum doesn't still carry a significant degree of danger, too. Why, one night during the holidays, the Lionel electric train in the Christmas display jumped the tracks, and he had to rise to the occasion once again. As he tells it, *"What else could I do? When the call came in, 'Train down,' I looked at my men and* said, 'I'm going in. Cover me, boys. I'm going in.'"

And the city (and electric-train lovers everywhere) sleeps in peace tonight.

Years may wrinkle the skin, but to give up enthusiasm wrinkles the soul.
—Samuel Ullman

Computer Signs for the Middle-Ager and Beyond

S :)   =   "So how do you like my new toupee?"

/ :)   =   "Can you tell I've got a comb over?"

{ }   =   "I don't remember these love handles being so prominent before."

: - x   =   "Who needs to count carbs when you've got duct tape?"

}} — I   =   "Drat! My forehead's in my eyes again."

:B - (=   "Is it just me or are the bags under my eyes getting worse?"

: - ()   =   "I just had Botox. Can you tell?"

8 -)   =   "Has anyone seen my glasses? I've been looking for them for the last—Oh, silly me. They're on my face."

X :)   =   "Fred, take the propeller hat off and act your age!"

W
. .   =   "I know they're only four hairs, but do
—   what you can with them."
///
. .   =   "What do you mean the air-conditioner's
O   broken?"

Gravity
(Parody of "Yesterday")

Gravity
Wish this wasn't how things had to be.
Body parts are falling off of me.
Oh, why did God make gravity?
Can you see
how my figure has dropped to my knees?
Not much else is where it used to be
since I lost out to gravity.
Why can't things just stay where God put them long ago?
All day long I'm warning folks to "Look out below!"
Gravity
I've been shrinking, now I'm half of me.
I might not stop until I'm four foot three.
Oh, why did God make gravity?

Let's Leave My Brain Out of This

Americans are getting stronger. Twenty years ago, it took two people to carry ten dollars worth of groceries. Today, a five-year-old can do it.

—Henny Youngman

I recently read about a new marketing concept called "neuro-marketing." Instead of merely taking our word on our opinions, companies will soon be able to use neuroimaging to determine whether our brains are backing up what our mouths are saying about their products. It's sort of like being hooked up to a lie-detector test for the Pepsi/Coke challenge. Companies want to be sure that when we say we like their products, we really *do* like their products. They don't want nice and polite. They want truth. Only honest to goodness feedback can help grow their business. Considering the advantages of such advanced technology, I'm sure there will be plenty of companies signing up for neuromarketing programs.

But has anyone thought about what could happen if the technology behind neuromarketing were to go beyond product analysis and become available to the general public? The ramifications could be enormous. Telephone solicitors would have to tell you the truth about that pyramid scheme they're pitching to you over the phone. And if you told them you were in the middle of dinner and couldn't talk right now, they would know by the neuroimaging whether or not you were telling the truth. When that waitress asks how your lunch is, instead of getting away with a simple but insincere "Fine," she would be able to read your brain and immediately know about all that gristle you're hiding under the parsley. And just imagine how quickly neuroimaging would reveal false friends and mother-in-law/son-in-law relationships. Yes, if this technology were available to the general public, there's no telling what kinds of changes it would make to our lives.

It would even affect marriage. There would be no more forgotten birthdays, anniversaries, or Christmas gifts because absolutely no excuse would get by the neuroimager. The only thing a husband or wife could say is the truth. "I forgot." Simple as that.

Politics would be affected, too. Imagine the next presidential debate with neuromarketing in action. One candidate might begin with, "With all due respect to my esteemed opponent," while the neuroimagining is indicating that what he's really saying is, *There's no way this doofus could run the country!*" (A few go ahead and say that now anyway.)

The technology wouldn't really be necessary on those of us over forty, though. By the time we've reached this age, most of us can't wait to share our true feelings. We've held our opinions in long enough. We realize life is much too short to mince words or beat around the bush. If we don't like a product, or if we think there is a better way to make it, we'll usually let the company know about it. We'll call and speak directly to the department head. We'll write letters to the corporate office. We'll tell our neighbors and friends. We'll share our opinions with anyone who'll listen. But by the same token, if we're impressed with a product, we're just as quick to let the company know about that, too. Middle-agers and beyond are a marketing team's dream.

Until the rest of the population can catch up on the sincerity of the middle-aged shopper, though, companies are going to have to depend on new techniques like neuro-marketing to do their research. After all, it's only through getting the honest opinion of their customers, young and old alike, that companies will be able to give us the products we truly want and can actually use.

And as far as neuroimaging's effect on mother-in-law/son-in-law relationships, well, sometimes it's best to just leave well enough alone.

My opinions may have changed, but not the fact that I am right.
—Ashleigh Brilliant

I Hereby Bequeath

**Death is not the end. There remains the
litigation over the estate.**
—Ambrose Bierce

There is a fear worse than knowing your children and grand-children will fight over all your possessions after your passing. And that is, *What if they don't?* What if all those souvenir trinkets you've carted around from house to house, all that stuff you couldn't bear to part with, all the pictures, furniture, books, dishes, rugs, and all the rest are set to be sold to the highest bidder as soon as you take your final breath? What if your family already has the garage sale signs printed up and they're just waiting to fill in the date? What if not one of your offspring is interested in hanging on to your hot-dog-shaped condiment tray? What if no one wants your elephant statue or your pink flamingo lamp? What if they can't wait to get rid of your Lone Ranger video series? What if no one wants your "stuff"?

No matter how many priceless treasures we've accumu-lated over the years, no matter how neatly we've displayed them, or how protective we have been of every single cherished item, in the end there is only one thing that we can do with any of it, and that's leave it behind. We can't take a single Tony Bennett album with us. We don't even get a two-suitcase allowance on our flight to eternity. We have to go out the same way we came in, empty-handed. All we can take with us is what is inside of us. It's like that old joke about never seeing a hearse towing a U-Haul trailer. No matter how much we might love our stuff, not one single item is making the trip to the hereafter with us. It's all staying behind, and it'll be up to those we leave behind to do with it as they so choose.

So maybe it's time to rip the protective plastic coverings off our sofas and start enjoying them in the here and now. Maybe it's time to start getting some use out of our priceless collectibles, instead of merely watching them accumulate dust. Maybe we should start building some memories of those things that we've been keeping up on our shelves. After all, a "keepsake" won't mean anything to your family unless there are some actual memories attached to it.

Going ahead and giving away a few of your things while you're still healthy might be a good idea, too. It helps us make sure we're giving the right mementos to the right people, and that we're not tossing out those things that mean the most to our families and hanging on to those things that mean the least. Too often we have no idea which items in our homes are most cherished by our children until they tell us years later that they would have liked that overstuffed chair we gave away for free to some stranger.

I'm not sure which of our things my children will want after my husband and I are no longer around. I hope they don't hold the mother of all garage sales and sell for mere pennies item after item, totally unaware of their real value. (The hot-dog-shaped condiment tray alone is number 346 of 1,000,000,000 and should be worth something.).

Like all of us who get to this point in life, I hope there are plenty of things around our house that do hold some special meaning to our children, regardless of any monetary value. Things that will bring to their minds heartwarming memories every time they look at them. Maybe it'll be the Christmas decorations (I am a certifiable Christmas fanatic), or the old photo albums (I am a picture junkie), or our book collection (both their father and I have a book collection that would rival the Library of Congress). Whatever items hold special memories for our children, I hope they'll recall those memories every time they see them.

If you are going to start giving away your things early, though, there is something to keep in mind. Don't give away those things that still give you pleasure. They're yours. You don't have to part with them until you're good and ready. Only give away those things that will give you greater pleasure watching someone else enjoy them for a while.

You might want to donate some of your possessions to a museum, church, or charity. Or you might even hold that mother of all garage sales yourself and take the money and go on a cruise. We've all seen estate sales of people who had died penniless, depressed, and all alone while they hung on to a houseful of possessions that weren't doing them any good at all. Possessions that were all too quickly sold to the highest bidder, raising a small fortune for the heirs, who had never taken the time to visit the deceased anyway.

It's like the old joke about an elderly man who, after many years of his family's complaining about his inability to hear, finally went out and bought himself a hearing aid. After wearing it for a few weeks, he went back to the doctor for a routine checkup. The doctor said, "Your hearing is perfect. It couldn't be better. I bet your family's pretty thrilled that you're hearing again, huh?" The man said, "My family? Are you kidding? I haven't told any of them yet. I just hang out in my recliner and listen to their conversations. I've changed my will three times!"

Junk or treasure, useless or collectible, the bottom line is they're your things. Keep them, give them away, do with them what you will. Then go about the business of enjoying your life.

I'm very proud of my gold pocket watch.
My grandfather, on his deathbed, sold me
this watch.
—Woody Allen

Today's Weather for the Menopausal Woman

Heat wave to continue, with intermittent volatility; some storms may be severe. An 80 percent chance of flash flooding, mostly indoors, during the overnight hours.

The Face-Lift-of-the-Month Club

I wish I had a twin, so I could know what I'd look like without plastic surgery.
—Joan Rivers

Television reality shows and magazine ads try to convince us that plastic surgery will give us back our youth and vitality, that it will put everything back in place and fix what may have needed fixing all along, that it is the answer to all our problems. But even though plastic surgery has become more routine and is helping more and more people look younger and younger, there is one other danger that plastic surgery candidates should be aware of. It's not always easy to know when to quit.

We have all seen those celebrities who seem to have a frequent-user pass for plastic surgery. Those stars who seem to spend so much time at their plastic surgeon's office, they get their fan mail there. The ones who are getting this nipped and that tucked and eventually end up looking like something out of a wax museum.

Some of these youth-seeking stars have had so much work done, their facial muscles don't even operate correctly anymore. They think they're smiling, but nothing on their face has moved to indicate that. They frown, but no one knows it. Their face is stuck with one expression, and it's like talking to a photograph.

After the sixth or seventh plastic surgery, you would think that friends and family of these desperate folks would try to arrange some sort of plastic surgery intervention.

"You've got to stop this, Beulah! Look what you're doing to yourself! Every time you blow your nose, it flies right off and you've got to spend twenty minutes looking for it. One of these days you're not going to be able to get it to stick back on. Stop this madness before it's too late!"

But these people don't stop. And thanks to the "makeover" reality shows, more people are getting plastic surgery than ever before. Men and women are lining up for every body part renovation you can think of, and now they're wanting to do it in package deals. They want their face lifted, their thighs liposuctioned, their chin reshaped, their teeth capped, their hair transplanted, and various other body parts enlarged, reduced, rearranged, and rejuvenated all during the same leave of absence from work. I guess they figure if *Trading Spaces* can give a room a complete makeover in two days, why can't a body remodel get done in the same amount of time?

But we're talking surgery here. There are health issues

that have to be taken into consideration. Sure, some of these televised body makeovers have been truly amazing, but we need to be careful that we're not just concentrating on the outside person, and forgetting about the remodeling job that often needs to take place on the inside.

If you're going to change something about your body, you need to be sure you're doing it for the right person—you. If you're happy with the way you look, that's all that matters. No one else's opinion counts.

If you're not happy and you do want to surgically change something about your body, then the best advice we can give you is to seek out the very best medical care you can find.

And know when to quit.

I recently watched one of those plastic surgery shows where a lady was having her lips redone because apparently they had gotten all lumpy from too many collagen injections. I guess I don't blame her for wanting the lumps out. After all, who wants lumpy lips? But why didn't someone stop her long before that point? Didn't they notice she was getting a little carried away? I don't think anyone is going for the lumpy lip or wax museum face on purpose. Some of these people have, to borrow Phyllis Diller's great line, had "more parts lifted than an abandoned Mercedes." They don't even look like themselves anymore. They've turned into a montage of coveted body parts of every celebrity they've ever admired. They got the nose of this star, the lips of that star, and the chin of someone else. They have so many mismatched parts, their driver's license photo could pass for a Picasso painting.

Some years ago a friend of mine underwent plastic surgery to have a bump removed from her nose. The surgery was successful in that she got the nose she'd always dreamed of. But a short time after the surgery her now perfectly bumpless nose began pulling to the right. I don't think it was a political statement or anything, it was just doing it for no apparent reason.

With each passing week her nose would slide farther and farther off center. In a weird sort of way, her nose had become a sort of nomad, traveling the surface of her face, and there was nothing that she could do about it short of another surgery. The nose finally came to rest so close to the side of her face, it gave new meaning to the term, "Blow it out your ear!"

She did eventually have the second surgery and it all turned out fine. But getting to that point was a long and embarrassing process. For a couple of years her Christmas card photos looked like Mrs. Potato Head. Each year's card showed her nose in a different place on her face.

It's because of stories like this that I've decided to keep my less-than-perfect body just the way it is. I'm happy with it, flaws and all. I don't really have any problem with anyone else getting plastic surgery. It's their choice. But for me for right now, I'm sticking with what I've got. Besides, whenever I need to blow my nose, I kinda like knowing where to find it.

I think your whole life shows in your face and you should be proud of that.
—Lauren Bacall

Top 20 Countdown for Middle-Agers and Beyond

20. "Stumbling in the Night" (Frank Sinatra)
19. "You Can't Hurry Me" (Diana Ross and the Supremes)
18. "Everything Goes" (Tony Bennett)
17. "Whole Lotta Sweatin' Goin' On" (Jerry Lee Lewis)
16. "These Orthopedic Boots Are Made for Walking" (Nancy Sinatra)
15. "Listen to the Rhythm of the EKG" (The Cascades)
14. "Eve of Reconstruction" (Barry McGuire)
13. "You've Lost That Nerve End Feeling" (The Righteous Brothers)
12. "Papa's Got a Brand New Spleen" (James Brown)
11. "Stairway to Arrhythmia" (Neil Sedaka)
10. "It Hurts to Be This Age" (Gene Pitney)
 9. "Blue Suede Sensible Shoes" (Elvis)
 8. "Catch A Falling Part" (Perry Como)

7. "Ache Around the Clock" (Bill Haley and His Comets)
6. "Where Did My Teeth Go?" (Diana Ross and the Supremes)
5. "It's My Bypass and I'll Cry If I Want To" (Lesley Gore)
4. "Where Has All the Firmness Gone?" (Pete Seeger)
3. "Harper Valley AARP" (Jeannie C. Riley)
2. "Splenda, Splenda" (The Archies)
1. "Bridge Over Night-Sweat Puddles" (Simon and Garfunkel)

19

Middle-Age Evolution

My life has a superb cast but I can't figure out the plot.
—Ashleigh Brilliant

I don't believe in evolution. I don't believe that man started out as a monkey, then continued to evolve until he could fit into a decent business suit. It just doesn't make sense to me. I do, however, believe in a form of reverse evolution. In other words, after decades of dealing with everything that life has to throw at him, man can certainly go from perfect posture in his twenties and thirties, to looking rather apelike by his forties, fifties, and beyond. For me, this "reverse evolution" makes far more sense than the evolution chart. I'll show you what I mean.

Man at marriage ceremony: head erect, shoulders back, perfect posture.

Man after one weekend of carrying around honey-do list:

hunched over shoulders, head leaning slightly forward.

Man after birth of first child: hunched over shoulders, droopy eyes, unshaven face, head leaning forward.

Man on second week of mother-in-law's visit: hunched over shoulders, head noticeably lowered, arms dragging floor, face and neck with seven-day growth, communicates with grunting sounds.

Man after birth of fourth child: hunched over shoulders, head bouncing back and forth uncontrollably, scratches backside and under armpit seemingly without control, grunts to self, bears a slight animal-like odor (also resembles the scent of soiled diapers and spoiled milk).

Man after five hours of outlet shopping: hunched over shoulders, chin touching chest, massive overgrowth on face, neck, and back that could use a good mowing, makes apelike movements as he drags packages from store to store for life mate.

Man on third day of babysitting grandchildren: hunched over shoulders, head and chest have both succumbed to the gravitational pull, hasn't shaved in so long that hair has taken over and is now even growing out his ears.

Man after seeing how much his retirement check really is after retiring: hunched over shoulders, head dragging the floor, swings from workout equipment at YMCA in a futile attempt to try to take his mind off his situation.

Man holding stack of relationship books that his wife wants him to read: hunched over shoulders and lowered head, suddenly appears to not understand a word of English.

He shakes his head "no" in an apelike fashion, jumping up and down on the books.

Man after three hours of searching for lost television remote control: extremely hunched over shoulders, chin dragging on the ground, arms swinging from side to side, hairy and unkempt appearance, makes loud grunting noises, will clumsily knock over furniture in attempt to find remote. If lost item is not found, subject is likely to sit in a corner, picking things out of his navel, and pine away for hours.

By this point, man has indeed become a full-blown primate.

> **_My wife has a slight impediment in her speech. Every now and then she stops to breathe._**
> —Jimmy Durante

Growing My Own Turtleneck

Some people try to turn back their odometers.
Not me, I want people to know why I look this
way. I've traveled a long way and some of the
roads weren't paved.
—Will Rogers

Some years ago while shopping at a local mall, I happened to catch a glimpse of myself in a mirror. That was when I first saw it. The Gathering. Skin Falls. Whatever you want to call it, all I know is somehow, some way, for some reason unbeknownst to me, I had managed to grow my own turtleneck.

It didn't matter how hard I tried not to look at it, there was no denying it. It was right there under my chin, plain as day. Where all that extra skin was coming from, I didn't have a clue. There was enough for a whole other person, maybe even a whole village, and some of it wasn't even my skin tone. But it was my skin nonetheless, and it was very much connected to me. Not tightly, but it was connected.

Sure, it was nice to know there was now enough skin there to keep me warm in the wintertime, but instinctively I knew there had to be some drawbacks. For one thing, I was now going to have to start rolling up my chin every time I ate soup.

Exactly where this flesh waterfall was originating from, I didn't have a clue. Layers and layers of what used to be taut, youthful skin had without warning started cascading down like a flesh-colored Niagara Falls.

As far as I could tell, this extra skin wasn't being pulled from other parts of my body. I regularly take inventory of my body (this is just something you do in middle age; the gravitational pull has a habit of relocating body parts on a regular basis, so I've found it's best to keep a log), but I couldn't find a gap anywhere. All of my original skin was present and accounted for. I had epidermis covering everything epidermis is supposed to be covering. Not one single internal organ was exposed. There was just a lot more skin than I had ever remembered having. It was like it had multiplied. And like I said, much of it had gathered under my neck.

So to this day, my "chin skirt," for lack of a better term, is still here and, short of surgery or duct tape, there isn't much I can do about it. I have, therefore, determined that since this book has now hit the bookstores and I've been able to spill my innermost feelings on the subject to you, my closest friends, I am not going to lose any more sleep over the issue. Why should I spend the rest of my life obsessing over changes that my body didn't even consult with me about? It's making these changes all on its own. All I can do is accept them and go on with my life.

According to some facial cream ads, the loosening of once perfectly fitting skin generally starts happening around forty years of age. For some of us, it might begin even sooner. If you've already experienced it, then you and I can commiserate together. If you haven't experienced it yet, count your blessings, but be assured the clock is ticking, and Chin Falls will eventually catch up to you. No one is immune.

Heredity and environmental factors have a lot to do with the degree of loosening that each person's skin might end up doing, but the bottom line is that at some point in our lives, we all have a date with gravity.

So learn from me. I, too, had taken my youthful, taut skin for granted. Every time I looked in the mirror, I counted on it being there. It had always been there before, a perfect fit. Until that one day in the mall when I was faced with the hard, cold, loose facts. My skin had let me down. It had let itself down. And it has been heading in that direction ever since.

My main complaint about all of this isn't so much the loose skin under my chin and elsewhere, but that all of this loosening took place without any warning whatsoever. It would have been nice to have had a warning. Why couldn't our bodies have come equipped with an alarm that would sound whenever these sorts of things are getting ready to take place, you know, like a tornado alert or a winter snowstorm advisory?

"Beep! Beep! Beep! Skin avalanche! Take cover immediately!"

Sure, it might get on people's nerves, like cell phones and car alarms do now, but at least we would have a warning for these sorts of bodily changes. And those standing near us would have the chance to take cover, too.

But there is no alarm system, so we'll just have to be on guard take our changes as they come. And realize that the best defense against the downside of aging is a sense of humor.

There is still no cure for the common birthday.
—John Glenn

21

Season's Greetings

The earth has music for those who listen.
—William Shakespeare

By the time you've reached middle age, you have no doubt celebrated, dreaded, enjoyed, and endured your share of holiday seasons. The holidays take on a whole new look, sound, and feel for those of us in the over-forty crowd, especially when it comes to holiday music. Christmas carols can undergo quite a change when they're adjusted for the middle-ager. Instead of the more traditional songs that we're all used to hearing, carols like "I'm Beginning to Look a Lot Like Grandma," "The Twelve Days of Ointment," and "Oatmeal Roasting On An Open Fire" start filling our homes and hearts. "All I Want For Christmas Is Some Estrogen" is another favorite, too. Even a new version of "Here Comes Santa Claus" can be heard in the malls, especially in stores like the menopausal version of Victoria's Secret, Victoria's Who Cares?

Here comes menopause, here comes menopause,
right down Menopause Lane.
All wet with night sweats
and hot flashes, too,
it's like our bodies rain!
Moods are swinging, clothes are clinging,
we're puffin' up like a bun.
Pack the quilt before we wilt
'cause menopause has begun!

It's not just Christmas carols that are getting rewritten for those of us in the over-forty crowd. Our Valentine's Day music is different, too. Instead of sitting in front of the fireplace listening to the usual romantic fare, you'll find us listening to songs like "Achy Breaky Bones," "Hunka Hunka Burnin' Me," "You Don't Bring Me Rolaids Anymore," and "I Just Called to Say . . . I Can't Remember."

Our Fourth of Julys are sounding different, too. Come to one of our barbeques and you might hear "Praise the Lord and Pass the Metamucil" or that ol' patriotic favorite "Let Eardrums Ring."

And we can't forget New Year's Eve:

Should old acquaintance be forgot
and never brought to mind?
Or should we take our ginseng now
to help with auld lang syne?

Life seems to go on without effort, when I am filled with music.
—George Eliot

Life in Reality

**Life is not a problem to be solved, but a reality
to be experienced.**
—Søren Kierkegaard

Reality shows are all fine and good, but if the producers are
looking for real heroism and adventure, they've missed the
biggest angle yet. Surviving the Australian outback or some
deserted, bug-infested island is nothing compared to what I
have in mind. So what's my show?

Menopause House.

Think about it. It's the perfect reality show. The idea is to
take ten menopausal women and put them in a trailer in the
hot Nevada desert and make them live together without air-
conditioning for two weeks. The last survivor would win a
million dollars and a lifetime supply of estrogen. Right now
I'm sure you're sitting there saying to yourself, *"Of course!
Why didn't I think of that!"* It doesn't take much television
savvy to realize this is an instant hit just waiting to happen.
Interested producers may feel free to contact me through my
Web site at *www.marthabolton.com,* or better yet, they can just

send me the estrogen to option the rights to it.

The main drawback on a show like this would be the insurance; it would no doubt be astronomical (there's no telling what kind of antics ten estrogen-deprived, mood-swinging, hot-flashing, crowded, cranky women could pull). But it would be a fun show to watch, wouldn't it? At least from the safety of your living room. And talk about suspense—viewers would never know who was going to go off at any given moment. Any one of them could start a menopausal rant, and the best part is there wouldn't even need to be an inciting incident. Nothing would have to be staged or instigated. The sparks would be flying for absolutely no reason at all. Throw in the fact that there's no air-conditioning and you have a potential hostage situation brewing.

Besides insurance, another major expense of the show would be tissue. *Menopause House* would be full of emotional moments. With ten menopausal women talking about their lives, their day, their bowl of cornflakes that just went soggy, why, the weeping could go on for days. But that's okay; the desert's used to flash floods.

And then there's the whole claustrophobia thing. What hot-flashing woman could bear to maneuver her way down the hallway of a trailer with nine other menopausal women trying to do the same thing? That many hot flashes happening simultaneously could not only set the trailer ablaze, but it could possibly set off a range fire, the likes of which no cowboy has ever seen.

So like I said, I'm just waiting for the television networks to contact me. I have a strong feeling this could be next season's big hit. That is, if the public is brave enough for it.

> *I find television very educating. Every time somebody turns on the set, I go into the other room and read a book.*
> —Groucho Marx

23

The Older We Get

The older we get, the more we realize that money, while certainly nice to have, is far from being everything.

The older we get, the more we appreciate our time- and crisis-tested friends. Unless you're a jogger, who needs friends who run?

The older we get, the more skeptical we become of the news and gossip. We've lived long enough to know that there are always two sides to a story. We also know that there is a lot more positive news out there than what they are telling us.

The older we get, the more we know that failure isn't permanent.

The older we get, the more we realize that the things we stress over are very seldom worth stressing over.

The older we get, the more we appreciate good days, even if they weren't quite as good as we're recalling them.

The older we get, the more we value our money and appreciate the good it can do.

The older we get, the more we want to mean something significant to someone.

The older we get, the more we realize that our time is far too valuable to waste.

The older we get, the more we know the healing power of laughter.

The Grandmother of Invention

An amazing invention—but who would ever want to use one?
—Rutherford B. Hayes after making a call from Washington to Pennsylvania with Alexander Graham Bell's telephone

I have what I believe are some good ideas for a few inventions. I realize I should probably go ahead and make a prototype and patent these myself, but I'm too busy. Or too giving. Okay, too lazy. If anyone out there wants to work on them though, I'd be happy to talk to you about sharing a portion of the profits. The fact is, I just want to see these inventions on the market.

Have you ever felt that way about an idea? You know it could make you wealthy, but *Jeopardy* is on and you just don't have the time or the energy to do the legwork for your million-dollar idea. Besides, what if it did earn you a million dollars? There would be all those bank deposits that you'd have to make, employees you'd have to hire, and you'd need a warehouse to store your product (your coffee table can only hold so much). If you ask me, it all sounds like one big headache. When you figure all the time it's going to consume of your life, sometimes what you'd really rather do is just go to the store, buy the product, and be done with it. Let someone else do the production and marketing work. Let someone else keep track of the sales. Let someone else make the infomercial and hype the audience into their "Oooohs" and "Ahhhhs." Let someone else deal with all the paper work and the wheeling and dealing. You just want to be able to go to Wal-Mart and buy the product.

That's how I feel about these ideas.

The first thing I wish someone would invent is a Husband Leash. Never mind those kiddie leashes. Most mothers and grandmothers have no problem keeping track of their offspring. What women really need is a leash for their husbands, especially in the mall. In fact, maybe malls could let you check them out like they do the kiddie strollers. When a husband leaves his wife in the sportswear department and goes to find a chair, he can easily end up two stores away without a clue in the world of where he is. Even broadcasting his name over the PA doesn't help because he may not be within earshot of the announcement. Some husbands have probably been divorced on the grounds of desertion, when all they did was wander into the wrong store at the mall.

I also think someone should invent a Cell Phone Disintegrator. This would work a lot like those laser guns that police use on speeders, except the Cell Phone Disintegrator would actually shoot a laser to the cell phone and instantly disintegrate it in the caller's hand, without harm or injury to the caller. Imagine the fun we'd have aiming it at those rudest of cell phone users that we encounter throughout our day, and watching the look on their faces as their phone mysteriously disintegrates right in their hands. You could use it in restaurants, in movie theaters, in elevators, in department stores; anywhere and everywhere you encounter people talking incessantly on their cell phone with no regard for those around them.

Another idea I would like to see invented is the Back of the Throat Scratcher. You know that scratchy feeling you can get in the back of your throat, especially during allergy season? The one that drives you to make that irritating noise with your throat, trying to make the vibrations "scratch" the area for you, but it only temporarily solves the problem? That's where the Back of the Throat Scratcher would come in. It would work like a back scratcher, only instead of scratching your back, you would be using it on your throat. The biggest problem I can see encountering with this invention is the gag reflex, but I'm sure that can be worked out.

And you know how car manufacturers now offer heated seats to warm you on those chilly mornings? Why can't that same technology give us heated clothes? Sure, we might have to stay near an outlet to plug in our pants or shirt, but the concept does have merit, don't you think? It'd be a tough sell to menopausal women, because of the heat issue, but men (especially the ones who tend to turn up the thermostat in their homes fourteen seconds after their hot-flashing wives have turned it down) would probably love it.

I also think someone should improve on the car wash. If we're going to be sitting in our car and going through the process anyway, why not make it a little more entertaining? Synchronize the giant brushes to '50s songs, add some laser lights, and make it a whole multi-media experience.

I can't help it, these million-dollar ideas just come to me.

I think the older we get, the more ideas like this pop into our heads. My father used to sit and draw out elaborate plans for all sorts of inventions, often on a dinner napkin. Some of the ideas and plans were pretty amazing. Maybe even brilliant. Unfortunately, he never did anything with those ideas. He passed away before trying to create it or applying for a patent. He never got past the napkin stage.

Who knows what kind of million-dollar ideas are floating around in your head, too. If you think you've got a good idea in you, do something with it. Who knows? Maybe your idea will be the next major discovery. Maybe it'll change life as we know it today.

Or maybe it'll just be another way to get rid of that throat itch. Whatever it is, don't let it just sit there on your napkin. Napkins are for wiping up messes. Not for genius.

The true creator is necessity, who is the mother of our invention.
—Plato

25

Dreaming Your Life Away

Never laugh at anyone's dreams. People who don't have dreams don't have much.
—Unknown

One of my father's favorite things to do was to browse through farm real estate catalogs and circle the ads of whatever properties happened to catch his eye. Some would be spreads of twenty acres, some fifty, and a few would be a hundred or more. It didn't matter how large or how small the farm was, my dad would dream about buying it and living there one day. Dad had grown up on a farm and spent a lot of time thinking about returning to his roots someday.

Unfortunately, he passed away before ever making that move and seeing his dream fulfilled. The closest he got to returning to farm life was those catalogs and his dreams.

My mother had dreams, too. One of those dreams was to see Washington, D.C. After my father passed away, leaving more circled ads in farmland magazines than footprints in green pastures, I determined that the same thing wasn't going to happen to at least one of my mother's dreams. So early one morning I "kidnapped" her and we flew to our nation's capital. It took some secretive planning on my part. I had to call her work and prearrange for her to have the time off. Then I needed to make the flight and hotel reservations and plan out our itinerary. It took a little extra effort, but looking back on it now, I am so glad that I did what I could to help fulfill this one particular dream of my mother's. Especially since a few years after that trip, she developed lymphoma, and due to her frequent chemotherapy treatments, travel was all too quickly out of the question.

Lesson learned? Life is too short not to fulfill or at least attempt to fulfill our dreams and the dreams of our loved ones. As long as our dreams are healthy, legal, and don't hurt anyone else, we should do everything we can to go after them. Too many people get to the end of their lives realizing that they did nothing except ponder the great "what might have beens" of their life.

Have you thought much about what dreams you might be postponing? What are you circling in catalogs and brochures and travel books? Where have you always wanted to visit or perhaps even move to? What have you dreamed of accomplishing? Or maybe just attempting? What talent lies within you that has yet to be released? What is your passion? What were you created to do that, for whatever reason, you have been postponing year after year after year? What is your dream and, more importantly, why are you waiting to do anything about fulfilling it?

Start putting your talents to work today, not tomorrow. Give your passion the attention it deserves. Whether it be teaching, singing, building, learning, traveling, or whatever else you've been longing to do, give yourself permission to do it. Your dream has waited long enough.

It's important to remember, though, that all you have power over is the pursuit of your dream, the attempt, and the perseverance. The outcome is not in your hands. Still, it's not the outcome that brings you all the satisfaction. There is a good feeling that comes from merely having attempted to follow your dreams. Succeed or fail, at least you know you tried.

Not one of us is going to get to the end of our lives and be handed a refund for our unfulfilled dreams and plans.

"Oh, I'm sorry. I see here on your life report that you never did fulfill that dream of becoming a professional baseball player. Okay, here's your youth back. Go give it another shot."

Life doesn't happen that way. If we want to fulfill our dreams, timing is everything. And there will be for all of us dreams that we can't go back and force to come true. We just have to accept that. It would be difficult for a sixty-five-year-old woman, no matter how attractive she may be, to fulfill her dream of becoming Miss America. By the same token, a fifty-five-year-old, 118-pound man will probably never fulfill his dream of becoming a professional football player, even if he can play a pretty good game with his grandchildren. Fifty-five-year-old bones are still fifty-five-year-old bones.

But the dreams that are still within our grasp, the ones that carry a degree of possibility, the ones that still burn inside us, those are the ones that we shouldn't give up on.

It comes down to this: While we're waiting for the "right" time, the *only* time we have is passing us by. While we're waiting for "perfect" circumstances, the *only* circumstances we're ever going to be offered are leaving us behind. We can plan all we want, dream all we want, hope all we want, but eventually it's up to us to take that first step. There is nothing sadder than someone reaching the final chapter of their life and having nothing to look back on except regrets.

So don't forget, there is more than one way of fulfilling your dreams. If you've always dreamed of becoming a doctor, but circumstances, responsibilities, and maybe your grade-point average has kept you from pursuing that career, you can still apply for a job or volunteer for a position in the medical industry. If you've always dreamed of traveling the world but don't have the funds to do it, maybe you could look into getting a part-time job at a travel agency. There are plenty of travel perks for people in the travel business. Who knows—you just might be able to earn money and see the world, too. Whatever it is you want to do, if you put your mind to it, you can probably find a way to either fulfill your dream or at least get a taste of it.

So go after your dreams. Celebrate the portion of your life that lies ahead of you, and don't fall into the trap of thinking it's too late. We may not have our yesterdays, but we have today and tomorrow. Don't waste them.

Whatever you can do, or dream you can, begin it. Boldness has genius, power, and magic in it. Begin it now.
—Goethe

26

Mind Games

Exercise is a dirty word. Every time I hear it,
I wash my mouth out with chocolate.
—Author Unknown

Have you ever watched another person do something physically straining, only to get worn out yourself? You haven't moved a muscle (unless you count eye muscles), but you're exhausted just from watching someone else get a workout.

Last Christmas I went with my daughter-in-law and granddaughter to a local ballet company's performance of *The Nutcracker Suite,* and I came home so weak I could barely put one foot in front of the other. For the duration of the ballet, I had been right there on stage with all the other dancers, doing every move they did. At least in my head. I was balancing myself on my toes, doing pirouettes, jumps, and leg lifts. By the next morning I was so sore I couldn't even get out of bed! My brain ballet had drained every ounce of energy out of me. I had leg cramps, and I think I even pulled a groin muscle. It's a good thing we didn't go see *Riverdance*; I could have ended up in traction.

This sort of thing always happens to me when I watch someone else do physically demanding activities. If I'm watching the World Series on television, I'll picture myself out there in the batter's box hitting a home run and running around the bases. I'm huffing and puffing so much by the second inning that I've got to take a nap.

If I watch basketball, in my mind I'm out there on the court, running with the team, making basket after basket, dribbling, shooting, guarding. I usually hold up pretty well until we get into the second minute of the game, and by then I'm so winded I have to imagine myself sitting on the bench for a while just so I can catch my breath.

If my neighbors are jogging down our street, I'll picture myself running alongside them (okay, a few blocks behind them), but I'm out there just the same. Then I imagine shin splints and have to stop.

I've had to give up watching the Olympics altogether. I almost blew a lung in the weightlifting competition. Luckily I turned the channel before I killed myself.

The problem is this—in my mind I have the ability to dance on my toes, jump rope for hours, lift weights, and run a four-hour marathon. No matter what I imagine myself doing, the realist in me fast-forwards to the end result, and that usually involves injury or extreme exhaustion. On one level I suppose it's a good quality. It keeps me from actually doing certain activities where I could get injured in real life. But on the other hand, it's taking all the enjoyment out of watching organized sports, ballet, or other physically demanding activities and competitions.

Long ago I accepted the fact that my face will never be on the cover of a box of Wheaties. Shredded Wheat, maybe, but Wheaties, no. I'm not the kind of person who inspires people to physical excellence. My motto isn't Feel the Burn, it's Feel the Bed. Last month I thought I'd found the perfect gym for me and bought a one-year membership, but the staff at Gymboree keep making me get off the plastic castle and let the kids have a turn.

Still, they tell us that at our age it's important to keep moving, to treat our bodies as a musical instrument and always keep it tuned. But I've seen myself from behind—I'm a set of bagpipes when I'd rather be a violin.

But facts don't lie, and the facts show that the more exercising we do, the healthier we're going to be. The problem I have, though, is figuring out what's the best exercise for me.

I've tried exercise equipment. My son bought his wife the Gazelle for her birthday, and she's been letting me use it. I really like it. It's a little like skiing, only without the frostbite. Once you learn how to balance yourself on it, it's a lot of fun.

I've also tried walking, biking, bowling, aerobics, Pilates, and just about everything else you can think of.

But I may have finally found the ideal exercise program for me. According to a new study by the Mayo Clinic, even those of us who live a sedentary lifestyle can burn around 350 calories a day from just all those routine movements we do every day, including fidgeting. That's right, fidgeting. So that's the exercise program I'm on now. The Fidget Plan. It's perfect for me. I might not be able to complete a single push-up, but I can fidget for hours. I could become a triathlon athlete in this competition. I can do all sorts of fidgeting. I can tap my fingers on the table, cross my legs, and swing my top leg back and forth faster and longer than most. I am a champion fidgeter.

But why not go for the gold? Why don't I increase all my nervous habits and movements and let them burn off even more calories and get me in shape? Eye twitches, fingernail biting, scratching, yawning, I can do it all!

But later. Right now I'm watching Wimbledon and I'm exhausted!

The human body was designed to walk, run or stop; it wasn't built for coasting.
—Cullen Hightower

Alma Maters Matter

The secret of life is honesty and fair dealing.
If you can fake that, you've got it made.
—Groucho Marx

I just read an article about an Internet "school" based in Texas that rewarded a college degree to a cat. The scam might have continued to go unnoticed, but apparently the cat was throwing fraternity parties and hanging out until all hours of the night.

All right, the cat only threw *one* fraternity party. But I'm serious about the degree. This six-year-old cat really did receive an MBA from an Internet "university" in Texas. As gifted as the cat might very well have been, the school, according to the article and lawsuit, didn't even offer classes. It was allegedly just a front for fake degrees. Poor cat. Now that the scam has been uncovered, he'll probably lose his accounting job.

It does bring up a good point, though. Scams are everywhere. And apparently, plenty of them are on the Internet. You can get just about anything you want in cyberspace these days. Want a Bachelor of Arts degree? Pay the money and print up a form. A doctorate? Pay the money and print up a form. Want to be valedictorian of your class, graduate with honors, be named "Most Likely to Succeed"? Pay a little extra and print up a form. If you've got the ink, apparently you can have the "degree," "certificate," or whatever else you happen to desire.

It doesn't only happen there, though. A writer friend of mine once filled out a biographical form for one of those generic *Who's Who* books. For laughs, he listed all sorts of outrageous credits, including serving a term as vice-president of the United States. Amazingly enough, they printed it! Now granted, many of *us* probably wouldn't be able to name all the vice-presidents from the past several decades, but you would think that a company would be required to do a little bit of research before they print whatever someone sends them. But since this probably wasn't a legitimate *Who's Who* book, no research was done. The book was printed, listing whatever credits he had sent them. For him it was just a prank to see if they really would print it, and he got a good laugh out of it all. For them, however, it seemed to be more of "if the check clears, you can have the credit."

Now, for the record, I'm listed in several *Who's Who* books myself. Well, actually my listings are just in a *Who?* book.

If getting all these "credits" is this easy, though, it does make you wonder about the "professional" people in your life, doesn't it? For instance, is that diploma that's hanging on the wall of your dentist's office one that he actually earned from an accredited dental school, or will your root canal involve garden tools? Is that plumber you found in the phone book someone with legitimate trade school training and twenty years of experience like his ad says, or will you have the next Old Faithful erupting in your living room? And what about the pilot on the airplane you're flying in? Did he get his license off the *i.r.a.pilot.com* Web site?

When did we get so gullible? Why don't we question more? If the doctor we go to has a degree from Phil's Medical Night School and Garage, maybe we should find someone else. If someone tries to tell us how to invest our money and they're driving a rusted '69 Volkswagen bus, maybe we ought to double-check their financial advice. If we meet someone who shares an unbelievable story of hardship, then asks us for a donation, maybe "unbelievable" should be the key word. It's up to us to check out their story before we write the check. Some people will do or say anything for attention or money. Middle-agers and seniors have been the target of scams for years, and the only way to stop it is to become more aware.

We shouldn't allow ourselves to get talked into car repairs we don't need, roofing projects that could have waited, a new vacuum cleaner when we have a perfectly good one that works, encyclopedias that we probably will never open, candy and cookies that cost twice the price of what you could get them for at a store, driveway cleaner that we use the first day and then put it away never to look at again, drums of laundry detergent too big to store in our laundry room, parcels of land we haven't even seen, gold mines and oil wells that probably dried up years ago. In so many situations we stand to lose a lot of our hard-earned money, or in some cases it could be our health, all because we didn't take the time to check things out for ourselves. Or we simply had trouble saying that one simple two-letter word: no.

If we don't do our part to help get a handle on these types of situations, who knows how bad things could get. I mean, if a cat can get an MBA, other animals might start trying to get degrees, too. Instead of being your best friend, your dog could soon be your boss. One day he could take you aside (after a course in English as a Second Language), and say,

"Sorry, pops, but I'm going to have to let you go."

"Let me go? But why? I thought you were my best friend."

"You've been late for walking me four nights in a row now. We haven't played Frisbee in over a month. And food from a can? Puh-leeeeeease. All this is completely unacceptable. Now pack your things and be out of the house by noon! I'll be interviewing replacement owners first thing tomorrow morning. And get out of that recliner. That's my seat now. You're shedding your hair all over it."

"I am not *shedding hair."*

"Hey, I'm just calling it like I see it. You're the one with the bald spot, not me!"

But before you move out, call the university and check out the legitimacy of his degree. If it's from a fraudulent Internet university, you can keep your seat. But now, if you find it's from a legitimate Internet school, well, your only recourse is to make him pay back his own student loans.

It is better to deserve an honor and not receive it, than to receive one, and not deserve it!
—Mark Twain

Of All Places

**Always have your bags packed; you never know
where life's journey is going to take you.**
—Appalachian saying

By the time you reach middle age, chances are you've done a
lot of housework. And that housework has no doubt included
cleaning that one item we all hate to clean—the toilet bowl.
But we do it because we realize that if we want to live in sani-
tary conditions, that's one chore that has to be done.

In the house where I grew up, my mother was usually the
one who cleaned the toilet. Every once in a while, though,
one of us kids would do it. It wasn't as much fun as playing a
game of Monopoly or Old Maid, but we did it and survived.

In the four houses that my husband and I have lived in
during our marriage, we've shared the toilet cleaning duties
in each one. I have also cleaned toilets in other people's
homes and at various churches, as the need arose. I've
cleaned all kinds of bowls—new ones, rusted ones, broken
ones, old-fashioned ones, elongated ones, and water-saving
ones. In all my years of cleaning toilets, however, nothing like

the story that I'm about to tell you has ever happened to me!

Apparently, a few years ago a woman in Longview, Texas, came home to find that her toilet was bubbling up oil. That's right—she struck *oil* right there in her toilet. This Longview, Texas, woman hit a gusher in her flusher!

Now, before you scoff, you should know that this wasn't an article that I read in some supermarket tabloid, nor is it one of those hoaxes that continually circle the Internet until we've all passed it around 487 times and have fallen for it 487 times. No, CNN, MSNBC, and the Associated Press all reported this story. It's true, down to the very last gooey drop of black Texas gold. The woman's years of cleaning toilets finally paid off for her. Instead of calling a plumber, the woman could call her accountant and tell him that she had finally found her pot of gold at the end of the rainbow, or in this case, at the end of the pot.

But why did this happen in the first place? And why don't more of us get a tip like this for our housecleaning services? All I've ever gotten for cleaning the bathroom is a backache.

Well, one theory is that the woman's house might have been built on top of an old abandoned well that wasn't adequately capped and suddenly started gushing oil out of whatever pipeline it could find. Whatever the reason, the bottom line is that the lady struck oil in the last place on earth anyone would be looking for it. Let's face it, when's the last time anyone ever listed their toilet as an asset on their balance sheet?

This discovery has to have a positive effect on families all across Texas, and perhaps even the world, though. Families will no longer fight over *not* doing the household chores.

"*Hey, it's my turn to clean the toilet!*"

"*No way! You got to clean it last time!*"

"*Mommmmmyyyyy! Rickey won't let me clean the toilet!*"

And now that I think about it, who knows how many other household chores might someday reap a similar benefit? Maybe there's a diamond mine in the midst of all those dust bunnies under our beds. Or gold nuggets just waiting to be panned in our dishwater. There might even be an abandoned silver mine in the back of our closet. Who knows what fortunes are waiting to be discovered with a little elbow grease? At long last our housecleaning duties just might be finally set to pay off!

Content makes poor men rich; discontentment makes rich men poor.
—Benjamin Franklin

Social Security

Parody of "Falling in Love Again," sung in the style of Marlene Dietrich:

> Social Security,
> paid our whole lives through,
> now that it's come due,
> *where is it?!*

30

What's in Your Pocket?

My doctor gave me six months to live, but when I couldn't pay the bill he gave me six months more.
—Walter Matthau

Perhaps you've seen it—the at-home defibrillator. They've been advertising it everywhere, and personally I think the idea is long overdue. There is no telling how many lives a product like this is going to save. Imagine not having to wait for emergency medical care to arrive. Now a defibrillator can be as close as your pocket.

As amazing as this new product is, though, it makes you wonder what other "pocket" medical equipment could follow, especially if the ever-expanding infomercial market starts getting in on the action and comes up with a few of these inventions. We might soon be seeing products like:

The Gall Bladder Eggstractor

The Arterial Blockage Blaster
The Post-Surgical Stitch and Buttoneer
Liver Spot Instagone
Pop-a-Dent Cellulite Removal Kit
Ginsu Face-Lift Surgical Knife Set
The Internal Organ Pocket Navigator (for all your at-home surgical needs)

And that's just the beginning. Whether we'll ever see any products like the above (probably not) or whether researchers are already working on something a whole lot better, one thing is for sure—incredible advances are being made in the field of home medical testing and monitoring. Millions of people living with chronic diseases such as diabetes, heart disease, high blood pressure, and more are all benefiting from these medical and technological breakthroughs.

But now if they ever do come out with Liver Spot Instagone, I'm ordering a five-gallon can and a paint roller.

> *Our doctor would never really operate unless it was necessary. He was just that way. If he didn't need the money, he wouldn't lay a hand on you.*
> —Herb Shriner

31

Tattoo to You, Too

*You don't stop laughing because you grow old;
you grow old because you stop laughing.*
—Michael Pritchard

I'm thinking about getting a tattoo. Now before you get the
impression that I'm some kind of middle-aged rebel, let me
explain. It's not really a tattoo, at least not in the anchor,
Harley, or "Mom" kind of way. It's not even a rose or a butter-
fly. The tattoo I'm wanting is, well, it's an eyebrow. No, not an
extra one; I'm not looking to start a new trend or anything
like that. It's just that I've been a half-eyebrow short for some
time now and I would very much like to have the missing
half permanently drawn back on. From what I understand,
they can do this now by sort of tattooing on permanent
makeup. An interesting, albeit not totally painless, idea. The
pain part isn't something I would look forward to, but I
would certainly welcome the opportunity to at long last wake
up in the morning and not look like a descendent of Spock
from *Star Trek*.

I don't know why fifty percent of my left eyebrow decided

to go AWOL in the first place. All I know is that some years ago, half of my left eyebrow took off to places unknown, and to this day it hasn't returned to camp. I've been having to fill it in with an eyebrow pencil, but the problem is some days I forget.

I remember this same thing happening to my father. His eyebrow suddenly stopped growing, too, so maybe it's hereditary. We've never been tested, but perhaps my family lacks the eyebrow gene. Or maybe we have a weak one floating around in our DNA. I suppose my own offspring could get their DNA genetically altered so that future descendents can have the eyebrows that God originally intended, but that could be expensive.

But I am a little apprehensive. Every once in a while the news will report a story of someone who tried to improve their looks by some procedure and never made it out of the clinic alive. Something went horribly wrong, and what should have been relatively minor and routine, turned deadly. Would I really want my cause of death to be listed as an eyebrow tattoo? Would my insurance policy even pay out on that? And what about my funeral? I could just imagine the comments.

"Why couldn't she have lived with it? It was just a lousy eyebrow, for crying out loud."

"I know, but she must have gone peacefully. Just look at how relaxed her good brow looks."

When you think about it, what do we really need our eyebrows for anyway? They don't provide a life-sustaining function or anything like that. They don't shade us from the sun. Most of the time our eyebrows just sit there on top of our eyes trying to stay out of the way of all the other facial parts. They're relatively passive. How else can they be? We make sure they don't dare grow beyond their borders. If they do, we women immediately get out the tweezers and start plucking them back into submission.

But since eyebrows do help balance out our faces, I'm looking into my options. It's either a tattoo or shave the other eyebrow to match.

> ***Nobody really cares if you're miserable, so you might as well be happy.***
> —Cynthia Nelms

32

It's All Downhill From Here

There is no thrill quite like doing something you didn't know you could.
—Marjorie Holmes

I did it. I never really wanted to do it, never thought I could do it, didn't even dream about doing it, but I did it. It's amazing the things you can talk yourself into doing when you're on a ladies' retreat with some forty-five other women in the mountains of Montana. You begin to feel courageous, daring, and maybe even a little bit coordinated. (Okay, maybe not coordinated. But definitely daring and courageous.)

Before that day the thought of going down the side of a mountain on a pair of skis had never even once appealed to me. Mainly because I instinctively knew I wouldn't look good in a body cast. (Body casts can make you look two sizes heavier.)

But then I saw the other ladies donning their snowsuits

and getting fitted for ski equipment, and something inside of me rose up and said, "*I shall not let the fear of landing upside down in the snow stand in my way! I shall not be a wimp! I shall prove to myself that I can do whatever I set my mind to do!*" (I didn't know what it was that rose up inside of me, but it sure was wordy.)

Before I knew it, me and my courage were in the rental shop trying on a pair of skis and filling out a form for whom to notify in case I died in some sort of freak ski entanglement accident on the bunny slope.

I didn't know the first thing about skiing, but our hostess, Kay Creech, had graciously offered a ski lesson to anyone who wanted one. Comforted by the support of about forty other women, I decided to take Kay up on the offer. When else would I ever sign up for a ski lesson?

So I dialed my husband on my cell phone. "I think I'll go skiing this afternoon, honey, maybe take a lesson," I said.

"You? On a pair of skis? Have you forgotten about *Les Misérables*?"

Les Misérables is our code word for, well, *Les Misérables*, and it's enough to snap me out of any physical activity requiring coordination. *Les Misérables* was another downhill experience, only without the skis, and it happened when my daughter-in-law and I were in New York to see the Broadway musical. During intermission, I walked upstairs to use the rest room. When they flashed the lights indicating that intermission was now over, I attempted to rush back to my seat, but my foot slipped as I began down the stairs, and my descent then picked up quite a bit of speed as I tumbled head over feet all the way down. And I was wearing a skirt. My body came to rest at the bottom of the stairs, at the foot of a security guard and dozens of onlookers. I was in pain, but thanks to the good time I had made due to the fall, I wasn't late for the next act.

But with friends like Sue Buchanan, Julie Barnhill, Kay Creech, Cindy Creech, and so many others encouraging me to give it a try, I got the courage to do it. After all, what hot-flashing middle-aged woman wouldn't want to spend an afternoon sliding around in snow and icy slush?

Our ski instructor, Link Neimark, is one of the top in the field. He's a PSIA Level III, a USSA Alpine Race Coach, and has over twenty-five years' experience. Or to put it another way, in the photos of our first lessons, he was always the one standing upright.

At first, the only coordination I had out there on the snow was my outfit. I had borrowed a black snowsuit from one of the ladies, and wore a black fleece jacket over it. (I figured black would be a suitable color. In case anything should go wrong, I would already be dressed for the funeral.) I also wore a tan jacket over the black one because they say when you're going to be out in the winter elements, it's best to layer your clothing. I was so layered, I was like a torte on skis.

And then there was the pink hat. All of the ladies in our group wore pink hats that we had decorated the night before with various pieces of costume jewelry and rhinestones and such. Gluing and stitching seemed like too much work, so all I did to decorate mine was write on it with a black Sharpie the words, "If found upside down with skis pointing heavenward, please call . . ." and I listed my phone number.

Link was very helpful and encouraging to each of us in the beginning group. He let us go at our own pace. It didn't take long for the other two gals in my group to advance and move on to bigger and better runs. I was a little more cautious. I knew that even though my pink hat did have my phone number listed on it, being buried in the snow would not be a good thing.

After a while I managed to actually take a few steps in the skis. Then I fell. I tried to get up, but my feet were stuck in one position, with my legs wanting to go in another. No matter how hard I tried, they refused to work together.

I finally did manage to get back up, and as it turned out, that was the only time I fell that day. Thanks to our encouraging instructor who never once laughed at me, and the fact that I was among friends and wanting to see my husband's face when he looked at the pictures of me "skiing," I hung in there and I can now say that I have skied.

Okay, the bunny slope.

Okay, the bottom third of the bunny slope.

I can also say that I learned a lot about myself that day. I learned that if I want to do something, I can achieve it at least on some level. I know that I'll never be an Olympic skier. I might not even ever ski again. But I did do it once, and I'm pretty proud of myself for that. I didn't break a single bone. By comparison, I once broke a toe just stepping up onto my front porch.

So maybe the motivational people are right. Maybe we shouldn't let our fears control our lives. Maybe life is really just a string of situations where we've faced our fears and learned that we could indeed do whatever it was we were afraid of.

Fear is a party pooper. What have you been letting it keep you from doing? Be courageous; who knows what exhilarating new experiences are awaiting you.

You must do the thing you think you cannot do.
—Eleanor Roosevelt

33

That Settles It

Avoid any diet which discourages the use of hot fudge.
—Don Kardong

I would like to know why I was awarded a little pouch in my midsection the minute I hit middle age. It's like I'm wearing a fanny pack around my waist. Only I'm not. It's all me. I am the fanny pack. Like my under-the-chin skin, this situation also appeared without warning, without permission, and definitely without a welcome. Overnight I went from being able to fit perfectly into my jeans to not even being able to fasten them. The button and buttonhole are farther apart than the Republicans and Democrats. No matter how hard I try to push the two sides together, I can't seem to get them to meet. There is just way too much of me in the way.

Some have referred to this as the middle-age spread, which makes sense, I suppose. After all, it's probably the result of a lot of spreads—butter, cream cheese, whipped topping, cake frosting . . .

I can recall a time when I never used to have to think

about my stomach. My father was tall and lean in his younger days, and I guess I had taken after him. My stomach has been perfectly flat for most of my life.

But now the pouch has arrived. I've tried to suck it in, but it won't budge. Apparently it likes it just fine where it's at.

It's a lot more prominent when I sit. Sometimes I feel like I'm holding a globe in my lap. It's round and protruding and whenever I look down at it, I can't help but wonder if I might be able to balance my coffee on it.

I guess the best way to describe what has happened to me is that I've "settled." You know how a house settles? Sometimes the repairs are merely cosmetic. Other times you need to call in the plumbers and hard-hat workers. Well, that's what it feels like my body has done. Some of the settling has required minor repairs. The rest has needed plumbers and hard-hat workers.

My body has even started making those settling noises, especially in the joints. You know that creaking sound that reminds you of a loose gate on an abandoned farm? My knees sound like that every time I get up from the sofa.

But even with all the settling, the creaking, the middle-age spreading, and the skin loosening, one thing's for certain: there is plenty to laugh about in the second half of our lives. And as long as our foundations don't crack, we're home free.

Old age is no place for sissies.
—Bette Davis

Relaxation Island

There cannot be a crisis next week.
My schedule is already full.
—Dr. Henry Kissinger

Some of the hottest merchandise on the market today is relaxation products. You can buy waterfall machines, neck massagers, back massagers, and sound therapy CDs that will play the sounds of a babbling brook, ocean waves, birds chirping, and just about any other relaxing sounds you can think of. (Funny, you never see a relaxation tape called "nagging wife" or "belching husband." But I digress.)

These products are great, and in our highly stressful world, probably very much needed.

But have you ever wondered how differently we would conduct our lives if we all had blood pressure and stress monitors hooked up to us twenty-four hours a day? If we knew the effect that high-stress situations had on our health, would we continue trying to right every wrong that is dealt us, or would we learn how to let a few of them slide? I have a feeling we'd start letting a *lot* of things slide.

Sure, it feels good to be right. But it also feels good to just *be*—as in being alive. Some disagreements and pettiness just aren't worth our getting involved in.

I wonder, too, how watching news programs affects our blood pressure and health. Every time the Homeland Security Alert rises to a new level, surely our stress indicators have to be rising right along with it. We can try to brush it off and go about our day, but it's not always easy to shake that feeling of impending doom. The "What if" scenarios are endless. What if there's anthrax on my mail? What if gas prices top three dollars a gallon? What if the terrorists attack Wal-Mart? There is so much more to worry about these days, it's a wonder we're not all hiding under our beds. What if. . . ? What if. . . ? What if. . . ? We can "What if?" ourselves right into a heart attack if we're not careful.

And what are all the political debates and commentaries doing to us? Tossing pillows at some politician or news anchor's image on the television screen might make us feel better for the moment, but it won't keep our blood pressure from rising over the long haul. Of course, even though we have the ability to turn off these news programs with the click of a remote control, many of us will stay glued to the television screen on a big news day, watching the same news story rerun itself into the wee hours of the morning, over and over and over again.

Maybe it would benefit us all if we would just go on a news-free diet, if even for a few days, just to see how much better we'd feel. This is a popular recommendation for people under stress, and I think it's a great idea. You don't even have to check with your doctor to begin this kind of health plan. Just turn off the news for one week and see how much brighter your outlook becomes and how much more relaxed you feel.

Another way to relax is to take a nice hot bath. There are all sorts of homemade soaps and bath additives that can turn your regular bathtub into a spa of sorts. You might also think about turning on some soft music and surrounding the bathtub with burning candles. Not only will this relax you, but if your hair happens to catch on fire from the candles, you've got plenty of water right there to put it out.

Aquariums are supposed to help lower our blood pressure and relax us, too. There's something soothing about watching fish with nothing better to do than swim around all day. They have it made. They're fed when they're hungry, and someone else even cleans their tank for them.

But we could learn a lot from aquarium fish. They know how to entertain themselves. You don't see them sitting in a corner looking bored with their life. All they do all day is swim around in circles, but they know how to make it interesting. They take a different path every time they go around the tank. It may be the same tank day in and day out, but they find creative ways to make the same-old same-old a little more interesting. Sometimes they'll dive to the bottom of the tank. Other times they'll swim up to the top. They'll go in and out of the underwater castle or the ceramic sunken ship.

They'll swim over to the light and check that out for a while. They might turn around and swim a different direction, then suddenly turn around again just for fun. They know how to make their restricted lives spontaneous and fun.

But how many of us humans are in a rut, doing the same old thing every day, with boredom written all over our faces? We drive the same road to the bank, walk the same path every night, go to the same grocery store, the same mall, the same gas station, and we're Bored with a capital B.

Perhaps we should try to be more like aquarium fish. Maybe we could start taking a different road into town. We could try out a new recipe, walk in a different park, go to a different grocery store, do something out of the ordinary. Who knows? We just might like it. At the very least, it will break up our monotony.

Another thing we can do is travel. If we have the health and the funds, we should start seeing those parts of the world that we've always wanted to see. If we have no one else to go with, we could go with a tour group. You know what they say—change your scenery and you'll change your outlook.

But whatever we do, however we relax, the important thing to remember is to keep our daily stresses down to a minimum. Deal with those situations that need to be dealt with, and leave alone the ones that are just time and energy drainers. We'll be a whole lot healthier for it.

I could go on and on about how to not let stress get the best of us, but the presidential debates just aired and now all the political pundits are putting in their two cents' worth. In other words, it's time to start tossing pillows at the television set again.

Worrying is like a rocking chair: it gives you something to do, but it doesn't get you anywhere.
—Anonymous

Tuesdays With Metamucil

I am a nutritional overachiever.
—Author Unknown

Have you ever wondered why it is that the older we get, the more preoccupied we become with our digestive and intestinal tracks? Take for instance roughage. Why do people our age obsess over roughage? I don't remember doing that when I was younger. I don't remember ever once asking my mother if she packed a bran muffin in my lunch pail because I wasn't really "feeling like myself" that day.

Frankly, I don't know anyone who truly likes bran. If bran were a popular flavor, we'd see bran-flavored chewing gum, bran-flavored Sno-Kones, Bran Coke and Bran Pepsi, and bran would be the thirty-second flavor of ice cream at Baskin-Robbins.

But bran isn't a popular flavor. Most of us wouldn't eat it if it wasn't for the health benefits of it. If the government were to issue a warning tomorrow admitting that they were wrong and bran in fact causes many health ailments and should not be eaten, we'd be tossing out our muffins so fast the sanitation workers couldn't keep up with it. (Or lift the bags either.)

That's never going to happen, though, because apparently bran is good for us.

I think I liked it better before all of this health consciousness. We could order the foods we liked, foods with high fat and low fiber content, foods with (I know I'm being politically incorrect here, but I have to be honest) *carbs*, and we didn't have a single ounce of guilt over any of it.

But then along came the carb counting, the good and bad cholesterol monitoring, and twenty-eight-grain breads, and all the fun shot right out of our whole dining experience. (By the way, just out of curiosity, exactly how many grains does a loaf of bread require before it is reclassified as lumber and sold at The Home Depot instead?)

Roughage isn't the only thing that we become obsessed with as we get older. We start paying closer attention to how much fat, sugar, sodium, carbs, cholesterol, and chili pepper we're putting into our mouths, too. We read the nutritional labels on packages like they're Grisham novels, and we carry bottles of drinking water around throughout our day to make sure we're getting all the fluids we need.

We try to stay up-to-date on all the latest nutritional discoveries, too. If we read an article about some new food item or vitamin or mineral supplement that's supposed to be healthy for us, we're at the grocery store buying a crate of it that same day.

Ever since I learned how healthy salmon is for us, I've been ordering it almost every time I go out to dinner. I don't even like salmon; I just eat it because I know it's good for me. Now I find out that there's a difference between farm-raised salmon and fished salmon, so I don't know if I've been helping myself or hurting myself. Who knows? I only know that I'm not going to be a happy camper if I've been opting for salmon when I could have been eating a cheeseburger and fries all this time.

If they do ever switch on us and confess that they were wrong about everything, wrong about carbs (we can have all we want), wrong about sugar (the more the merrier), wrong about fat (go ahead, indulge!), wrong about sodium, cholesterol, chili pepper, and all the rest, there's going to be a revolt in this country the likes of which we've never seen before. Riots will break out in front of health food stores! People will be having bran bonfires, and considering the woody texture, the fire might burn for years. Posters of famous nutritionists and diet book writers, with a giant circle drawn around their faces with a line through it, will be carried through the streets! Exercise equipment will be thrown through the glass doors at gym and health clubs! Unless cooler heads prevail, it is not going to be pretty, people.

Husband to his wife: "You could lose a lot of weight if you'd just carry all your diet books around the block once a day."
—Bill Hoest (*The Lockhorns*)

Thanks, But No Thanks

Gratitude is not only the greatest of virtues,
but the parent of all others.
—Cicero

Not long ago, Oprah Winfrey and Pontiac gave away G6
sedans to Oprah's entire studio audience, consisting of 276
people. Apparently, this incredible display of generosity rang
in at a price of around seven million dollars. When presented
with their gift, tears of joy overwhelmed the recipients. That
is, until they discovered they would need to pay the taxes on
the cars out of their own pockets. It was then that a few of
the recipients seemed to change their attitude and decided to
bite or at least nibble on the hand that extended the car keys.

Now granted, paying the taxes on a brand-new car would
certainly be a problem for someone who couldn't afford to
buy the car in the first place. So on one level the complaints
might be a little understandable. But weren't there other ways

to remedy the situation other than complaining to the news media? Selling the car, taking the equally needed cash, and buying a less expensive used car might have been one choice. As far as I know, no one was forcing anyone to keep their brand-new cars. I may be wrong, but I'm pretty sure it was their option to either accept the gift, give it back, or trade it in for something else, just like any of us could do with any of the gifts we receive. If your Aunt Agnes gives you a pair of armadillo bedroom slippers next Christmas, you would probably exercise your right to take the slippers back to the store and use the cash or store credit for whatever else you might want (if your dignity can handle walking back into the store carrying armadillo bedroom slippers, that is). I'm assuming these people were free to have done the same thing with Oprah's gift.

To me, complaining about a gift of a brand-new car is a little like winning the Publisher's Clearing House Sweepstakes, then handing the van driver a bill for running over your azaleas. You might have every right to do so (after all, they were *your* azaleas), but the driver also just brought you a check for a million dollars. With that kind of money, you could buy your own nursery!

Maybe it's just me, but in our day it seemed people were far more appreciative of what they had been given. Maybe that was because we, or our parents and grandparents, had gone through times of war, famine, recessions and, for some, a major depression.

Today some people think they're "doing without" if they can't afford to buy dessert. Back then "thank you" didn't sound like a foreign language. People instinctively said it whenever someone did something nice for them. In fact, people even routinely sent thank-you cards to acknowledge someone's generosity. They didn't ignore gifts or the kindnesses shown to them. There wasn't such a sense of entitlement. They were more grateful and they showed it more often and more sincerely. They also had good memories of the generosity of others. There was far less of that "what has anyone done for me lately?" attitude.

But don't misunderstand. I'm not at all implying that any of the people who were given those new cars on Oprah's show had a sense of entitlement. I'm sure they are all good, hardworking folks who just needed a little help. I am also sure that down deep they were all thankful for the gift, even in spite of any problems or misunderstandings.

The point I'm making is simply this—there does seem to be a growing number of people today who are going through their lives joyless and unsatisfied, complaining about what they don't have without taking an honest inventory of everything they do have. Martin Luther once said, "Unthankfulness is theft." I think he might have been right. When we complain about what we lack without acknowledging all we have right in front of us, it is a little like stealing. And the sad part is, when we live our lives this way, the one we're ultimately robbing is ourselves.

***If the only prayer you ever say in your entire life
is thank you, it will be enough.***
—Meister Eckhart

Retirement Community

**How beautiful it is to do nothing,
and then rest afterward.**
—Spanish Proverb

I have to say that the thought of moving to a retirement community has never really interested me. I haven't reached retirement age yet, but for years I've been convinced that to feel youthful and vital, one needs to be surrounded by young people.

But I think I might need to back up and rethink that for a moment.

After having lived next door to teenagers who seemed to have no direction in their lives, throwing parties while their parents are away, playing loud music till all hours of the night, walking down the street with their boom boxes blaring, and constantly revving their car engines, a retirement community doesn't seem so bad anymore.

Also in a retirement community you usually don't have people "trying to find themselves." Most of the residents are pretty comfortable with who they are. By the time you reach retirement age, you don't have to prove anything to anyone. You're comfortable in your skin. It might not be as tight a fit as it once was, but you're comfortable.

Retirement communities don't have to deal with gangs either. You won't see "AARP" spray-painted on the side of buildings, and no one will be standing on the corner peddling B_{12} shots.

Another advantage to living in a retirement community is that older citizens usually do realize the importance of showing good manners and consideration for one's neighbors. Their wild parties are over by nine o'clock, and the only mess they make is when someone pours too much Epsom salt in the Jacuzzi.

I have to admit the advertisements for some of these retirement communities today are pretty enticing. They picture golf courses, waterfalls, gardens, community centers with monthly guest speakers covering a variety of interesting topics, holiday parties, and much more. Some of these places offer restaurant facilities and shopping, as well as a post office, drug store, and other business offices. They are their own village. Some even offer gyms and personal trainers.

And the people pictured on the brochures don't even look old anymore. They look youthful and vibrant, and they seem to be having the time of their lives enjoying all the activities and spending their children's inheritance.

So on second thought, when my husband and I get ready

to retire, maybe we'll look into moving to a retirement community. We like peace and quiet. We like mannerly neighbors. And we're usually in bed by nine o'clock, anyway. As for the Epsom-salt Jacuzzi? I guess it's like they say: You don't know if you'll like it unless you try.

The best time to start thinking about your retirement is before the boss does.
—Source unknown

Road Signs for the Middle-Ager and Beyond

No Outlet (shopping)

Watch Out for Falling Parts

Reduced Estrogen Ahead

No Dumping (We've all got enough problems of our own.)

No Passing Zone (Looks like you'll have to keep your kidney stone a little longer.)

Bridge May Freeze (Dentures, too, so use caution when eating ice cream.)

Watch Downhill Speed (You may be over the hill, but you haven't come to the Stop sign yet. So slow down and enjoy the rest of the journey.)

Welcome Mat

We cannot always oblige; but we can always speak obligingly.
—Voltaire

I live in Tennessee now. I grew up, married, and raised our family in California, but we moved to Tennessee a few years ago. They're polite here in Tennessee. In fact, the national news recently covered a robbery that took place here in the Volunteer State, where the alleged perpetrator, an elderly man, apologized to the clerk before robbing the store. Talk about Southern hospitality. It isn't something you just read about in books. It's real. People out here really do take their manners seriously.

When we first moved to the South, we were amazed at all the kindnesses that were so generously shown to us by the various people we encountered. Once, when my husband and I were needing a large dogwood tree (an anniversary/house-warming gift from good friend Diantha Ain) delivered to our house, a man at the nursery pulled up next to us in his pickup truck and asked if we were the ones who needed help transporting a tree to our home. When we told him we were, he loaded it into his truck and then followed us to our house. The entire time that he was loading it up and driving behind us en route to our home, we just assumed that he worked for the nursery. But come to find out, he was just another customer! We tried to tip him for his kindness and time, but he refused. He did it, he said, just to "help out."

Another time, when my daughter-in-law, Crystal, and I had bought a television set and were trying to load the giant box into our car, a lady driving down the parking aisle noticed us struggling, then pulled up and asked if we wanted to put the box in the back of her truck so she could take it to our house for us. Just at that moment, though, we had finally managed to get the box to fit into the car, so we turned down her offer. In Los Angeles, if someone had offered to drive a newly purchased television set to our house, we probably would have just heard the sound of burning rubber as they peeled out of the parking lot with the box, heading in the opposite direction of our home. But the woman who offered to help us was just showing us her natural Southern hospitality.

I like living in a place where friendly, considerate people abound, where the notion of folks helping other folks isn't just a fantasy, where strangers are made to feel comfortable and welcome in an unfamiliar setting. Sure, there are plenty of people who use and abuse the kindness of others, who take advantage of someone's generosity and kindness, who may even exaggerate or fabricate their need or desperation and prey on the goodwill of society. But that still shouldn't stop us from showing good ol' Southern hospitality to others no matter what part of the country, or world, we happen to live in. It's wise to ask questions, and certainly, if we've been burned before, it might make us more selective of where and to whom we offer our help, but it shouldn't make us stop meeting the real needs of those who happen to cross our path throughout our day.

My mother was always hospitable. She never cared if more people than she had planned on showed up for dinner. She would simply "throw some more beans in the pot." And she always put herself last, believing that guests should have the best of whatever you had to offer. For every one person who might have taken unfair advantage of that quality, there were a host of other appreciative ones who will be eternally grateful for her kindness.

So yes, I must say that all of this Southern hospitality has been nice. The older we get, the more kindness and respect seem to matter. But the South doesn't hold the patent on those qualities. I've met nice people in the North, in the East, and in the West. There are plenty of nice people in big cities like Los Angeles, Chicago, and New York, too. It just seems to be a little more of an epidemic in the South. And that's one epidemic I don't think any of us would want to stop.

*Clothes and manners do not make the man;
but, when he is made,
they greatly improve his appearance.*
—Henry Ward Beecher

40

Not Looking Back

*Save the Earth, it's the only planet
with chocolate.*
—Bumper sticker

Have you fallen into the trap of saying to yourself that as
soon as this or that happens, then you'll be happy? If only my
daughter would get her life straightened out. If only my son
called a little more often. If only my neighbor wasn't such a
grump. If only I didn't have so many bills. If only I had a better car. If only I could afford to take that trip I've always
dreamed about. If only my husband didn't leave. If only my
wife was less critical. If only my friends were more caring. If
only, if only, if only.

Do you know that while you're busy waiting for life to be
"perfect," your imperfect life keeps marching on day after day,
week after week, year after year? Time doesn't stop for life to
straighten itself out. We just have to accept the fact that life is
very rarely a perfect proposition. So don't waste another minute waiting for it to be. Those "perfect" circumstances might

not ever come along, and while you're wasting your time waiting for them, all you're going to get is older and less happy.

And don't waste another minute pining about yesterday and what might have been. It very well might have been, but it wasn't. No matter how much we beg for yesterday to return, it's irretrievable. Life offers no rewrites. Even a minute ago is too far gone to ever bring back. Whatever happened, good or bad, fun or boring, worthwhile or wasted, is now history. The only thing we have the power over is today. Even tomorrow is unpredictable.

That's the nice thing, though, about middle age. By the time we've made it this far, we've (hopefully) learned a lot from the past—to influence the decisions we make today and to improve our lives tomorrow. We've learned not to let other people's opinions affect us as much as they did in our youth. By this stage in our lives we've had to maneuver our way through some of life's more rocky places. We've won a few and lost some, too. We've been praised, blamed, uplifted, demeaned, coddled, kicked around, loved, and rejected. If we were paying attention through it all, we've learned a thing or two about ourselves, others, and life.

One of the most important things we've learned is that all those losses and hurts, the ones that were so painful it felt like we might not ever survive them, somehow didn't destroy us. We survived not one, not two, not twenty, but every single one of them. We wouldn't still be here if we hadn't. Like Reinhold Niebuhr said in his oft-quoted prayer, we accepted those things that we could not change, changed those things that we could, and had the wisdom (most of the time) to know the difference. Maybe life didn't turn out exactly the way we wanted it, and maybe some of our survival may have required setting boundaries that were necessary for our own health and peace of mind. But through God's mercy, we made it to this point of our life. That is no small accomplishment. It's called endurance, and if we're still around today, we were apparently blessed with a good deal of it.

Our parents and grandparents knew how to endure. When the going got rough, they hung tough. They didn't pull over to the side of life's road and whine about how tricky the lane changes were or how many times they got cut off by another driver. They knew the road of life was treacherous for all of us at some point. They didn't expect it to be otherwise. They just taught themselves how to adapt and take things as they come. Many of them lived through the Great Depression. They survived two world wars. They lived through political scandals, weather disasters, and black-and-white TV. They knew how to adjust their sails. They knew how to persevere, hang on to hope, and never ever give in to doubt or fear. They were true survivors.

So don't give away any more of today's energy and promise fretting over the pain or disappointment of the past. Deal with it if you haven't already, face the truth of your hurts and failures, confront who you must, forgive who you need to, set healthy boundaries with those who have a history of hurting you, and then move on. Be a survivor, too.

Finish each day and be done with it. You have done what you could; some blunders and absurdities have crept in; forget them as soon as you can. Tomorrow is a new day; you shall begin it serenely and with too high a spirit to be encumbered with your old nonsense.
—Ralph Waldo Emerson

Vote for Who?

Being president is a lot like running a cemetery.
You've got a lot of people under you and
nobody's listening.
—Bill Clinton

I don't think I'll run for president. Nobody has asked me yet, but even if I were to be approached by the nominating committee of either political party, I don't think I'd accept the invitation. The pay is fine. Actually, it's more than fine. But there are too many requirements for running the most powerful nation in the world. For one thing, I'm pretty sure you can't sleep in. If you're still in bed past noon, someone is bound to be looking for you. And if you try to catch a quick catnap between your thoughts during a State of the Union address, the picture is sure to hit the front page of every newspaper in the country.

I've also come to realize that it's virtually impossible to please everyone, no matter how hard you work at it. If you sign this bill, the Republicans get mad. If you sign that bill, the Democrats get upset. If you don't do anything, the independents will be picketing in front of the White House. You can do your best to make everyone happy, and you're still going to make someone unhappy. Sometimes you might even make half the country unhappy. Like Lyndon Johnson once said, "If one morning I walked on top of the water across the Potomac River, the headline that afternoon would read, 'President Can't Swim.'"

I am, however, fascinated with how the political machine works. It's fun to look for spin in the press or try to see the bigger picture in difficult decisions made by either party. I also find it quite interesting to see how hard all the political parties work to win the senior and baby boomer vote. Beyond playing oldies tunes at some of their rallies, the candidates will address topics like whether or not Social Security will be there for us when we retire (even though many of us have been paying into it for decades), and they'll make pledges to make our streets safer, cut our taxes, keep interest rates at a reasonable level, give us better prescription drug coverage, fund more medical research, build better roads, and control the rate of inflation. The list goes on and on.

It's hard to keep track of all the promises the candidates routinely make to us when they're running for office. So why do they go to so much trouble to get our votes? Because we are a force to be reckoned with. Not only are we great in number, but we vote. We actually show up at the polls and go through the process. We don't let much of anything keep us away from the polls. We send donations to our respective political parties. We tune in to the debates. We call up the talk shows. We read (sometimes word for word) the political literature that is mailed to us. Most of us are very much involved in the political process.

MTV can hype the youth vote, run super-slick ads trying to get millions of young adults to register, but on election night, we're still the ones showing up. In rain, snow, or rush-hour traffic. Or we mail in our ballots ahead of time. When it comes to our right to vote, we take it very seriously. Maybe that's because we have a very good understanding of what went into winning that right, and we don't take the sacrifice of those who went before us lightly.

But I still don't think I'd ever want to be president. It's just too hard to run a country and still keep up with all my soaps.

There are advantages to being president. The day after I was elected, I had my high school grades classified.
—Ronald Reagan

On Purpose

Life is a promise; fulfill it.
—Mother Teresa

How many times in our lives have we apologized or had someone apologize to us for things that weren't done "on purpose"?

"I didn't hurt your feelings on purpose," someone will say to us. *"But I had to tell you the truth about your hair. Was it really your intention for it to come out that particular shade of orange?"*

Or they'll run over our toes with their grocery cart and then apologize. *"I'm sorry. I didn't do that on purpose. Let me just back up over them again and then I'll be out of your way."*

Whether the apology is sincere or not, we may never really know for sure. Without getting inside someone's head, it's hard to know what they do on purpose and what they truly do accidentally. Some of us don't even see when our own actions are very much on purpose.

There is something, though, that we should all do "on purpose," and that's live our lives. None of us should want to just wander about from decade to decade, career to career, relationship to relationship. We should want, even demand, more out of our lives. We are here for a reason, and we should find that reason.

What is it that you feel driven to accomplish in your life? It doesn't matter how old you are. It's never too late to fulfill your purpose.

Ask yourself this: If you were to make a "To-Do" list for your life, what would be on it? Where would you like to go? Whom would you like to meet? What would you like to learn? What have you always wanted to do? What field have you always wanted to work in? What charity have you always had a heart for?

Think about it, then jot down some of your goals, aspirations, and things that you still hope to accomplish in your lifetime. This is your "To-Do List for Life":

1.
2.
3.
4.
5.
6.
7.
8.
9.
10.

Now that you know at least ten of your lifelong desires, start doing them one at a time, or at least attempting them, and as you accomplish each one, check it off. What you do

with your life is up to you. It will be as fulfilling or as unful-
filling as you allow it to be. If you've got today, you've got the
time to make a difference.

Dost thou love life? Then do not squander time,
for that is the stuff life is made of.
—Benjamin Franklin

43

How to Have a Happy Birthday

❀ Give yourself a present.
❀ Call an old friend that you haven't talked to in a long time.
❀ Take a few of your favorite old photos out of their albums or shoe boxes and prominently display them somewhere in your home.
❀ Have someone else take your picture. If no one is around, go to a studio (Wal-Mart, Sears, and many other discount department stores have reasonably priced photo studios) and get your picture taken. Even those photo booths at malls would cost you only a few dollars for four poses. Or if you have a camera, stroll to a nearby park and ask someone to take your picture. Most people will gladly accommodate your request. It doesn't matter how you get your picture taken, but document this special day with a photo.

✿ Make this day a day of favorites. Wear your favorite shirt, watch your favorite television shows, eat your favorite foods, talk to your favorite people, read your favorite book. It's your day—treat yourself to the things you enjoy.

✿ Tell others what you'd like for your birthday. If you don't get it, don't be disappointed. Just look at it as an opportunity to treat your own body and mind with a little "thank-you gift" for all they've done for you, then go out and buy it yourself.

✿ If whoever you're hoping will call you today doesn't call by 6 P.M., call him or her. Once the two of you start talking, you'll forget all about which one of you had to do the dialing.

✿ Look in the mirror and tell yourself that you are one fine-looking person for whatever age you happen to be.

✿ Buy a birthday card or gift for someone else whose birthday is close to yours. Giving to others has a residual effect of making you feel good, too.

✿ Pick some flowers, put them in a vase, and display them where you can see them all day long.

✿ Look through catalogs and circle everything you'd like to have. You may never buy any of it, but it's fun to dream.

✿ Share at least one good memory with someone, even if it's your pharmacist.

✿ Write in your journal what you learned about yourself and life throughout the previous year.

✿ Sing "Happy Birthday" to yourself at least one time all the way through, and smile while you're doing this.

✿ Hide a dollar in your house for you to find next year on your birthday. It'll be good exercise for your brain to spend the next 365 days trying to remember where you hid it. If you do this every year for the rest of your life, and always forget where you've hidden the money, think of all the fun your heirs will have discovering all those dollar bills.

✿ Never forget that on this day someone very special was born. You.

44

Without You

"One man's life touches so many others, when he's not there it leaves an awfully big hole."
—Clarence from *It's A Wonderful Life*

Have you ever been in one of those melancholy moods where you found yourself feeling insignificant? Maybe you've even wondered what life might have been like had you never been born. You've asked yourself if there would be, as Clarence said in *It's a Wonderful Life*, an awfully big hole where you were meant to be.

The answer is yes, there would be an awfully big hole. We don't always realize that, though. Too often we think if we didn't make some amazing medical discovery, or were instrumental in achieving world peace, or some other incredible feat, then we had no worth. But the proof of our importance to this world is most often found in small ways.

In the movie *Saving Private Ryan*, Private Ryan spent his life trying to prove to himself that he was worthy of the ultimate sacrifice that was paid by the soldiers who lost their lives trying to save his. He carried tremendous guilt and never quite felt worthy of the trade. But by the end of the movie, his wife assures him that the sacrifice of those men wasn't in vain, because Private Ryan was a good man. He was important in the lives of his family.

No, we may not change the world by discovering the cure for cancer, but those cards, phone calls, and visits that we gave to a friend who was diagnosed with cancer may have been the hope he or she needed to hang on, to keep fighting and ultimately win the battle. Maybe we never held a political office that enabled us to create policies that would help save the world, but those toys we gave away to a needy child that one Christmas may have meant the whole world to that boy or girl.

We don't always see the importance of the small acts of kindnesses that we do. We brush off these little niceties, almost embarrassed at their apparent insignificance, telling ourselves that anybody could have done what we did. But the simple truth is, nobody else was doing it, at least not at that time. We saw the need of one single person in one single moment and we acted.

If a survey was ever taken of people whose lives had been miraculously changed, we might be surprised at how many of them would say that the turning point came as a result of one small act of kindness, either given by someone they knew or a total stranger.

Do you remember how the "buddy system" worked when you were younger? If a group of you were going swimming, hiking, mountain biking, or doing some other outdoor sport, the leader always made sure that everyone had a buddy with them at all times. You were assigned someone to watch out for you in case anything went wrong, and you watched out for them. That's because no one person could keep their eye on the entire group at every moment.

The same is true in life. None of us can be there for everyone. It's a physical, financial, and emotional impossibility. But I'm sure those we have helped, either financially or emotionally, those we gave a kind word to, or a monetary gift, or showed any kindness in any way, are forever grateful that we happened to come along at the precise moment of their need. And we'll be forever grateful for those who happened along in our times of need.

So, yes, there would be an awfully big hole. From the very first day of your life, you've been affecting people. Your parents, your extended family, your friends, even people you didn't know that well, or at all for that matter. Your birth may have meant everything to your parents. That first home run you hit in Little League may have been the proudest moment in your father's life. When you were in the eighth grade you may have thought you were just warming a chair, but that smile you gave to the boy sitting behind you in class may have been the only one he got all semester. The time you defended a friend who was being picked on in school was no small thing. It took courage to stand up for someone whom everyone else was making fun of. Think it went unnoticed? That girl is forty-eight now, and to this day she can still recite your words verbatim. You've been making an impact on people your entire life, you just don't know it.

We may not know until we get to heaven just how many lives we've positively affected simply by our being here. And since we're all still around, that can only mean there are plenty more lives waiting to be affected by our presence, too.

An insignificant life? Hardly.

> **"You see, George, you really have had a wonderful life."**
> —Clarence from *It's A Wonderful Life*